NEW ACCENTS

General Editor: TERENCE HAWKES

The Politics of Postmodernism

IN THE SAME SERIES

Literature, Politics and Theory: Papers from the Essex
    Conference 1976–84   ed. *Francis Barker, Peter Hulme, Margaret
    Iversen, and Diana Loxley*
Translation Studies   *Susan Bassnett-McGuire*
Rewriting English: Cultural politics of gender and class   *Janet
    Batsleer, Tony Davies, Rebecca O'Rourke, and Chris Weedon*
Critical Practice   *Catherine Belsey*
Formalism and Marxism   *Tony Bennett*
Sexual Fiction   *Maurice Charney*
Alternative Shakespeares   ed. *John Drakakis*
Poetry as Discourse   *Antony Easthope*
The Semiotics of Theatre and Drama   *Keir Elam*
Language and Style   *E.L. Epstein*
Reading Television   *John Fiske and John Hartley*
Literature and Propaganda   *A.P. Foulkes*
Linguistics and the Novel   *Roger Fowler*
The Return of the Reader: Reader-response
    criticism   *Elizabeth Freund*
Superstructuralism: The philosophy of structuralism and
    post-structuralism   *Richard Harland*
Structuralism and Semiotics   *Terence Hawkes*
Subculture: The meaning of style   *Dick Hebdige*
Reception Theory: A critical introduction   *Robert C. Holub*
Popular Fictions: Essays in Literature and History   ed. *Peter
    Humm, Paul Stigant, and Peter Widdowson*
Fantasy: The literature of subversion   *Rosemary Jackson*
Deconstruction: Theory and practice   *Christopher Norris*
Orality and Literacy   *Walter J. Ong*
Science Fiction: Its criticism and teaching   *Patrick Parrinder*
The Unusable Past: Theory and the study of American
    literature   *Russell J. Reising*
Narrative Fiction: Contemporary poetics   *Shlomith Rimmon-Kenan*
Criticism in Society   *Imre Salusinszky*
Re-reading English   ed. *Peter Widdowson*
Metafiction   *Patricia Waugh*
Psychoanalytic Criticism   *Elizabeth Wright*
The Empire Writes Back: Theory and practice in post-colonial
    literature   *Bill Ashcroft, Gareth Griffiths, and Helen Tiffin*
Dialogue and Difference: English into the nineties   *Peter Brooker
    and Peter Humm*
English and Englishness   *Brian Doyle*

The Politics of Postmodernism

LINDA HUTCHEON

ROUTLEDGE
London and New York

First published 1989
by Routledge
11 New Fetter Lane, London EC4P 4EE
29 West 35th Street, New York, NY 10001

© *1989 Linda Hutcheon*

Photoset by Rowland Phototypesetting Ltd,
Bury St Edmunds, Suffolk
Printed in Great Britain by Richard Clay,
Bungay, Suffolk

British Library Cataloguing in Publication Data

Hutcheon, Linda
    The politics of postmodernism. – (New accents)
    1. Culture.   Postmodernism
    I. Title   II. Series
    306

Library of Congress Cataloging in Publication Data

Hutcheon, Linda
    The politics of postmodernism.
    (New accents)
    Bibliography: p.
    Includes index.
    1. Fiction – 20th century – History and criticism.
2. Postmodernism.   3. Photography and literature.
I. Title.   II. Series: New accents (Routledge (Firm))
PN3503.H84   1989   809.3'04   89-5904

ISBN 0 415 03991 6
ISBN 0 415 03992 4 (pbk.)

Contents

General editor's preface   vii

Acknowledgements   ix

1   Representing the postmodern   1

    What is postmodernism?   1

    Representation and its politics   2

    Whose postmodernism?   11

    Postmodernity, postmodernism, and modernism   23

2   Postmodernist representation   31

    De-naturalizing the natural   31

    Photographic discourse   42

    Telling stories: fiction and history   47

3   Re-presenting the past   62

    'Total history' de-totalized   62

Knowing the past in the present   70

The archive as text   78

4   The politics of parody   93

Parodic postmodern representation   93

Double-coded politics   101

Postmodern film?   107

5   Text/image border tensions   118

The paradoxes of photography   118

The ideological arena of photo-graphy   124

The politics of address   134

6   Postmodernism and feminisms   141

Politicizing desire   141

Feminist postmodernist parody   151

The private and the public   160

Concluding note: some directed reading   169

Bibliography   171

Index   189

General editor's preface

It is easy to see that we are living in a time of rapid and radical social change. It is much less easy to grasp the fact that such change will inevitably affect the nature of those disciplines that both reflect our society and help to shape it.

Yet this is nowhere more apparent than in the central field of what may, in general terms, be called literary studies. Here, among large numbers of students at all levels of education, the erosion of the assumptions and presuppositions that support the literary disciplines in their conventional form has proved fundamental. Modes and categories inherited from the past no longer seem to fit the reality experienced by a new generation.

New Accents is intended as a positive response to the initiative offered by such a situation. Each volume in the series will seek to encourage rather than resist the process of change; to stretch rather than reinforce the boundaries that currently define literature and its academic study.

Some important areas of interest immediately present themselves. In various parts of the world, new methods of analysis have been developed whose conclusions reveal the limitations of the Anglo-American outlook we inherit. New concepts of literary forms and modes have been proposed; new notions of the nature of literature itself and of how it communicates are current; new views of literature's role in relation to society flourish. *New Accents* will aim to expound and comment upon the most notable of these.

In the broad field of the study of human communication, more and more emphasis has been placed upon the nature and function of the new electronic media. *New Accents* will try to identify and discuss the challenge these offer to our traditional modes of critical response.

The same interest in communication suggests that the series should also concern itself with those wider anthropological and sociological areas of investigation which have begun to involve scrutiny of the nature of art itself and of its relation to our whole way of life. And this will ultimately require attention to be focused on some of those activities which in our society have hitherto been excluded from the prestigious realms of Culture. The disturbing realignment of values involved and the disconcerting nature of the pressures that work to bring it about both constitute areas that *New Accents* will seek to explore.

Finally, as its title suggests, one aspect of *New Accents* will be firmly located in contemporary approaches to language, and a continuing concern of the series will be to examine the extent to which relevant branches of linguistic studies can illuminate specific literary areas. The volumes with this particular interest will nevertheless presume no prior technical knowledge on the part of their readers, and will aim to rehearse the linguistics appropriate to the matter in hand, rather than to embark on general theoretical matters.

Each volume in the series will attempt an objective exposition of significant developments in its field up to the present as well as an account of its author's own views of the matter. Each will culminate in an informative bibliography as a guide to further study. And, while each will be primarily concerned with matters relevant to its own specific interests, we can hope that a kind of conversation will be heard to develop between them; one whose accents may perhaps suggest the distinctive discourse of the future.

TERENCE HAWKES

Acknowledgements

This book should probably be entitled *Re-presenting Postmodernism*, for it literally presents once again certain core notions about the postmodern that I first developed in different contexts and with a different focus in two earlier studies – *A Poetics of Postmodernism: History, Theory, Fiction* (1988) and *The Canadian Postmodern: A Study of Contemporary English–Canadian Fiction* (1988). But what was missing from both these books is the subject of this one: that is, a general introductory overview of both postmodernism and its politics and an investigation of their challenges to the notion of representation in the verbal and visual arts.

In the other books, I always thanked my spouse, Michael Hutcheon, *last*, but this time my debt to him must be acknowledged from the start, for he is in a very real sense responsible for this work: his talent as a photographer and his abiding interest in photography as an art form and a semiotic practice provide the background for this entire book. In addition, his continued support and enthusiasm, his critical acumen and his fine sense of humor and his *aequinimitas* have never been more welcome. To him therefore go my deepest gratitude and affection.

Because of the cumulative nature of this study, I feel I ought also to thank once again all those I have already mentioned by name in the first two books – all those colleagues, students, and friends, all those artists, critics, and theorists who have contributed to my understanding of postmodernism and to the sheer enjoyment I have experienced working on these projects. I hope they will accept one more time my thanks, this time collectively. A special debt is owed to Terry Hawkes whose idea this book was and whose wit, warmth, and wisdom make him the fine editor and critic he is. To Janice Price, as always, my sincerest thanks for her unfailing confidence and friendship. Finally I must express my gratitude to the Isaac Walton Killam Foundation of the Canada Council whose Research Fellowship (1986–8) enabled this and the other books to be written: the generosity and faith the foundation shows toward its fellows makes scholarly work particularly rewarding.

Some of the ideas in this book have appeared elsewhere in print, though usually with a very different focus, depending on the occasion and the state of development of the ideas at the time of writing. I would like to thank the editors and publishers of the following journals and collections of essays for their support of work in progress: *Texte*; *Signature: A Journal of Theory and Canadian Literature*; *Style* (special issue editor: Mieke Bal); *Canadian Review of Comparative Literature* (special issue editor: Alain Goldschläger); *Quarterly Review of Film and Video* (ed. Ronald Gottesman); *Bulletin of the Humanities Institute at Stony Brook* (ed. E. Ann Kaplan); *Postmodernism* (ed. Hans Bertens, London: Macmillan); *Intertextuality* (ed. Heinrich F. Plett, Berlin and New York: Walter de Gruyter).

Special thanks go to the early audiences who helped me refine these ideas through their acute and discerning responses and to those who invited me to speak at their conferences or universities: SUNY-Stony Brook (E. Ann Kaplan); University of Western Ontario (Martin Kreiswirth); Queen's University (Clive Thomson); Toronto Semiotic Circle (Ian Lancashire); Victoria College (Barbara Havercroft) and University College (Hans de Groot), University of Toronto; International Summer Institute for Semiotic and Structural Studies (Paul Bouissac); McMaster University (Nina Kolesnikoff); American Comparative Literature Association (Daniel Javitch).

Representing the postmodern

What is postmodernism?

Few words are more used and abused in discussions of contemporary culture than the word 'postmodernism.' As a result, any attempt to define the word will necessarily and simultaneously have both positive and negative dimensions. It will aim to say what postmodernism is but at the same time it will have to say what it is not. Perhaps this is an appropriate condition, for postmodernism is a phenomenon whose mode is resolutely contradictory as well as unavoidably political.

Postmodernism manifests itself in many fields of cultural endeavor – architecture, literature, photography, film, painting, video, dance, music, and elsewhere. In general terms it takes the form of self-conscious, self-contradictory, self-undermining statement. It is rather like saying something whilst at the same time putting inverted commas around what is being said. The effect is to highlight, or 'highlight,' and to subvert, or 'subvert,' and the mode is therefore a 'knowing' and an ironic – or even 'ironic' – one. Postmodernism's distinctive character lies in this kind of wholesale 'nudging' commitment to doubleness, or duplicity. In many ways it is an even-handed process because postmodernism ultimately manages to install and reinforce as much as undermine and subvert the conventions and presuppositions it appears to challenge. Nevertheless, it seems reasonable to say that the postmodern's initial concern is to de-naturalize some of the dominant features of our way of life; to point out that those entities that we unthinkingly experience as 'natural' (they might even include capitalism, patriarchy, liberal humanism) are in fact 'cultural'; made by us, not given to us. Even nature, postmodernism might point out, doesn't grow on trees.

This kind of definition may seem to run counter to the majority of those discussed in the opening chapter of this book. But its roots lie in the sphere in which the term 'postmodern' first found general usage: architecture. And there we find a further contradiction. It is one which juxtaposes and gives equal value to the self-reflexive and the historically grounded: to that which is inward-directed and belongs to the world of art (such as parody) and that which is outward-directed and belongs to 'real life' (such as history). The tension between these apparent opposites finally defines the paradoxically worldly texts of postmodernism. And it sparks, just as powerfully, their no less real, if ultimately compromised politics. Indeed it is their compromised stance which makes those politics recognizable and familiar to us. After all, their mode – that of complicitous critique – is for the most part our own.

Representation and its politics

A decade or so ago a German writer stated: 'I cannot keep politics out of the question of post-modernism' (Müller 1979: 58). Nor should he. The intervening years have shown that politics and postmodernism have made curious, if inevitable, bedfellows. For one thing, the debates on the definition and evaluation of the postmodern have been conducted largely in political – and negative – terms: primarily neoconservative (Newman 1985; Kramer 1982) and neoMarxist (Eagleton 1985; Jameson 1983, 1984a). Others on the left (Caute 1972; Russell 1985) have seen, instead, its radical political *potential*, if not actuality, while feminist artists and theorists have resisted the incorporation of their work into postmodernism for fear of recuperation and the attendant de-fusing of their own political agendas.

While these debates will not be the main focus of this study, they do form its unavoidable background. This is not so much a book about the representation of politics as an investigation of what postmodern theorist and photographer Victor Burgin calls the 'politics of representation' (Burgin 1986b: 85). Roland Barthes once claimed that it is impossible to represent the political, for it resists all mimetic copying. Rather, he said, 'where politics begins is where imitation ceases' (Barthes 1977b: 154). And this is where the self-reflexive, parodic art of the postmodern comes in, underlining in its ironic way the realization that all cultural forms of representation – literary, visual, aural – in high art or the mass media are ideologically grounded, that they cannot avoid involvement with social and political relations and apparatuses (Burgin 1986b: 55).

In saying this, I realize that I am going against a dominant trend in contemporary criticism that asserts that the postmodern is disqualified from political involvement because of its narcissistic and ironic appropriation of existing images and stories and its seemingly limited accessibility – to those who recognize the sources of parodic appropriation and understand the theory that motivates it. But, what this study of the forms and politics of postmodern representation aims to show is that such a stand is probably politically naive and, in fact, quite impossible to take in the light of the actual art of postmodernism. Postmodern art cannot but be political, at least in the sense that its representations – its images and stories – are anything but neutral, however 'aestheticized' they may appear to be in their parodic self-reflexivity. While the postmodern has no effective theory of agency that enables a move into political action, it does work to turn its inevitable ideological grounding into a site of de-naturalizing critique. To adapt Barthes's general notion of the 'doxa' as public opinion or the 'Voice of Nature' and consensus (Barthes 1977b: 47), postmodernism works to 'de-doxify' our cultural representations and their undeniable political import.

Umberto Eco has written that he considers postmodern 'the orientation of anyone who has learned the lesson of Foucault, i.e., that power is not something unitary that exists outside us' (in Rosso 1983: 4). He might well have added to this, as others have, the lessons learned from Derrida about textuality and deferral, or from Vattimo and Lyotard about intellectual mastery and its limits. In other words, it is difficult to separate the 'de-doxifying' impulse of postmodern art and culture from the deconstructing impulse of what we have labelled poststructuralist theory. A symptom of this inseparability can be seen in the way in which postmodern artists and critics speak about their 'discourses' – by which they mean to signal the inescapably political contexts in which they speak and work. When discourse is defined as the 'system of relations between parties engaged in communicative activity' (Sekula 1982: 84), it points to politically un-innocent things – like the expectation of shared meaning – and it does so within a dynamic social context that acknowledges the inevitability of the existence of power relations in any social relations. As one postmodern theorist has put it: 'Postmodern aesthetic experimentation should be viewed as having an irreducible political dimension. It is inextricably bound up with a critique of domination' (Wellbery 1985: 235).

Yet, it must be admitted from the start that this is a strange kind of critique, one bound up, too, with its own complicity with power and domination, one that acknowledges that it cannot escape implication in that which it nevertheless still wants to analyze and maybe even undermine. The ambiguities of this kind of position are translated into both the content and the form of postmodern art, which thus at once purveys and challenges ideology – but always self-consciously. The untraditional 'political' novels of Günter Grass, E.L. Doctorow, or any number of Latin American writers today are good examples. So too is Nigel Williams's *Star Turn* in which we find a simultaneous inscription and 'de-doxification' of both bourgeois and Marxist notions of class. The working-class narrator, Amos Barking, likes to hide his class origins: he goes by the name of Henry Swansea at work (in the wartime Ministry of Information). The novel takes place in 1945, however, a year in which, as Amos ironically notes, 'all working-class people are alleged to be heroes (perhaps because they are being killed in extremely large numbers)' (Williams 1985: 15).

This novel never lets its readers forget the issue of class; it never lets us avoid the (often unacknowledged) class assumptions we might possess. While a number of historical personages – Marcel Proust, Douglas Haig, Sigmund Freud – are presented

as (acceptably) mad (thanks to their protective class identities),
Amos announces:

> Difficult as it may seem to you, dear reader, there are
> probably still people out there in the East End of London
> quite unaware that, when worn down by the problems of the
> world, a quick and simple solution is often to lie on a couch
> and talk about one's mother to a highly qualified stranger. In
> 1927 in the Whitechapel area, if you allowed the world to get
> you down, you tended to go and jump under a bus – still a
> popular option for members of the working class foolish
> enough to opt for neurosis.
>
> (Williams 1985: 203)

But what is most obviously postmodern about the politics of this
novel's mode of representation is that it does not stop at an
analysis of class difference: race is shown to enter into complicity with class on both the formal and the thematic levels of
the novel. The plot action revolves around Isaac Rabinowitz,
the Jewish boy who wants to be known as Tom Shadbolt,
all-English lad, and who ends up (ironically and tragically) as a
stand-in look-alike for the fascist and racist Oswald Mosley.
Not only are fiction and history mixed here in what I will argue
to be a typically postmodern way, but class and race and
nationality as well. Difference and ex-centricity replace
homogeneity and centrality as the foci of postmodern social
analysis. But even this focus on the 'marginal' gets called into
question in this self-undercutting novel.

Amos calls England a 'complacent, marginal little kingdom'
(Williams 1985: 17) and its marginality and complacency
mirror his own: he witnesses the First World War from the
sidelines; he meets D.H. Lawrence, Marcel Proust, Virginia
Woolf, Freud, Churchill, Goebbels, Lord Haw Haw (William
Joyce), but somehow always remains peripheral to history.
Fittingly, he spends the Second World War at home cynically
writing propaganda. When he is forced to witness the firebomb-
ing of Dresden, his first reaction, not surprisingly, is evasion:

> Don't think just because I'm British, Anglo-Saxon and the
> rest of it that I am party to all that. I'm not responsible for
> English history, thank you very much. I don't actually like

very much in this rotten little island, including, as it happens, the present war.

(Williams 1985: 304–5)

It is his German Jewish boss, however, who refuses to let him avoid public responsibility, attacking him for feeling he has the liberty (and luxury) in a democracy to decide what is true and what is not (such as the concentration camps). He derides Amos's contempt of history and tries to show him the real pain and atrocity of war: 'You're a typical Englishman. . . . You've a marvellous talent for hypocrisy. You have a way with language that spells away your true feelings' (Williams 1985: 306). The overt self-consciousness about language and (hi)story-writing in the novel is tied directly to the political, as Amos is taught that '[y]ou can't hide behind your country and abuse it at the same time, any more than you can dodge history' (307). And not dodging history would mean taking into account class, race, gender, and nationality. It would mean de-naturalizing English social assumptions about each.

This is the kind of novel – both historical and self-reflexive – that enacts yet another of the ambiguities of the postmodern position. This paradoxical mixing of seeming opposites often results in its representations – be they fictive or historical – being offered as overtly politicized, as inevitably ideological. The conceptual grounding of such a postmodern view of the politics of representation can be found in many theories today. In fact there exists a journal, *boundary 2*, which clearly sees theory, postmodernism, and politics as being at the very heart of its agenda. However, the single most influential theoretical statement on the topic might well be Louis Althusser's much cited notion of ideology both as a system of representation and as a necessary and unavoidable part of every social totality (Althusser 1969: 231–2). Both points are important to any discussion of postmodernism and, indeed, inform the theoretical orientation of this book.

While it may indeed be the case that criticism in the literary and visual arts has traditionally been based on foundations that are expressive (artist-oriented), mimetic (world-imitative), or formalist (art as object), the impact of feminist, gay, Marxist, black, postcolonial, and poststructuralist theory has meant the

de - doxify = denormalize

addition of something else to these historical foundations and
has effected a kind of merger of their concerns, but now with a
new focus: the investigation of the social and ideological production of meaning. From this perspective what we call 'culture' is seen as the *effect* of representations, not their source. Yet,
from another point of view, western capitalist culture has also
shown an amazing power to normalize (or 'doxify') signs and
images, however disparate (or contesting) they may be. The
work of Jean-François Lyotard and Jean Baudrillard has zeroed
in on the socio-economics of our production and reproduction of
signs. These studies have been influential in our understanding
of postmodern culture. But it is specifically the politics of
postmodern representation – the ideological values and interests that inform any representation – that will be the main
focus of this book.

Underlying this notion of a postmodern process of cultural
'de-doxification' is a theoretical position that seems to assert
that we can only know the world through 'a network of socially
established meaning systems, the discourses of our culture'
(Russell 1980: 183). And indeed I have chosen to concentrate
here on two art forms which most self-consciously foreground
precisely this awareness of the discursive and signifying nature
of cultural knowledge and they do so by raising the question of
the supposed transparency of representation. These are fiction
and photography, the two forms whose histories are firmly
rooted in realist representation but which, since their reinter-
pretation in modernist formalist terms, are now in a position to
confront both their documentary and formal impulses. This is
the confrontation that I shall be calling postmodernist: where
documentary historical actuality meets formalist self-reflexivity
and parody. At this conjuncture, a study of representation
becomes, not a study of mimetic mirroring or subjective projecting, but an exploration of the way in which narratives and
images structure how we see ourselves and how we construct
our notions of self, in the present and in the past.

Of course, the postmodern return both to figuration in painting and to narrative in avant-garde film has had an important
impact on the question of representation in photography and
fiction in recent years. Feminist theory and practice have also
problematized the same issue, pointing to the construction of

gender as both the effect and the 'excess' of representation
(de Lauretis 1987: 3). Less obvious, perhaps, but just as significant to postmodernism have been the current debates about
the nature and politics of representation in history-writing
(LaCapra 1985, 1987; White 1973, 1978b, 1987). Of course
many other factors must be taken into account, but generally
speaking, the postmodern appears to coincide with a general
cultural awareness of the existence and power of systems of
representation which do not *reflect* society so much as *grant*
meaning and value within a particular society.

However, if we believe current social scientific theory, there is
a paradox involved in this awareness. On the one hand, there is
a sense that we can never get out from under the weight of a long
tradition of visual and narrative representations and, on the
other hand, we also seem to be losing faith in both the inexhaus-
tibility and the power of those existing representations. And
parody is often the postmodern form this particular paradox
takes. By both using and ironically abusing general conventions
and specific forms of representation, postmodern art works to
de-naturalize them, giving what Rosalind Krauss has called the
strange sense of 'loosening the glue by which labels used to
adhere to the products of convention' (Krauss 1979: 121). I am
not referring here to the kind of ahistorical kitsch seen in some
New York or Toronto restaurants or at Disneyland; rather, the
postmodern parody in the work of Salman Rushdie or Angela
Carter or Manuel Puig has become one of the means by which
culture deals with both its social concerns and its aesthetic
needs – and the two are not unrelated.

A slight detour is in order before proceeding, because I do not
want to give the impression that representation is *not* problematized by other forms of postmodern art. As the next section will
show, I want to model postmodernism in general on the example of postmodern architecture, where it is not just the representation of the historical past of architectural styles that gets
de-naturalized, but also, e.g. in the work of Lars Lerup, even the
representational notions of 'house' and the (North American)
economic and social structures that engender them. Those
social concerns and aesthetic needs once again come together in
an interrogation of the ideology of the stable family unit and of
the 'built as the vehicle of referentiality' (Lerup 1987: 99).

Much has been written about postmodernism in architecture (see bibliography entries on Jencks and Portoghesi) and of course the term 'postmodern' itself has been extended to cover most other art forms, as shown best by Stanley Trachtenberg's useful anthology of studies, *The Postmodern Moment: A Handbook of Contemporary Innovation in the Arts*. In some art forms, such as film, the word postmodern is often restricted to avant-garde production. But, given the relative inaccessibility of such films for general viewing, perhaps we should not ignore those commercial films that are nevertheless quite deconstructive, quite parodic yet historically grounded – films like *Zelig*, *The Mozart Brothers*, or *Marlene* – for they could be said to illustrate just as well the paradox of postmodern complicitous critique. This is not to deny that feminist avant-garde film, in particular, is not equally (or more) parodically contesting. We need only think of the miming of Kleist's play in Peter Wollen and Laura Mulvey's *Penthesilea* or Sally Potter's retelling of *La Bohème* in her *Thriller*. This is simply a plea to widen the scope of the term postmodernism in film studies, in order to include, for instance, the sorts of things which (under the influence, perhaps, of performance art) are considered postmodern in dance: 'irony, playfulness, historical reference, the use of vernacular materials, the continuity of cultures, an interest in process over product, breakdowns of boundaries between art forms and between art and life, and new relationships between artist and audience' (Banes 1985: 82). (See chapter 4.)

'Postmodern' is a term that is not used very often in music criticism, yet there are analogies between postmodern architecture or dance and contemporary music: in music too we find a stress on communication with the audience through simple repetitive harmonies (offered in complex rhythmic forms) in the work of Phil Glass or through a parodic return to tonality and to the past of music, not as a source of embarrassment or inspiration, but with ironic distance, as in the work of Lukas Foss or Luciano Berio. What I shall argue to be typically postmodern genre-boundary crossings can also be found in music: Phil Glass's *The Photographer* is a dramatic musical piece on the life and work of photographer Eadweard Muybridge. And, going in another direction, his 'cross-over' *Songs from Liquid Days* is both a song cycle and a pop album. Much of what might be called postmodern music requires of its listeners a certain theoretical sophistication and historical memory. So too does the postmodern poetry of John Ashbery and others. There are other art forms that operate more directly (if equally self-consciously) on the representations of mass culture which surround us daily, such as the plays of Sam Shepard.

The one medium that is consistently referred to as postmodern, however, is television. Jean Baudrillard calls it the paradigmatic form of postmodern signification because its transparent sign seemingly offers direct access to a signified reality. While there is some truth in this description, its relation to postmodernism as I see it is tangential. Most television, in its *unproblematized* reliance on realist narrative and transparent representational conventions, is pure commodified complicity, without the critique needed to define the postmodern paradox. That critique, I will argue, is crucial to the definition of the postmodern, whatever its acknowledged complicity; it is part of what some see as the unfinished project of the 1960s, for, at the very least, those years left in their wake a specific and historically determined distrust of ideologies of power and a more general suspicion of the power of ideology.

The word 'postmodernism' has been bandied about in artistic circles since the 1960s, of course, most often used too generally and vaguely to be very useful, encompassing things as diverse as Susan Sontag's camp, Leslie Fiedler's pop, and Ihab Hassan's literature of silence. Gerald Graff has distinguished two strains in the 1960s' version of 'postmodernism' – one of apocalyptic despair and another of visionary celebration. But the postmodernism of the 1970s and 1980s offers little cause for either despair or celebration; it does leave a lot of room for questioning. Deriving its ideological grounding from a general 1960s' challenging of authority and its historical consciousness (and conscience) from the inscription into history of women and ethnic/racial minorities during those years, today's postmodernism is both interrogative in mode and 'de-doxifying' in intent. But, less oppositional and less idealistic than the culture of the (formative) 1960s, the postmodern we know has to acknowledge its own complicity with the very values upon which it seeks to comment.

But what exactly is this 'postmodern we know?'

Whose postmodernism?

In his book, *Postmodernist Fiction*, Brian McHale points out that every critic 'constructs' postmodernism in his or her own way from different perspectives, none more right or wrong than the others. The point is that all are 'finally fictions.' He goes on to say:

> Thus, there is John Barth's postmodernism, the literature of replenishment; Charles Newman's postmodernism, the literature of an inflationary economy; Jean-François Lyotard's postmodernism, a general condition of knowledge in the contemporary informational régime; Ihab Hassan's postmodernism, a stage on the road to the spiritual unification of humankind; and so on. There is even Kermode's construction of postmodernism, which in effect constructs it right out of existence.
>
> (McHale 1987: 4)

To this, we could add McHale's postmodernism, with its ontological 'dominant' in reaction to the epistemological 'dominant' of modernism. But we should also include Fredric Jameson's postmodernism, the cultural logic of late capitalism; Jean Baudrillard's postmodernism, in which the simulacrum gloats over the body of the deceased referent; Kroker and Cook's (related) hyperreal dark side of postmodernism; Sloterdijk's postmodernism of cynicism or 'enlightened false consciousness'; and Alan Wilde's literary 'middle grounds' of the postmodern.

As you will no doubt have noticed, since the prefatory note there is another fiction or construct operating here too: my own paradoxical postmodernism of complicity and critique, of reflexivity and historicity, that at once inscribes and subverts the conventions and ideologies of the dominant cultural and social forces of the twentieth-century western world. My model for this definition is always that of postmodern architecture and its response to the ahistorical purism of the modernism of the International Style. Modernism may have begun as an ideological rejection of the historical city because of the dominant class view of territoriality and of history as hierarchical, but its deliberate break with history meant a destruction of the connection to the way human society had come to relate to space over time. Along with this came a rupture of the relations between public street and private space. All this was intentional, but it also proved to be politically naive and even socially destructive: Le Corbusier's great radiant city became Jane Jacobs's great dead city. Postmodernism has called into question the messianic faith of modernism, the faith that technical innovation and purity of form can assure social order, even if that faith disregards the social and aesthetic values of those who must inhabit those modernist buildings. Postmodern architecture is plural and historical, not pluralist and historicist; it neither ignores nor condemns the long heritage of its built culture – including the modern. It uses the reappropriated forms of the past to speak to a society from within the values and history of that society, while still questioning it. It is in this way that its historical representations, however parodic, get politicized.

To make this claim is not to deny the all too evident, trendy commercial exploitation of these postmodern parodic strategies in contemporary design: hardly a shopping plaza or office building gets constructed today that does not have a classical keystone or column. These usually vague and unfocused references to the past should be distinguished from the motivated historical echoes found, for example, in Charles Moore's Piazza d'Italia, intended as a center for the Italian community of New Orleans: to signal 'Italianness' Moore respectfully parodied the Trevi Fountain, Roman classical arches, even the geographical shape of the country itself, transcoding their historical forms into contemporary materials (neon, stainless steel) as befits a symbolic representation of modern Italian–American society. No doubt Douglas Davis (1987) is right to deplore the existence of those kitschy shopping plazas or even the gratuitous (or unconsciously ironic?) architectural citations of the Acropolis and the Vatican in a (Kohn Pedersen Fox) Madison Avenue office complex. But we should not forget that this commodification (and demotivating) of postmodern strategies was preceded by the same watering-down of heroic modern ideals by what could be called 'corporate modernism.' Such is life in advanced capitalist culture. But the inevitability of commercial co-option should still not invalidate the aims and successes of either modernism or postmodernism. Nor should it excuse their failings.

However our culture may eventually come to evaluate postmodern architecture, it certainly began and has continued to be seen by many as politically inspired. The only disagreement is over the direction of its politics: is it neoconservatively nostalgic or is it radically revolutionary? Modeling postmodernism as a general cultural enterprise from postmodern architecture, I would have to argue that it is both and neither: it sits on the fence between a need (often ironic) to recall the past of our lived cultural environment and a desire (often ironized too) to change its present. In Anne Friedberg's parodic terms, there is here a paradox worthy of Dickens: 'it was conservative politics, it was subversive politics, it was the return of tradition, it was the final revolt of tradition, it was the unmooring of patriarchy, it was the reassertion of patriarchy' (Friedberg 1988: 12). This is the paradox of art forms that want to (or feel they have to) speak to a culture from inside it, that believe this to be the only way to reach that culture and make it question its values and its self-constructing representations. Postmodernism aims to be accessible through its overt and self-conscious parodic, historical, and reflexive forms and thus to be an effective force in our culture. Its complicitous critique, then, situates the postmodern squarely within both economic capitalism and cultural humanism – two of the major dominants of much of the western world.

What these two dominants have in common, as many have pointed out, are their patriarchal underpinnings. They also share a view of the relation of the individual to the social whole which is rather contradictory, to say the least. In the context of humanism, the individual is unique and autonomous, yet also partakes of that general human essence, human nature. In a capitalist context, as Adorno argued, the pretence of individualism (and thus, of choice) is in fact proportional to the 'liquidation of the individual' (Adorno 1978: 280) in mass manipulation, carried out, of course, in the name of democratic ideals – the masks of conformity. If, as is frequently the case, postmodernism is identified with a 'decentering' of this particular notion of the individual, then both humanist and capitalist notions of selfhood or subjectivity will necessarily be called into question. But I have been arguing that the postmodern involves a paradoxical installing as well as subverting of conventions – including conventions of the representation of the subject. The complicitous inscribing is as evident as the subverting challenge in, for example, Cindy Sherman's early self-posed self-portraits modeled on Hollywood film stills. They are considerably less complicitous than Madonna's appropriation of the same (masculine-coded) images in *her* self-construction, in that Sherman's images foreground femininity as construction and even masquerade (Friedberg 1988), but they are hardly innocent or uncompromised.

Recently the same kind of questions about the complicity that goes hand in hand with the challenges of postmodern art have been asked of postmodern theory. Is the theorizing of Derrida, Lacan, Lyotard, Foucault, and others not, in a very real sense, entangled in its own de-doxifying logic? Is there not a center to even the most decentered of these theories? What is power to Foucault, writing to Derrida, or class to Marxism? Each of these theoretical perspectives can be argued to be deeply – and knowingly – implicated in that notion of center they attempt to subvert. It is this paradox that makes them postmodern. Teresa de Lauretis has put the case of the feminist version of this paradox in terms of the 'subject of feminism,' as it is being constructed in feminist discourse today, being both inside and outside the ideology of gender – and aware of the double pull (de Lauretis 1987: 10). But complicity is not full affirmation or strict adherence; the awareness of difference and contradiction, of being inside and outside, is never lost in the feminist, as in the postmodern.

A few examples of the form this paradox can take might be helpful. Sherrie Levine challenges the romantic/modernist notions of self-expression, authenticity, and originality (as well as the capitalist belief in proprietorship) in her re-photographing of famous art photos by male artists. However, as her critics never tire of saying, in her representations she still remains complicitous with the idea of 'photography-as-art,' even while undermining both this and those attendant ideological presuppositions. Narrative representation – fictive and historical – comes under similar subversive scrutiny in the paradoxical postmodern form I would like to call 'historiographic metafiction.' Perhaps, as Lennard Davis (1987: 225) has convincingly

argued, the novel has been inherently ambivalent since its
inception: it has always been both fictional and worldly. If this is
so, then postmodern historiographic metafiction merely foregrounds this inherent paradox by having its historical and
socio-political grounding sit uneasily alongside its self-
reflexivity. Recently, many commentators have noticed an
uneasy mix of parody and history, metafiction and politics. This
particular combination is probably historically determined by
postmodernism's conflictual response to literary modernism.
On the one hand, the postmodern obviously was made possible
by the self-referentiality, irony, ambiguity, and parody that
characterize much of the art of modernism, as well as by its
explorations of language and its challenges to the classic realist
system of representation; on the other hand, postmodern fiction
has come to contest the modernist ideology of artistic autonomy, individual expression, and the deliberate separation of art
from mass culture and everyday life (Huyssen 1986: 53–4).

Postmodernism paradoxically manages to legitimize culture
(high and mass) even as it subverts it. It is this doubleness that
avoids the danger Jameson (1985: 52) sees in the subverting or
deconstructing impulse operating alone: that is, the danger (for
the critic) of the illusion of critical distance. It is the function of
irony in postmodern discourse to posit that critical distance and
then undo it. It is also this doubleness that prevents any possible
critical urge to ignore or trivialize historical-political questions.
As producers or receivers of postmodern art, we are all implicated in the legitimization of our culture. Postmodern art
openly investigates the critical possibilities open to art, without
denying that its critique is inevitably in the name of its own
contradictory ideology.

I have offered my definition of postmodernism here at the
start because it will unavoidably condition everything I say
about postmodern representation in this study. Many a theorist
has noted the problems of saying anything enlightening about
postmodernism without acknowledging the perspective from
which it is said, a perspective that will inevitably be limited, if
only because it will come from within the postmodern. The
postmodern is seemingly not so much a concept as a problematic: 'a complex of heterogeneous but interrelated questions
which will not be silenced by any spuriously *unitary* answer'

(Burgin 1986a: 163–4). The political and the artistic are not separable in this problematic. This is not always considered a positive, of course. For the neoconservative critic, postmodernism is fundamentally destabilizing, a threat to the preservation of tradition (and the status quo). But when Charles Newman in *The Postmodern Aura* accuses the postmodern of fearing stability, he mistakes stability for what he himself calls stasis. It is indeed the case that the postmodern does not advocate the 'restoration of faith in institutions' (Newman 1985: 107), as Newman desires, but it refuses to do so because it must ask important questions instead: In whose institutions will faith be restored? In whose interest will such a restoration be? Do these institutions deserve our faith? Can they be changed? Should they be? While postmodernism may offer no answers, these are questions perhaps worth asking – or so goes the lesson of the 1960s. In other words, it is not postmodernism (at least, as I have been defining it) that masks stasis, as Newman claims (184), but rather neoconservativism – which does so in the name of stability and tradition. This kind of confusion of definition offers a good example of the difficulties involved in discussing postmodernism in general: no one seems to be able to agree, not only on the interpretation, but often on what cultural phenomena are to be interpreted.

Nevertheless, we do seem to be stuck with the word. While 'fastidious academics' once shunned the term 'postmodernism,' as Ihab Hassan has noted, now it has become 'a shibboleth for tendencies in film, theater, dance, music, art, and architecture; in literature and criticism; in philosophy, theology, psychoanalysis, and historiography; in new sciences, cybernetic technologies, and various cultural life styles' (Hassan 1987: xi). The history and complexity of the term's usage have been carefully traced by many scholars working in architecture, in the visual arts, in literature and criticism, and in social and cultural studies in general (see the Concluding Note, p. 169). There is little sense repeating here this fine work, just as there is little sense in trying to find a definition of postmodernism that would encompass all the varying usages of the term. That route would only lead to further confusion and contribute to the already apparent lack of clarity and consistency of meaning in the use of the word. Instead this study offers an investigation of one particular definition of postmodernism from the point of view of its politicized challenges to the conventions of representation.

Whatever the confusion over the definition of the term, however, in terms of evaluation there are two clearly opposed 'camps' in the postmodern wars: the radically antagonistic and the provisionally supportive. The tone of the former group ranges from sly irony to rabid rage. Curiously, this camp encompasses the opposition of the neoconservative right, the liberal center, and the Marxist left. However positioned politically, the objections seem to be consistently to what are perceived as, on the one hand, the ahistoricism and pastiched depthlessness of the postmodern and, on the other, its crossing of boundaries of genre and discourse once considered discrete and firm. While these objections will be addressed in specific chapters later in this study, it should be noted here that this camp tends to see only the complicity and never the critique – yet together these two are constitutive of the postmodern as I have been defining it. Furthermore, as many commentators have remarked, the often unconscious ethnocentrism and phallocentrism (not to mention heterocentrism) of many in this camp lead to a devaluing or ignoring of the 'marginalized' challenges (aesthetic and political) of the 'ex-centric,' those relegated to the fringes of the dominant culture – the women, blacks, gays, Native Peoples, and others who have made us aware of the politics of all – not just postmodern – representations.

The work of those provisionally or tentatively supportive of postmodernism ranges from descriptive accounts of the postmodern in terms of its incredulity toward grand totalizing narratives to more tendentiously rueful acknowledgements that we are all part of the postmodern, whether we like it or not. Few critics outside the field of architecture seem willing to be thoroughly positive about postmodernism: its complicity always interferes with their evaluation of the efficacy of its critique. Hal Foster deals with the political ambivalence of the postmodern by positing two kinds: one, a postmodernism of resistance, and the other, of reaction, one poststructuralist and the other neoconservative (Foster 1985: 121). I would argue that the postmodern enterprise actually includes both Foster's types: it is a critique both of the view of representation as reflective (rather than as constitutive) of reality and of the accepted idea of 'man' as the centered subject of representation; but it is also an exploitation of those same challenged foundations of representation. Postmodern texts paradoxically point to the opaque nature of their representational strategies and at the same time to their complicity with the notion of the transparency of representation – a complicity shared, of course, by anyone who pretends even to describe their 'de-doxifying' tactics.

Many of the disagreements about the evaluation of postmodern strategies can be seen as the result of a denial of the doubleness of postmodernist discourse's politics of representation. To Alan Wilde, irony is a positive and defining characteristic of the postmodern; to Terry Eagleton, irony is what condemns postmodernism to triviality and kitsch. To some, postmodernism's inevitable implication in the high art/mass culture debate is significant; to others, it is lamentable. To M.H. Abrams (1981: 110), the 'irresolvable indeterminacies' by which he defines the postmodern are implicitly related to meaninglessness and the undermining of cultural foundations, whereas to Ihab Hassan those same indeterminacies are part of 'a vast, revisionary will in the Western world, unsettling/resettling codes, canons, procedures, beliefs' (1987: xvi).

Despite the polarized camps in the evaluation of the postmodern, there does seem to be some agreement about certain of its characteristics. For example, many point to its parody and self-reflexivity; others to the opposite, its worldliness. Some, like myself, want to argue that these two qualities co-exist in an uneasy and problematizing tension that provokes an investigation of how we make meaning in culture, how we 'de-doxify' the systems of meaning (and representation) by which we know our culture and ourselves. The tension between the worldly and the reflexive, the historical and the parodic, acts to remind us of 'the historicity of textuality' (Spanos 1987: 7).

There are other kinds of border tension in the postmodern too: the ones created by the transgression of the boundaries between genres, between disciplines or discourses, between high and mass culture, and most problematically, perhaps, between practice and theory. While there is arguably never any practice without theory, an overtly theoretical component has become a notable aspect of postmodern art, displayed within the works themselves as well as in the artists' statements about their work. The postmodern artist is no longer the inarticulate, silent, alienated creator of the romantic/modernist tradition. Nor is the theorist the dry, detached, dispassionate writer of the academic tradition: think of Peter Sloterdijk's *Critique of Cynical Reason* with its mixture of satire, complex philosophical discourse, aphoristic play, anecdote, and the history of ideas and of literature.

There is little doubt that a certain kind of theory has supported and even created a certain kind of art and that the academy, art institutions, and the publishing industry have, in part, *constructed* postmodernism. As an editor of *October*, a curator, and a critic, Douglas Crimp has effectively defined photographic postmodernism (Andre 1984: 18–20). But so have Victor Burgin, Barbara Kruger, Martha Rosler, Allan Sekula, and others who both theorize and make the photographs that I want to call postmodern. We should perhaps also keep in mind that art has never been free of institutional constraints and even construction – not even (or especially not) the so-called autonomous art of modernism. We need only think of the role of New York's Museum of Modern Art in the promotion and validation of both abstract expressionist painting and formalist art-photography.

Many have pointed to the recent conjuncture of postmodern art and either poststructuralist or psychoanalytic theory, but few have noted the even more important impact of various forms of feminism on the need to investigate the complexity of aesthetic/political interactions on the level of representation (see, however, Owens 1983 and Creed 1987). Given the focus of this book on the politics of representation, a feminist perspective has proved to be literally unavoidable. As Andreas Huyssen puts it:

The ways in which we now raise questions of gender and sexuality, reading and writing, subjectivity and enunciation, voice and performance are unthinkable without the impact of feminism, even though many of these activities may take place on the margin or even outside the movement proper.

(Huyssen 1986: 220)

Feminist perspectives have brought about a major shift in our ways of thinking about culture, knowledge, and art and also about the way in which the political impinges upon and infuses all of our thinking and acting, both public and private.

Yet there has been considerable resistance to any identification of the postmodern with the feminist. There has been an understandable suspicion of the deconstructing and undermining impulse of postmodernism at a historic moment when construction and support seem more important agendas for women. Yet, as the work of Christa Wolf, Angela Carter, Susan Daitch, Audrey Thomas, and Maxine Hong Kingston shows, 'de-doxification' is as inherently a part of feminist as it is of postmodernist discourse. This is not to deny the gender blindness of much postmodern writing. But many writers, from John Berger to Margaret Atwood, are set upon investigating the perhaps unavoidable binary opposition of gender. For example, in Christa Wolf's *No Place on Earth*, two historical personages – a man and a woman, the poets Kleist and Günderrode – are made to meet in fictional space. Their initial perception of the gender roles they must each fulfil differs. Kleist looks at the woman poet and sees only her security:

> She is provided for, whatever that may mean; she is not compelled to concentrate her thoughts on the most trivial demands of everyday life. It seemed to him a kind of advantage that she has no choice in the matter. As a woman she is not placed under the law of having to achieve everything or to regard everything as nothing.
>
> (Wolf 1982: 107)

Günderrode's version of her fate as a woman is different:

> By the age of seventeen we must have accepted our fate, which is a man, and must learn to accept the penalty should we behave so improbably as to resist. How often I have wanted to be a man, longed for the real wounds, to which you men expose yourselves.
>
> (Wolf 1982: 112)

In fact, as the two poets come to realize, 'man and woman have a hostile relationship' within each of them: 'Woman. Man. Untenable words. We two, each imprisoned in his sex' (108). The postmodern and feminist reply to binary oppositions as unresolvable as this one is to problematize, to acknowledge contradiction and difference, and to theorize and actualize the site of their representation.

In the visual arts too, feminist work has meant that representation can no longer be considered a politically neutral and theoretically innocent activity:

> The question of representation locates itself between feminism and art. It is an interrogation into the way the repetition inherent in cultural imagery (whether in visual arts, mass media, or advertising) has the particular ideological function of presenting and positioning 'feminine' or 'masculine' subjectivity as stable and fixed.
>
> (Gagnon 1987: 116)

To accept unquestioningly such fixed representations is to condone social systems of power which validate and authorize some images of women (or blacks, Asians, gays, etc.) and not others. Cultural production is carried on within a social context and an ideology – a lived value system – and it is this that feminist work has helped teach us. In photographic and cinematic art and theory much has been done to investigate the maleness of the representing camera eye. For instance, Mary Kelly's *Post-Partum Document* (1983) stresses the production of sexual difference through systems of representation, while contesting the forms that the mastering male gaze has traditionally created: this is no familiar figuration of the mother/madonna and child, but a visualization through words and objects of the mother–child relationship as a complex psycho-social process that is anything but simple, serene, and natural – at least from a woman's point of view. Similarly, Hans Haacke's fourteen informational panels about Seurat's *Les Poseuses*, tracing the history of the painting's ownership from 1888 to 1975, foreground the tradition of the female nude and the male heterosexual viewer who, through mastering vision, 'possesses' the posed and viewed women as surely as if it were an act of sexual possession, an act analogous to the economic ownership whose history is the subject of Haacke's work. This is art that still works within the conventions of patriarchy, but in order to contest them, for they are now problematized by a new and complex socio-political context.

I have chosen to concentrate in this study on photography, among the visual arts, for much the same reason that I have chosen narrative fiction among the literary: they are equally omnipresent in both high art and mass culture and their very ubiquity has tended to grant their representations both a certain transparency and a definite complexity. What Annette Kuhn says of photography applies, with the appropriate adaptations of medium, to fictive narrative today:

> Representations are productive: photographs, far from merely reproducing a pre-existing world, constitute a highly coded discourse which, among other things, constructs whatever is in the image as object of consumption – consumption by looking, as well as often quite literally by purchase. It is no coincidence, therefore, that in many highly socially visible (and profitable) forms of photography women dominate the image. Where photography takes women as its subject matter, it also constructs 'woman' as a set of meanings which then enter cultural and economic circulation on their own account.

(Kuhn 1985: 19)

Power of the Image

The same is true of its construction of 'man' or of race, ethnicity, or sexual orientation. Postmodern photography and fiction both foreground the productive, constructing aspects of their acts of representing. Nevertheless their political complicity is as evident as their de-naturalizing critique. The difference between the postmodern and the feminist can be seen in the potential quietism of the political ambiguities or paradoxes of postmodernism. The many feminist social agendas demand a theory of agency, but such a theory is visibly lacking in postmodernism, caught as it is in a certain negativity that may be inherent in any critique of cultural dominants. It has no theory of positive action on a social level; all feminist positions do. To 'de-doxify' is not to act, even if it might be a step toward action or even a necessary precondition of it.

This relation between the feminist and the postmodern is the topic of the final chapter of this study, but it is important to note from the start both the impact of the feminist on the postmodern and their shared deconstructing impulses. It is not accidental that postmodernism coincides with the feminist re-evaluation of non-canonical forms of discourse, that a very postmodern auto-biography (*Roland Barthes by Roland Barthes*) and a very postmod-ern family biography (Michael Ondaatje's *Running in the Family*) have a lot in common with Christa Wolf's *Patterns of Childhood* or Maxine Hong Kingston's *The Woman Warrior*. They all not only challenge what we consider to be literature (or rather, Litera-ture) but also what was once assumed to be the seamless, unified narrative representations of subjectivity in life-writing. Of course, it is also not accidental that feminist theory's recent self-positioning both inside and outside dominant ideologies, using representation both to reveal misrepresentation and to offer new possibilities, coincides with the (admittedly more) complicitous critique of postmodernism. Both try to avoid the bad faith of believing they can stand outside ideology, but both want to reclaim their right to contest the power of a dominant one, even if from a compromised position. Victor Burgin has claimed that he wants his art and theory to show the meaning of sexual difference (for others, it is difference of class, race, ethnicity, or sexual preference) as a process of production, as 'something mutable, something historical, and therefore some-thing we can do *something* about' (Burgin 1986a: 108). Post-modernism may not *do* that something, but it may at least show what needs undoing first.

Postmodernity, postmodernism, and modernism

Much of the confusion surrounding the usage of the term postmodernism is due to the conflation of the cultural notion of postmodern*ism* (and its inherent relationship to modernism) and postmodern*ity* as the designation of a social and philo-sophical period or 'condition.' The latter has been variously defined in terms of the relationship between intellectual and state discourses; as a condition determined by universal, diffuse cynicism, by a panic sense of the hyperreal and the simulacrum. The manifest contradictions between some of these desig-nations of postmodernity will not surprise anyone who enjoys generalizations about the present age. Nevertheless many do see postmodernity as involving a critique of humanism and positivism, and an investigation of the relation of both to our notions of subjectivity.

In philosophical circles, postmodernity has been the term used to situate theoretical positions as apparently diverse as Derrida's challenges to the western metaphysics of presence; Foucault's investigations of the complicities of discourse, knowledge, and power; Vattimo's paradoxically potent 'weak thought'; and Lyotard's questioning of the validity of the metanarratives of legitimation and emancipation. In the broadest of terms, these all share a view of discourse as problematic and of ordering systems as suspect (and as humanly constructed). The debate about postmodernity – and the confusion with postmodernism – seems to have begun with the exchange on the topic of modernity between Jürgen Habermas and Jean-François Lyotard. Both agreed that modernity could not be separated from notions of unity and universality or what Lyotard dubbed 'metanarratives.' Habermas argued that the project of modernity, rooted in the context of Enlightenment rationality, was still unfinished and required completion; Lyotard countered with the view that modernity has actually been liquidated by history, a history whose tragic paradigm was the Nazi concentration camp and whose ultimate delegitimizing force was that of capitalist 'technoscience' which has changed for ever our concepts of knowledge. Therefore, for Lyotard, postmodernity is characterized by no grand totalizing narrative, but by smaller and multiple narratives which seek no universalizing stabilization or legitimation. Fredric Jameson has pointed out that both Lyotard and Habermas are clearly working from different, though equally strong, legitimating 'narrative archetypes' – one French and (1789) Revolutionary in inspiration, the other Germanic and Hegelian; one valuing commitment, the other consensus. Richard Rorty has offered a trenchant critique of both positions, ironically noting that what they share is an almost overblown sense of the role of philosophy today. Attempting a more modest role that is ultimately postmodern – that of accepting the complicity of knowledge with power – Rorty's neopragmatism has been seen as bravely trying to bridge the seeming opposites.

In a very real sense, though, such oppositions cannot be bridged quite so easily. Part of the difficulty is a matter of history: modernity in Habermas's Germany could be said to have been cut short by Nazism and thus indeed to be 'incomplete.' It would seem to be for this reason that Habermas opposes what he sees as postmodern historicism: for him, the 'radicalized consciousness of modernity' (Habermas 1983: 4) was able to free itself from history and therein lay its glory and its explosive content. In the specifically German context of this revolutionary view of modernity, the postmodern might well look neoconservative, as Habermas has claimed. But many have objected to Habermas's extension of his critique of local forces of anti-modernity outside that specific German context to include all postmodernity and postmodernism.

Lyotard's challenge to Habermas's definition of the postmodern has also come under serious scrutiny. In his introductory remarks to the English translation of *La Condition Postmoderne*, Jameson makes an attempt to rescue the notion of metanarrative from Lyotard's Habermas-inspired attack, partly because his own notion of postmodernity is itself a metanarrative one, based on Mandel's cultural periodization: in its simplest terms, market capitalism begat realism; monopoly capitalism begat modernism; and therefore multinational capitalism begets postmodernism (Jameson 1984a: 78). The slippage from postmodern*ity* to postmodern*ism* is constant and deliberate in Jameson's work: for him postmodernism *is* the 'cultural logic of late capitalism.' It replicates, reinforces, and intensifies the 'deplorable and reprehensible' (85) socioeconomic effects of postmodernity. Perhaps. But I want to argue that it also critiques those effects, while never pretending to be able to operate outside them.

The slippage to postmodern*ism* from postmodern*ity* is replicated in the very title of Jameson's influential 1984 article, 'Postmodernism, or the cultural logic of late capitalism.' Yet what is confusing is that Jameson retains the word postmodern*ism* for both the socio-economic periodization and the cultural designation. In his more recent work, he is adamant about defining postmodernism as both 'a whole set of aesthetic and cultural features and procedures' and 'the socioeconomic organization of our society commonly called late capitalism'

(Jameson 1986–7: 38–9). While the two are no doubt inextricably related, I would want to argue for their separation in the context of discourse. The verbal similarity of the terms postmodernity and postmodernism signals their relationship overtly enough without either confusing the issue by using the same word to denote both or evading the issue by conflating the two in some sort of transparent causality. The relationship must be *argued*, not *assumed* by some verbal sleight of hand. My exhortation to keep the two separate is conditioned by my desire to show that critique is as important as complicity in the response of cultural postmodernism to the philosophical and socioeconomic realities of postmodernity: postmodernism here is not so much what Jameson sees as a systemic form of capitalism as the name given to cultural practices which acknowledge their inevitable implication in capitalism, without relinquishing the power or will to intervene critically in it.

Habermas, Lyotard, and Jameson, from their very different perspectives, have all raised the important issue of the socioeconomic and philosophical grounding of postmodernism in postmodernity. But to assume an equation of the culture and its ground, rather than allowing for at least the possibility of a relation of contestation and subversion, is to forget the lesson of postmodernism's complex relation to modernism: its retention of modernism's initial oppositional impulses, both ideological and aesthetic, and its equally strong rejection of its founding notion of formalist autonomy.

Much serious scholarly work has already been done on the complexity of the relationship between postmodernism and modernism. Certainly many of the attacks on the postmodern come from the implicit or explicit vantage point of what Walter Moser once wittily called 'a relapsarian modernism.' Others – less negatively – want to root postmodernism historically in the oppositionality of the modernist avant-garde. For the Marxist critic, the attraction of modernism lies in what Jameson calls its 'Utopian compensation' (1981: 42) and its 'commitments to radical change' (1985: 87). While the postmodern has indeed no such impulse, it is none the less fundamentally demystifying and critical, and among the things of which it is critical are modernism's elitist and sometimes almost totalitarian modes of effecting that 'radical change' – from those of Mies van der Rohe to those of Pound and Eliot, not to mention Céline. The oppositional politics to which modernism laid claim were not always leftist, as defenders like Eagleton and Jameson appear to suggest. We must not forget, as Andreas Huyssen has put it, that modernism has also been 'chided by the left as the elitist, arrogant and mystifying master-code of bourgeois culture while demonized by the right as the Agent Orange of natural social cohesion' (Huyssen 1986: 16–17). Huyssen goes on to explain that the historical (or modernist) avant-garde too was, in its turn, condemned by both the right (as a threat to the bourgeois desire for cultural legitimation) and the left (by the Second International's and by Lukács's valorizing of classical bourgeois realism).

Among the crypto-modernist anti-postmodernists, there is a strong sense that postmodernism somehow represents a lowering of standards or that it is the lamentable consequence of the institutionalization and acculturation of the radical potential of modernism. In other words, it would seem to be difficult to discuss postmodernism without somehow engaging in a debate about the value and even identity of modernism. Jameson (1984c: 62) has claimed that there are four possible positions: pro-postmodernist and anti-modernist; pro-postmodernist and pro-modernist; anti-postmodernist and anti-modernist; and anti-postmodernist and pro-modernist. But however you break down the positions, there is still an even more basic underlying opposition between those who believe postmodernism represents a break from modernism, and those who see it in a relation of continuity. The latter position stresses what the two share: their self-consciousness or their reliance, however ironic, on tradition. Contrary to the tendency of some critics to label as typically postmodern both American surfiction and the French texts of *Tel Quel*, I would see these as extensions of modernist notions of autonomy and auto-referentiality and thus as 'late modernist.' These formalist extremes are precisely what are called into question by the historical and social grounding of postmodern fiction and photography. To use Stanley Trachtenberg's terms, the postmodern is not (or perhaps not only) an 'intransitive art, which constitutes an act in itself'; it is also 'transitive or purposive' (in Preface to Trachtenberg 1985: xii). From those committed to a model of rupture rather than continuity between the modernist and the postmodernist come arguments based on any number of fundamental differences: in socio-economic organization; in the aesthetic and moral position of the artist; in the concept of knowledge and its relation to power; in philosophical orientation; in the notion of where meaning inheres in art; in the relation of message to addressee/addresser. For some critics, the modernist and the postmodernist can in fact be opposed point by point (see Hassan 1980b). But one of the most contentious of these points seems to be that of the relation of mass culture to both modernism and postmodernism. The Marxist attacks on the postmodern are often in terms of its conflation of high art and mass culture, a conflation modernism rejected with great firmness. It is precisely this rejection that Andreas Huyssen addresses so cogently in his *After the Great Divide* (1986), arguing that modernism defined itself through the exclusion of mass culture and was driven, by its fear of contamination by the consumer culture burgeoning around it, into an elitist and exclusive view of aesthetic formalism and the autonomy of art. It is certainly the historical avant-garde that prepares the way for postmodernism's renegotiation of the different possible relations (of complicity and critique) between high and popular forms of culture. Huyssen does much to upset the view (presented by Jameson and Eagleton, among others) of mass culture as, in his words, 'the homogeneously sinister background on which the achievements of modernism can shine in their glory' (Huyssen 1986: ix). It is not that the modernist exclusion was not historically understandable in the context of, say, fascist spectacle, but Huyssen claims that this is now a 'historically superseded protest' (x) which needs rethinking precisely in the context of late capitalism.

Much influential work has been done on high/popular cultural oppositions and their interactions in order to show that the crossing of such borders does not necessarily mean the destruction of all order or the intrinsic devaluation of all received ideas, as Charles Newman thinks, or an increasing dehumanization of life, as Jameson seems to believe. There is still a tendency to see ethnic, local, or generally popular forms of art as 'subcultural' (Foster 1985: 25) and it is for this reason that I have deliberately chosen to focus on those two most consistently omnipresent and problematic forms of postmodern representation – still photography and narrative fiction. Between them they constitute a statistically significant number of the representations of both mass culture and high art today. The photography of postmodernism challenges the ideological underpinnings of both the high-art photography of modernism and the mass- (advertising, newspapers, magazines) and popular- (snapshots) cultural photographic forms. It moves out of the hermeticism and narcissism that is always possible in self-referentiality and into the cultural and social world, a world bombarded daily with photographic images. And it manages to point at once to the contingency of art and to the primacy of social codes, making the invisible visible, 'de-doxifying' the doxa – be it either modernist/formalist or realist/documentary. In postmodern fiction, too, the documentary impulse of realism meets the problematizing of reference seen earlier in self-reflexive modernism. Postmodern narrative is filtered through the history of both. And this is where the question of representation and its politics enters.

2

Postmodernist representation

De-naturalizing the natural

> Like every great word, 'representation/s' is a stew. A
> scrambled menu, it serves up several meanings at once. For a
> representation can be an image – visual, verbal, or aural. . . .
> A representation can also be a narrative, a sequence of
> images and ideas. . . . Or, a representation can be the product
> of ideology, that vast scheme for showing forth the world and
> justifying its dealings.
>
> (Stimpson 1988: 223)

Postmodern representation is self-consciously all of these –
image, narrative, product of (and producer of) ideology. It is a
truism of sociology and cultural studies today to say that life in
the postmodern world is utterly mediated through representations and that our age of satellites and computers has gone
well beyond Benjamin's 'Age of Mechanical Reproduction' and
its particular philosophical and artistic consequences and
moved into a state of crisis in representation. Nevertheless, in
literary and art critical circles there is still a tendency to see
postmodern theory and practice either as simply replacing
representation with the idea of textuality or as denying our
intricate involvement with representation, even though much
postmodern thought has disputed this tendency: think of

Derrida's statements about the inescapability of the logic of representation, and Foucault's problematization, though never repudiation, of our traditional modes of representation in our discourses of knowledge.

I suppose the very word 'representation' unavoidably suggests a given which the act of representing duplicates in some way. This is normally considered the realm of mimesis. Yet, by simply making representation into an issue again postmodernism challenges our mimetic assumptions about representation (in any of its 'scrambled menu' meanings): assumptions about its transparency and common-sense naturalness. And it is not just postmodern *theory* that has provoked this rethinking. Take, for instance, Angela Carter's story, 'The Loves of Lady Purple.' The plot details are derived from literalizations of these same mimetic assumptions – and their politics. It begins as the story of a master puppet-maker. The more life-like his marionettes can be made to seem, the more 'god-like' he becomes (Carter 1974: 23). He is said to speculate 'in a no-man's limbo between the real and that which, although we know very well it is not, nevertheless seems to be real' (23). He makes puppets which 'cannot live' yet can 'mimic the living' and even 'project signals of signification.' The precise imitation of these representations is said to be 'all the more disturbing because we know it to be false' (24). His 'didactic vedette,' Lady Purple, is such a success that she is said to have 'transcended the notion she was dependent on his hands and appeared wholly real and yet entirely other' (26). She did not so much imitate as distill and intensify the actions of real women: 'and so she could become the quintessence of eroticism, for no woman born would have dared be so blatantly seductive' (26–7).

The handbills advertising her show speak of her 'unappeaseable appetites,' for she is said to have once been a famous (living) prostitute who, 'pulled only by the strings of lust' (Carter 1974: 28), was reduced to this puppet status. The prostitute's tale is the narrative represented in the show. What Carter's text reveals is that women (as prostitutes, in particular) are never real; they are but representations of male erotic fantasies and of male desire, 'a metaphysical abstraction of the female' (30). Lady Purple was figuratively a puppet even in her living incarnation; she was always 'her own replica' (33) in a sense. The short story ends with the puppet returning to life, sucking her master's breath and drinking his blood. But what does she do with her new-found life and freedom? The only thing she can do: she heads for the brothel in the town. The question we are left with is: 'had the marionette all the time parodied the living or was she, now living, to parody her own performance as a marionette?' (38). But there is another question too: to what extent are all representations of women 'the simulacra of the living' (25)? While there are obvious references in this story to Hoffman's 'Sandman' story and thus to Freud's Uncanny, to Pygmalion and even to Mozart (Lady Purple is called 'Queen of Night'), there is clearly a more contemporary allusion here to Jean Baudrillard's theory of the postmodern simulacrum.

In an article entitled 'The precession of simulacra,' Baudrillard argued that today the mass media have neutralized reality by stages: first they *reflected* it; then they *masked* and perverted it; next they had to *mask its absence*; and finally they produced instead the *simulacrum* of the real, the destruction of meaning and of all relation to reality. Baudrillard's model has come under attack for the metaphysical idealism of its view of the 'real,' for its nostalgia for pre-mass-media authenticity, and for its apocalyptic nihilism. But, as Carter's story suggests, there is a more basic objection to his assumption that it is (or was) ever possible to have unmediated access to reality: have we ever known the 'real' except through representations? We may see, hear, feel, smell, and touch it, but do we *know* it in the sense that we give meaning to it? In Lisa Tickner's succinct terms, the real is '*enabled to mean* through systems of signs organized into discourses on the world' (Tickner 1984: 19). This is obviously where the politics of representation enters for, according to the Althusserian view, ideology is a production of representations. Our common-sense presuppositions about the 'real' depend upon how that 'real' is described, how it is put into discourse and interpreted. There is nothing natural about the 'real' and there never was – even before the existence of mass media.

This said, it is also true that – whatever the naivety of its view of the innocent and stable representation once possible – Baudrillard's notion of the simulacrum has been immensely influential. Witness the unacknowledged but none the less real debt to it in Jameson's own version of pre-mass-media nostalgia:

> In the form of the logic of the image or the spectacle of the simulacrum, everything has become 'cultural' in some sense. A whole new house of mirrors of visual replication and of textual reproduction has replaced the older stable reality of reference and of the non-cultural 'real.'

(Jameson 1986–7: 42)

What postmodern theory and practice together suggest is that everything always was 'cultural' in this sense, that is, always mediated by representations. They suggest that notions of truth, reference, and the non-cultural real have not ceased to exist, as Baudrillard claims, but that they are no longer unproblematic issues, assumed to be self-evident and self-justifying. The postmodern, as I have been defining it, is not a degeneration into 'hyperreality' but a questioning of what reality can mean and how we can come to know it. It is not that representation now dominates or effaces the referent, but rather that it now self-consciously acknowledges its existence as representation – that is, as interpeting (indeed as creating) its referent, not as offering direct and immediate access to it.

This is not to say that what Jameson calls 'the older logic of the referent (or realism)' (1986–7: 43) is not historically important to postmodernist representation. In fact, many postmodern strategies are openly premised on a challenge to the realist notion of representation that presumes the transparency of the medium and thus the direct and natural link between sign and referent or between word and world. Of course, modernist art, in all its forms, challenged this notion as well, but it deliberately did so to the detriment of the referent, that is, by emphasizing the opacity of the medium and the self-sufficiency of the signifying system. What postmodernism does is to de-naturalize both realism's transparency and modernism's reflexive response, while retaining (in its typically complicitously critical way) the historically attested power of both. This is the ambivalent politics of postmodern representation.

With the problematizing and 'de-doxifying' of both realist reference and modernist autonomy, postmodern representation opens up other possible relations between art and the world:

gone is the Benjaminian 'aura' with its notions of originality, authenticity, and uniqueness, and with these go all the taboos against strategies that rely on the parody and reappropriation of already existing representations. In other words, the history of representation itself can become a valid subject of art, and not just its history in high art. The borders between high art and mass or popular culture and those between the discourses of art and the discourses of the world (especially history) are regularly crossed in postmodern theory and practice. But it must be admitted that this crossing is rarely done without considerable border tension.

As we shall see in later chapters, postmodern photography's parodic appropriation of various forms of mass-media representation has come under severe attack by the (still largely modernist) art establishment. The equivalent on the literary scene has been the hostile response of some critics to the mixing of historical and fictive representation in historiographic metafiction. It is not that the fact of the mixing is new: the historical novel, not to mention the epic, should have habituated readers to that. The problem seems to reside in its manner, in the self-consciousness of the fictionality, the lack of the familiar pretence of transparency, and the calling into question of the factual grounding of history-writing. The self-reflexivity of postmodern fiction does indeed foreground many of the usually unacknowledged and naturalized implications of narrative representation. In *The Politics of Reflexivity*, Robert Siegle lists some of these:

> the codes by which we organize reality, the means by which we organize words about it into narrative, the implications of the linguistic medium we use to do so, the means by which readers are drawn into narrative, and the nature of our relation to 'actual' states of reality.
>
> (Siegle 1986: 3)

Siegle further argues that textual reflexivity itself is 'highly charged ideologically precisely because it denaturalizes far more than merely literary codes and pertains to more than the aesthetic "heterocosm" to which some theorists might wish to restrict it' (11). In other words, a self-reflexive text suggests that perhaps narrative does not derive its authority from any reality it represents, but from 'the cultural conventions that define both narrative and the construct we call "reality"' (225). If this is so, the mixing of the reflexively fictional with the verifiably historical might well be doubly upsetting for some critics. Historiographic metafiction represents not just a world of fiction, however self-consciously presented as a constructed one, but also a world of public experience. The difference between this and the realist logic of reference is that here that public world is rendered specifically as discourse. How do we know the past today? Through its discourses, through its texts – that is, through the traces of its historical events: the archival materials, the documents, the narratives of witnesses . . . and historians. On one level, then, postmodern fiction merely makes overt the processes of narrative representation – of the real or the fictive and of their interrelations.

Esquire's recent publishing of what its editor clearly feels is an anomaly for the magazine attests to both the interest and the unease provoked by this kind of problematizing. Peter Davis's 'Prince Charles narrowly escapes beheading' is introduced to readers as an exploration of fact and fantasy. In his editorial, Lee Eisenberg calls it 'a work of the imagination' yet 'woven of facts – some of which are true and accurate, others of which are unverifiable.' No doubt part of his motivation here is legal protection, but he significantly has recourse to Doctorow's fictionalized historical version of the ragtime era and Coover's of Richard Nixon in *The Public Burning* as precedents. Davis is said to have walked where Prince Charles walks, tried to 'dream his dreams, to think his thoughts.' In a more traditional journalistic fashion, he has also spoken to 'those who have tried to know him' and read 'both the tomes and the tabs' (P. Davis 1988: 93). Before the piece even begins, the reader is told: 'He came away with a real-life fiction. For the Lonely Prince is a man, you see, but the Lonely Prince is a story, too.' Davis is careful to signal the fictionality of what, on the whole, is a realist narrative (even if in fragments) of the life and work of the heir to the British throne. He opens with a section called 'Masque' which is a parody of a Renaissance dramatic dialogue between Charles and Lady Diana, complete with Shakespearean and Donnean punning (on 'Di,' for instance). In the rest of the text, there are other literary echoes to point to both literary fabulation and narratorial interpretation. After citing Charles on his political position and its present limitations ('I serve'), the text offers a Prufrockian comment: 'One is not Prince Hamlet nor was meant to be. Neither is one a courtier, though one can be deferential, glad to be of use' (96).

This is not really a blurring of boundaries between fact and fiction, but more a hybridizing mix, where the borders are kept clear, even if they are frequently crossed. The same is true of the other postmodern border tensions between, say, the literary and the theoretical. It is a truism of contemporary criticism that the seriously playful textuality of the writing of Derrida or the fanciful fragments of the later works of Barthes, for instance, are as literary as they are theoretical. Postmodernism has provoked many of its critics into similar deviations from traditional academic critical norms: Ihab Hassan, Peter Sloterdijk, even novelist Mario Vargas Llosa, whose *Perpetual Orgy* is divided into three parts – a 'tête-à-tête with Emma Bovary,' a critical study of the genesis and text of Flaubert's novel (in the form of question and answer), and an investigation into the heritage of the novel that reveals the writer's intense personal engagement with it.

Postmodern representational practices that refuse to stay neatly within accepted conventions and traditions and that deploy hybrid forms and seemingly mutually contradictory strategies frustrate critical attempts (including this one) to systematize them, to order them with an eye to control and mastery – that is, to totalize. Roland Barthes once asked: 'Is it not the characteristic of reality to be *unmasterable*? And is it not the characteristic of system to *master* it? What then, confronting reality, can one do who rejects mastery?' (1977b: 172). Postmodern representation itself contests mastery and totalization, often by unmasking both their powers and their limitations. We watch the process of what Foucault once called the interrogating of limits that is now replacing the search for totality. On the level of representation, this postmodern questioning overlaps with similarly pointed challenges by those working in, for example, postcolonial and feminist contexts. How is the 'other' represented in, say, imperialist or patriarchal discourses? But a *caveat* is in order. It may be true that postmodern thought 'refuses to turn the Other into the Same' (During 1987: 33), but there is also a very real sense in which the postmodernist notions of difference and a positively valorized marginality often reveal the same familiar totalizing strategies of domination, though usually masked by the liberating rhetoric of First World critics who appropriate Third World cultures to their own ends (Chow 1986–7: 91). Postmodernist critique is always compromised. The ex-centric 'other' itself may have different (and less complicitous) modes of representation and may therefore require different methods of study.

The standard negative evaluation of postmodernism asserts that it is without an ordered and coherent vision of 'truth': 'To the postmodernist mind, everything is empty at the center. Our vision is not integrated – and it lacks form and definition' (Gablik 1984: 17). Actually, that center is not so much empty as called into question, interrogated as to its power and its politics. And if the notion of center – be it seen as 'Man' or Truth or whatever – is challenged in postmodernism, what happens to the idea of the 'centered' subjectivity, the subject of representation? In Catherine Stimpson's terms, the

> theory that representational machineries were reality's synonyms, not a window (often cracked) onto reality, eroded the immediate security of another lovely gift of Western humanism: the belief in a conscious self that generates texts, meanings, and a substantial identity.
>
> (Stimpson 1988: 236)

That sense of the coherent, continuous, autonomous, and free subject is, as Foucault too suggested in *The Order of Things*, a historically conditioned and historically determined construct, with its analogue in the representation of the individual in fiction. In historiographic metafiction, written from the perspective of a different historical moment, one which at least queries that 'lovely gift of Western humanism,' character gets represented rather differently.

In John Fowles's *A Maggot*, for instance, the self-consciously contemporary narrator introduces the eighteenth-century prophet John Lee as, in his words, an 'innocently self-believing . . . ignorant mystic.' He then adds, however:

To speak so is anachronistic. Like so many of his class at this time, he still lacks what even the least intelligent human today, far stupider even than he, would recognize – an unmistakable sense of personal identity set in a world to some degree, however small, manipulable or controllable by that identity. John Lee would not have understood *Cogito, ergo sum*; and far less its even terser modern equivalent, *I* am. The contemporary I does not need to think, to know it exists. To be sure the intelligentsia of John Lee's time had a clear, almost but not quite modern, sense of self.

(Fowles 1985: 385)

This kind of historical situating of the notion of subjectivity is presented in the most metafictively self-reflexive of ways: 'John Lee *is*, of course; but as a tool or a beast is, in a world so entirely pre-ordained it might be written, like this book' (385). The text's representational self-consciousness points to a very postmodern awareness of both the nature and historicity of our discursive representations of the self (see Smith 1988). And it is not simply poststructuralist theory that has engendered this complex awareness. As we saw in the first chapter, feminist theory and practice have problematized poststructuralism's (unconsciously, perhaps, phallocentric) tendency to see the subject in apocalyptic terms of loss or dispersal, for they refuse to foreclose the question of identity and do so in the name of the (different) history of women: 'Because women have not had the same historical relation of identity to origin, institution, production, that men have had, women have not, I think, (collectively) felt burdened by too much Self, Ego, Cogito, etc.' (Miller 1986: 106). It is the feminist need to inscribe first – and only then subvert – that I think has influenced most the postmodern complicitously critical stand of underlining and undermining received notions of the represented subject.

Whether it be in the photography of Victor Burgin or Barbara Kruger or in the fiction of John Fowles or Angela Carter, subjectivity is represented as something in process, never as fixed and never as autonomous, outside history. It is always a gendered subjectivity, rooted also in class, race, ethnicity, and sexual orientation. And it is usually textual self-reflexivity that paradoxically calls these worldly particularities

to our attention by foregrounding the doxa, the unacknowledged politics, behind the dominant representations of the self –
and the other – in visual images or in narratives. Of course, not
only photography and fiction do this. Films like *Zelig* or *Sammy
and Rosie Get Laid* unmask representation as the process of
constructing the self, but they also show the role of the 'other' in
mediating that sense of self. Similarly Canadian composer R.
Murray Schafer's *Patria 1: The Characteristics Man* is a theatrical/
operatic/rock performance work that thematizes and actualizes
the problematic nature of postmodern subjectivity. A silent
anonymous immigrant ('D.P.'), introduced to the audience as
'victim' (a large sign with the word and an arrow follows him
about the stage), seeks to define a self in a new and hostile world
that denies him his speech (it is not English) and leaves him
with only the symbolic voice of the ethnically coded accordion.
A strategically placed wall of mirrors facing the audience
prevents any self-distancing and any denial of complicity.

Another way of problematizing the notion of the 'centered
self' can be seen in the challenges to the conventions of self-
representation in postmodern autobiographical writing, most
infamously exemplified, perhaps, by *Roland Barthes by Roland
Barthes*. From its title alone, this calls attention to itself as a
parody of the French series of *X par lui-même* to which Barthes
contributed the volume on Michelet. When the text opens with
a hand-written facsimile representation of a note warning that
everything we are about to read must be considered as if spoken
by a character in a novel, we know we have entered the
problematized zone of postmodern self-representation. Given
my focus here on photographic and narrative representation,
this is a particularly important book, for it opens with photographs of Barthes and his family. Yet, the opening of the verbal
text reverses the readers' perceiving order, telling us that
the visuals are 'the author's treat to himself, for finishing his
book. His pleasure is a matter of fascination (and thereby
quite selfish). I have kept only the images which enthrall me'
(Barthes 1977b: 3).

This sliding from the third to the first person is a constant in
the text and it always serves to emphasize Barthes's awareness
of the doubleness of the self, as both narrator and narrated: *I see
the fissure in the subject (the very thing about which he can say

nothing)' (Barthes 1977b: 3). And it is the representation of self in the photographs, as much as in the act of writing, that provokes this double vision. In addition, there is another split, that between the self-image and the imaged self, between representation to the self and representation of the self, between the childhood self represented in the pictures and in memory and the adult self writing in words: '"But I never looked like that!" How do you know? What is the "you" you might or might not look like?' (36).

It is hard to imagine a text that would address the issue of representation-as-construction more directly than this post-modern autobiography: 'I do not say: "I am going to describe myself" but: "I am writing a text, and I call it R.B."' (Barthes 1977b: 56). He then adds: 'Do I not know that, *in the field of the subject, there is no referent?*' To represent the self is to 'constitute' the self (82), be it in images or in stories. Even if the chronological linearity or the causality of the *Bildungsroman* are to be rejected, even if fragments with no center are to structure the text, there is still a story of a self, a construction of a subject, however 'deconstructed, taken apart, shifted, without anchorage' (168) it may be. As Barthes puts it: 'nothing is reported without making it signify' (151).

His self-consciousness about the act of representing in both writing and photography undoes the mimetic assumptions of transparency that underpin the realist project, while refusing as well the anti-representationalism of modernist and late modernist abstraction and textuality. *Roland Barthes by Roland Barthes* manages to de-naturalize both the 'copying' apparatus of photography and the realist reflecting mirror of narrative, while still acknowledging – and exploiting – their shared power of inscription and construction. Its simultaneous use and abuse of both realist reference and modernist self-reflexivity is typically postmodern, as is its deployment of both photographic and narrative representation. Both forms have traditionally been assumed to be transparent media which paradoxically could master/capture/fix the real. Yet the modernist formalist reaction to this transparent instrumentality revealed photography and fiction to be, in fact, highly coded forms of representation. This is the history behind the postmodern view of representation as a matter of construction, not reflection. After modernism, one might well ask, does this still have to be argued? I think the answer is yes, because realism and its attendant ideology have found renewed vigor in popular fiction and film, just as the transparency of visual representation is generally assumed in the ubiquitous advertising images that surround us and in the snapshots we take.

This last point provides another reason for the linking of photography and fiction in this study: both are unavoidably connected to mass-media representations today and, even in their high-art manifestations, they tend to acknowledge this inevitable (if compromising) implication. This is most obvious in the appropriation of film and ad. images in postmodern photography, but a similar process occurs in the use, for example, of detective-story structures in 'serious' fiction like *The Name of the Rose* or *Hawksmoor*. Lennard Davis has even suggested that the question of narrative representation was already problematized in the earliest examples of the novel as a genre:

> After all, the novel, as the first wave in the sweep of mass media and the entertainment industry, stands as an example of how large, controlled, cultural forms came to be used by large numbers of people who wished or were taught to have a different relation to reality than those who preceded them. As the first powerful, broad, and hegemonic literary form, the novel served to blur, in a way never before experienced, the distinction between illusion and reality, between fact and fiction, between symbol and what is represented.
>
> (L. Davis 1987: 3)

Postmodern historiographic metafiction simply does all of this overtly, asking us to question how we represent – how we construct – our view of reality and of our selves. Along with the photographic practices of Martha Rosler, Hans Haacke, and Silvia Kolbowski, as we shall see, these novels ask us to acknowledge that representation has a politics.

Photographic discourse

As a visual medium, photography has a long history of being both politically useful and politically suspect: think of Brecht or Benjamin, or of Heartfield's photomontages. A recent show of three Vancouver photographers (Arni Runar Haraldsson, Harold Ursuliak, and Michael Lawlor) called *A Linear Narration: Post Phallocentrism* offered examples of sophisticated satirical socio-political critiques of dominant cultural representations. Lawlor's media-derived photomontages are most reminiscent of Heartfield's technique, if not his virulence: *Two Queens* features roughly torn-out images of Warhol's Marilyn Monroe and of a newspaper photo of Queen Elizabeth II. This conjunction suggests a particularly Canadian irony directed against Canada's double colonialization, historical (British royalty) and present (American media).

Photography today is one of the major forms of discourse through which we are seen and see ourselves. Frequently what I want to call postmodern photography foregrounds the notion of ideology as representation by appropriating recognizable images from that omnipresent visual discourse, almost as an act of retaliation for its (unacknowledged) political nature or its (unacknowledged) constructing of those images of ourselves and our world. Photography, precisely because of its mass-media ubiquity, allows what are considered high-art representations – like those of Nigel Scott, Barbara Kruger, or Richard Prince – to speak to and against those of the more visible vernacular and to exploit the seduction of those images. But postmodern photography also addresses the medium's history and it does so in a way that goes beyond obvious journalistic instrumentality and capitalist seduction: for instance, modernism's formalist art-photography and the documentary 'victim' photography of the 1930s are made rather politically problematic in the work of Sherrie Levine and Martha Rosler, respectively; the transparently referential conventions of portraiture get both installed and subverted in Cindy Sherman's self-posed self-portraits; the relation of narrative to photographic sequences gets destabilized in the work of Duane Michals and Victor Burgin (see Crimp 1980; Starenko 1983; Thornton 1979).

What is common to all these postmodern challenges to convention is their simultaneous exploitation of the power of that convention and their reliance on the viewers' knowledge of its particulars. In most cases, this reliance does not necessarily lead to elitist exclusion, because the convention being evoked has usually become part of the common representational vocabulary of newspapers, magazines, and advertising – even if its history is more extensive. In photographer Sarah Charlesworth's words: 'The reason why I use what are commonly called "appropriated images", images drawn from popular culture, is that I wish to describe and address a state of mind that is a direct product of living in a common world' (in Clarkson 1987–8: 14). Many video and performance artists have used similar methods to address social and political issues from within the discourse of that larger field of cultural representations that includes television, Hollywood movies, and commercial advertising. There are, of course, other ways of achieving this end, ones that artists in other media have explored: the theory-informed art of postmodern painting is a good example, but it is also one that does indeed raise the question of exclusivity. As we shall see in a later chapter, postmodern photographers have often tried to avoid this danger by introducing didactic verbal texts into their works.

Reappropriating existing representations that are effective precisely because they are loaded with pre-existing meaning and putting them into new and ironic contexts is a typical form of postmodern photographic complicitous critique: while exploiting the power of familiar images, it also de-naturalizes them, makes visible the concealed mechanisms which work to make them seem transparent, and brings to the fore their politics, that is to say, the interests in which they operate and the power they wield (Folland 1988: 60). Both any (realist) documentary value and any formal (modernist) pleasure that such a practice may invoke are inscribed, even as they are undercut. So too is any notion of individuality or authenticity – for work or artist – but that has always been problematic for photography as a mechanically reproductive medium. This technological aspect has other implications too. Commentators as diverse as Annette Kuhn, Susan Sontag, and Roland Barthes have remarked on photography's ambivalences: it is in no way innocent of cultural formation (or innocent of forming culture) yet it is in a very real sense technically tied to the real, or at least, to the visual and the actual. And this is what postmodernist use of this medium exposes, even as it exploits what Kuhn calls the ideology of 'the visible as evidence.' It also exposes what may be the major photographic code, the one that pretends to look uncoded.

If the postmodern photographer is more the manipulator of signs than the producer of an art object and the viewer is more the active decoder of messages than the passive consumer or contemplator of aesthetic beauty (Foster 1985: 100), the difference is one of the politics of representation. However, postmodern photography is often overtly about the representation of politics too. The work of Hans Haacke on multinational corporations or of Martha Rosler on the poverty of New York's Bowery suggests a material and maybe even materialist critique of the modernist art establishment's separation of the political and the aesthetic and of the art gallery/museum's neutralization of any possible sense of art as resistance, much less revolution. Yet Barbara Kruger's use of the lenticular screen, in which viewers see two different images depending on their position, directly addresses this issue. It is a literalization and materialization of the notion of the positioning of the body in ideology: what we see depends on where we are. As mentioned earlier, Sherrie Levine's re-presentation of famous photos of both the modernist-formalist and realist-documentary traditions suggests that what we see depends on context and perhaps even that we cannot avoid approaching some subjects primarily through our culturally accepted representations of them. This is not only true of poor farmers in 1930s' America or of blacks or Asians or Native Peoples, but of women too.

In *Ways of Seeing*, John Berger argued that a woman 'comes to consider the *surveyor* and the *surveyed* within her as the two constituent yet always distinct elements of her identity as woman' (Berger 1972a: 46). That 'I/her' or even 'I/you' split is exactly what a feminist and postmodern photographer like Barbara Kruger explores in her enigmatic but powerful verbal/visual photographic collages: the words 'You thrive on mistaken identity' sit atop an image of a stereotypically glamorous woman, but as photographed through distorting patterned glass. The word 'mistaken' is placed directly over her eyes. Kruger's black and white works clearly echo Russian constructivism, Heartfield's photomontages, generic 1940s and 1950s images (Bois *et al.* 1987: 199), and their message about the politics of representation is as explicit as that of some of the even more didactic postmodern representations of politics: Hans Haacke's attacks on Mobil or Alcan or Klaus Staeck's ironic photomontages in aid of causes like the lack of housing for the elderly (a photo of Dürer's famous drawing of his aged mother with the caption: 'Would you rent a room to this woman?') or the social inequalities in 1980s' Britain (a parody of a political poster, featuring the photo of an enormous Rolls Royce driving down a narrow alley in a poor area, accompanied by the text: 'For wider streets vote Conservative'). Photography may legitimize and normalize existing power relations, but it can also be used against itself to 'de-doxify' that authority and power and to reveal how its representational strategies construct an 'imaginary economy' (Sekula 1987: 115) that might usefully be deconstructed.

Once again I should repeat that it is not only photography that both does and undoes this 'economy.' Canadian artist Stan Douglas uses multi-media installations to study representation in terms of the relations of culture to technology, especially film technology. He disassembles film into its constituent parts (sounds; stills projected as slides) in order to make opaque the supposed ability of film to be a transparent recording/representation of reality. The artists known as General Idea (A.A. Bronson, Felix Partz, and Jorge Zontal) have taken a different tack: their *1984 Miss General Idea Pageant* made the high-art world into a beauty pageant, literalizing art's relation to displaced desire and to commodity acquisition and in the process problematizing our culture's notions of the erotic and of sexual 'possession' in relation to capitalist values.

What these artists share with the postmodern photographers I have mentioned is a focus on the ways in which art overlaps and interacts with the social system of the present and the past. All representations have a politics; they also have a history. The conjunction of these two concerns in what has been called the New Art History has meant that issues like gender, class, race, ethnicity, and sexual orientation are now part of the discourse of the visual arts, as they are of the literary ones. Social history cannot be separated from the history of art; there is no value-neutral, much less value-free, place from which to represent in any art form. And there never was.

Telling stories: fiction and history

In *Postmodernist Fiction*, Brian McHale has noted that both modernist and postmodernist fiction show an affinity for cinematic models, and certainly the work of Manuel Puig or Salman Rushdie would support such a claim. But historiographic metafiction, obsessed with the question of how we can come to know the past today, also shows an attraction to photographic models – and to photographs – either as physically present (in Michael Ondaatje's *Coming Through Slaughter*) or as the narrativized trappings of the historical archive (in Timothy Findley's *The Wars*, Maxine Hong Kingston's *China Men*, or Gayl Jones's *Corregidora*). In raising (and making problematic) the issue of photographic representation, postmodern fiction often points metaphorically to the related issue of narrative representation – its powers and its limitations. Here, too, there is no transparency, only opacity. The narrator in John Berger's novel *G.* tries to describe an actual historical and political event, but ends up in despair: 'Write anything. Truth or untruth, it is unimportant. Speak but speak with tenderness, for that is all that you can do that may help a little. Build a barricade of words, no matter what they mean' (Berger 1972b: 75). The politics of narrative representation can apparently sometimes be of limited efficacy when it comes to the representation of politics.

It is not surprising that this should be the case, especially with historical representation, for the question of historiography's representational powers is a matter of current concern in a number of discourses but most obviously, perhaps, in historiographic metafiction. Roa Bastos's *I the Supreme* is a typical, if extreme, example of this. El Supremo (José Gaspar Rodríguez Francia) did exist and did rule Paraguay from 1814 to 1840, but the novel we read opens with a story about the instability of even a dictator's power over his self-representation in the documents of history: he discovers that his decrees are frequently parodied so well and so thoroughly that 'even the truth appears to be a lie' (Roa Bastos 1986: 5) and the competence of the scribe to whom the dictator 'dictates' his text is suspect. This novel disorients its readers on the level of its narration (who speaks? is the text written? oral? transcribed?), its plot and temporal structures, and even its material existence (parts of the text are said to have been burned): 'Forms disappear, words remain, to signify the impossible. No story can ever be told' (11), especially, perhaps, the story of absolute power.

'I the Supreme' and *I the Supreme* equally distrust history's ability and will to convey 'truth': 'The words of power, of authority, words above words, will be transformed into clever words, lying words. Words below words' (Roa Bastos 1986: 29). Historians, like novelists, are said to be interested not in 'recounting the facts, but [in] recounting that they are recounting them' (32). Yet the text does provide a narrative of the historical past of Paraguay, albeit one recounted in anachronistic wording that underlines the present time of the recounting to the (doubly dictated-to) scribe who writes down what he is told to. Or does he? He openly admits to not understanding the meaning of what he transcribes, and, therefore, to misplacing words, to writing 'backwards' (35). The text metafictionally includes even a reference to Roa Bastos and his novel: 'One or another of those émigré-scribblers will doubtless take advantage of the impunity of distance and be so bold as to cynically affix his signature' to the text we read (35). And so he does.

I the Supreme is a novel about power, about history-writing, and about the oral tradition of story-telling. It thematizes the postmodern concern with the radically indeterminate and unstable nature of textuality and subjectivity, two notions seen as inseparable: 'I must dictate/write; note it down somewhere. That is the only way I have of proving that I still exist' (Roa Bastos 1986: 45). Writing here is not 'the art of tracing flowery figures' but that of 'deflowering signs' (58). Or, as the text explicitly states: 'This is representation. Literature. Representation of writing as representation' (60). However, the power of literary representation is as provisional as that of historiography: 'readers do not know if they [Don Quixote and Sancho Panza] are fables, true stories, pretended truths. The same will come to pass with us. We too will pass for real-unreal beings' (60).

The entire novel is full of such remarks about representation – in the narratives of both fiction and history. The 'Final Compiler's Note' states:

The reader will already have noted that, unlike ordinary texts, this one was read first and written later. Instead of saying and writing something new, it merely faithfully copies what has already been said and composed by others. . . . [T]he re-scriptor declares, in the words of a contemporary author, that the history contained in these *Notes* is reduced to the fact that the story that should have been told in them has not been told. As a consequence, the characters and facts that figure in them have earned, through the fatality of the written language, the right to a fictitious and autonomous existence in the service of the no less fictitious and autonomous reader.

(Roa Bastos 1986: 435)

This is postmodern de-naturalizing – the simultaneous inscribing and subverting of the conventions of narrative.

Coinciding with this kind of challenge in the novels themselves, there have been many theoretical examinations of the nature of narrative as a major human system of understanding – in fiction, but also in history, philosophy, anthropology, and so on. Peter Brooks (1984: xii) has claimed that with the advent of romanticism, narrative became a dominant mode of representation, though one might wonder what the status of the classical epic and the Bible might be. He is likely right to say, however, that in the twentieth century there has been an increasing suspicion of narrative plot and its artifice, yet no diminishing of our reliance on plotting, however ironized or parodied (7). We may no longer have recourse to the grand narratives that once made sense of life for us, but we still have recourse to narrative representations of some kind in most of our verbal discourses, and one of the reasons may be political.

Lennard Davis describes the politics of novelistic narrative representation in this way: 'Novels do not depict life, they depict life as it is represented by ideology' (L. Davis 1987: 24). Ideology – how a culture represents itself to itself – 'doxifies' or naturalizes narrative representation, making it appear as natural or common-sensical (25); it presents what is really *constructed* meaning as something *inherent* in that which is being represented. But this is precisely what postmodern novels like Peter Ackroyd's *Chatterton* or Roa Bastos's *I the Supreme* or Graham Swift's *Waterland* are about. And in none of these cases is there

ever what Jameson associates with the postmodern: 'a repudiation of representation, a "revolutionary" break with the
(repressive) ideology of storytelling generally' (Jameson
1984c: 54). This misconception shows the danger of defining
the postmodern in terms of (French or American) anti-repre-
sentational late modernism, as so many do. In these novels,
there is no dissolution or repudiation of representation; but
there *is* a problematizing of it.

Historiographic metafiction is written today in the context of
a serious contemporary interrogating of the nature of representation in historiography. There has been much interest
recently in narrative – its forms, its function, its powers, and its
limitations – in many fields, but especially in history. Hayden
White has even asserted that the postmodern is 'informed by a
programmatic, if ironic, commitment to the return to narrative
as one of its enabling presuppositions' (White 1987: xi). If this is
the case, his own work has done much to make it so. Articles like
'The value of narrativity in the representation of reality' have
been influential in raising questions about narrative representation and its politics in both history and literature. From a
different angle, the work of Dominick LaCapra has acted to
de-naturalize notions of historical documents as representations of the past and of the way such archival traces of historical
events are used within historiographic and fictive representations. Documents are not inert or innocent, but may indeed
have 'critical or even potentially transformative relations to
phenomena "represented" in them' (LaCapra 1985: 38). But
this is the subject of the next chapter.

Of course, it is not just historiographic theory that has
deconstructed narrative representation. Feminist thought, such
as that of Teresa de Lauretis, has done much to deconstruct it as
well. It has explored how 'narrative and narrativity . . . are
mechanisms to be employed strategically and tactically in the
effort to construct other forms of coherence, to shift the terms of
representation, to produce the conditions of representability of
another – and gendered – social subject' (de Lauretis 1987:
109). Narrative is indeed a 'socially symbolic act,' as Jameson
claims, but it is also the outcome of social interaction. In the
work of Maxine Hong Kingston or Gayl Jones, story-telling is
not presented as a privatized form of experience but as asserting

a communicational bond between the teller and the told within a context that is historical, social, and political, as well as intertextual.

The same is true in the postmodern fiction of Salman Rushdie or Gabriel García Márquez. It is not simply a case of novels metafictionally revelling in their own narrativity or fabulation; here narrative representation – story-telling – is a historical and a political act. Perhaps it always is. Peter Brooks argues: 'We live immersed in narrative, recounting and reassessing the meaning of our past actions, anticipating the outcome of our future projects, situating ourselves at the intersection of several stories not yet completed' (1984: 3). In Fowles's *The French Lieutenant's Woman*, the hero does just this – at great length – and the contemporary narrator interrupts to forestall our objections in the name of a kind of postmodern mimesis of process, reminding us that we too do this constantly. While it is un-doubtedly true that modernism had already challenged the conventions of what could/should be narrated and had already explored the limits of narrative's ability to represent 'life,' it is postmodern culture at large that may have become 'novelistic.' As Stephen Heath has argued, it mass-produces narratives (for television, radio, film, video, magazines, comic books, novels), thereby creating a situation in which we must consume 'the constant narration of the social relations of individuals, the ordering of meanings for the individual in society' (Heath 1982: 85). Perhaps this is why story-telling has returned – but as a problem, not as a given.

It is still a truism of anti-postmodernist criticism that this return has been at the expense of a sense of history. But perhaps it just depends on your definition of history – or History. We may indeed get few postmodern narrative representations of the heroic victors who have traditionally defined who and what made it into History. Often we get instead both the story and the story-telling of the non-combatants or the losers: the Canadian Indians of Rudy Wiebe's *The Temptations of Big Bear* or Leonard Cohen's *Beautiful Losers*; the women of Troy in Christa Wolf's *Cassandra*; the blacks of South Africa or America in the work of J.M. Coetzee, André Brink, Toni Morrison, or Ishmael Reed.

Equally interesting are the postmodern attempts to go beyond the traditional representational forms of both fictional and historical narration: Patrick Süskind's *Perfume* offers the fictionalized history of eighteenth-century France in all its *olfactory* glory, though it must do so through verbal representations of the physical sense that narrative so rarely records. The novel offers the sense of smell as the vehicle not only for its historical and social contextualizing but also for its metafictional commentary, since this is the tale of Jean-Baptiste Grenouille, the product of French peasant misery who is born an 'abomination' – with no bodily odor himself, but with the most discerning nose in the world. The story's narrator is omniscient and controlling, as well as being our contemporary and in complicity with us as readers. He uses this power and position to emphasize from the start the limits of his (and our) language. As a boy Grenouille has trouble learning the words of things that have no smell: 'He could not retain them, confused them with one another, and even as an adult used them unwillingly and often incorrectly: justice, conscience, God, joy, responsibility, humility, gratitude, etc. – what these were meant to express remained a mystery to him' (Süskind 1986: 25). This may not be surprising, perhaps, for the protagonist of a novel subtitled: *The Story of a Murderer*.

Grenouille is constantly aware of the discrepancy between the 'richness of the world perceivable by smell' and 'the poverty of language' (Süskind 1986: 26). The narrator suggests that this linguistic impoverishment accounts for our normal inability to make anything other than gross distinctions in the 'smellable world' (125). The text links the failure of language to Grenouille's creativity as the distiller and creator of the greatest perfumes in the world, and yet, as readers, we can never forget that we know of this only through the very language of the novel. The postmodern paradox of inscription and subversion governs the metafictive reflexivity. It also structures the plot, for this is a novel about power: the power the poor peasant was not born into; the power he acquires in serving others with his gifts (as a master of scents); the power to kill (for the perfect scent); the power that perfect scent wields over others. His executioners and the crowd gathered to witness justice done to this multiple murderer suddenly fall into an ecstatic orgy of love for their victim – when he applies the 'perfume' distilled from the murdered girl who had possessed the most powerful smell in the world: 'A power stronger than the power of money or the power of terror or the power of death: the invincible power to command the love of mankind' (252).

Perfume points to the absence of the representation of the sense of smell in historical, social, or fictional narratives. The olfactory density of the novel – recounted through verbal representation, of course – is historically specific and accurate and also socially significant. This is historiographic metafiction, fictionalized history with a parodic twist. The form this twist takes may vary from novel to novel, but it is always present: Mario Vargas Llosa's *The War of the End of the World* represents the history of the 1896 Canudos War in northeastern Brazil, but its parody shows how traditional narrative models – both historiographical and fictional – that are based on European models of continuous chronology and cause-and-effect relations are utterly inadequate to the task of narrating the history of the New World.

Such a clashing of various possible discourses of narrative representation is one way of signalling the postmodern use and abuse of convention that works to 'de-doxify' any sense of the seamlessness of the join between the natural and the cultural, the world and the text, thereby making us aware of the irreducible ideological nature of every representation – of past or present. This complexity of clashing discourses can be seen in many historiographic metafictions. In Angela Carter's 'Black Venus,' as we shall see in the last chapter, the discourses of male erotic representation of woman and those of female and colonial self-representations are juxtaposed with a certain political efficacy. Similarly, confrontations between contemporary narrators and their narrated historical contexts occur in novels as diverse as Banville's *Doctor Copernicus* and Fowles's *The French Lieutenant's Woman* or *A Maggot*.

In challenging the seamless quality of the history/fiction (or world/art) join implied by realist narrative, postmodern fiction does not, however, disconnect itself from history or the world. It foregrounds and thus contests the conventionality and unacknowledged ideology of that assumption of seamlessness and asks its readers to question the processes by which we represent our selves and our world to ourselves and to become aware of the means by which we *make* sense of and *construct* order out of

experience in our particular culture. We cannot avoid representation. We *can* try to avoid fixing our notion of it and
assuming it to be transhistorical and transcultural. We can also
study how representation legitimizes and privileges certain
kinds of knowledge – including certain kinds of historical
knowledge. As *Perfume* implies, our access through narrative to
the world of experience – past or present – is always mediated by
the powers and limits of our representations of it. This is as true
of historiographical narrative as it is of fictional.

In his review article, 'The question of narrative in contemporary historical theory,' Hayden White outlines the role
assigned to narrative representation in the various schools of
thought about the theory of history. Given that narrative has
become problematic in historiography as well as fiction, what is
interesting is that the same issues arise: narrative representation as a mode of knowledge and explanation, as unavoidably
ideological, as a localizable code. One way of outlining some of
these parallel concerns would be to look at a historiographic
metafiction that directly addresses the intersection of the debates about representation in both the novel and history:
Graham Swift's *Waterland*, a didactic fictive lesson or a medita-
tion on history – or both. No historical characters populate this
book, but it is a profoundly historical work none the less, in both
form and content.

Its first (unattributed) epigraph conditions our entry into the
novel and prepares us for the 'de-doxifying' of narrative representation that it proceeds to enact: '*Historia*, ae, f. 1. inquiry,
investigation, learning. 2. a) a narrative of past events, history.
b) any kind of narrative: account, tale, story.' The novel's action
opens in the 'fairy tale' landscape of the fen country of England,
a land so flat that it drives its inhabitants either to 'unquiet' or to
telling stories, especially to calm the fears of children. This is a
land 'both palpable and unreal' (Swift 1983: 6), an apt, self-
reflexive setting for any fiction. The narrator, Tom Crick, comes
from a family that has the 'knack for telling stories' of all kinds:
true or made up, believable or unbelievable – 'stories which
were neither one thing nor another' (1–2). This is a fitting
description, too, of *Waterland* itself.

However, the second chapter is called 'About the end of
history.' It is addressed to the second-person plural 'Children'

by Crick, their history teacher, who has spent his life trying to 'unravel the mysteries of the past' (Swift 1983: 4), but who is now to be retired because of some personal embarrassment, though the official reason is that his school is 'cutting back on history.' Crick's response is to defend his discipline – and his personal past: 'sack *me*, don't dismiss what I stand for. Don't banish my history' (18). But his students seem little interested in his subject; for them history is a 'fairy tale' (5) and they prefer to learn of the 'here and now' of a world threatened by nuclear annihilation. From the opening pages of the novel, both history-telling and story-telling are thus linked to fear.

They are also connected to the marshy, reclaimed land of the fen country, primarily through the major historical metaphor of the novel: 'Silt: which shapes and undermines continents; which demolishes as it builds; which is simultaneous accretion and erosion; neither progress nor decay' (Swift 1983: 7). A more perfect image of postmodern paradox would be hard to find. In terms of history, the allegorical, slow 'process of human silta-tion' is contrasted with that of revolution and of 'grand meta-morphoses.' To Crick, reality is what the monotonous fens provide: reality is 'that nothing happens.' Historiography's causality is only a construct: 'How many of the events of history have occurred . . . for this or for that reason, but for no other reason, fundamentally, than the desire to make things happen? I present to you History, the fabrication, the diversion, the reality-obscuring drama. History, and its near relative, His-trionics' (34). He would like to replace the heroes of history with the silenced crowds who do the 'donkey-work of coping with reality' (34).

Nevertheless, Crick realizes that we all imitate 'the grand repertoire of history' in miniature and endorse 'its longing for presence, for feature, for purpose, for content' (Swift 1983: 34–5) in order to convince ourselves that reality means some-thing. He himself attributes his becoming a history teacher to the tales his mother told him when he was afraid of the dark as a child. Later, when he wanted 'an Explanation,' he studied history as an academic discipline, only to 'uncover in this dedicated search more mysteries, more fantasticalities, more wonders and grounds for astonishment' (53). In other words, as it had begun for him, history continues to be 'a yarn': 'History itself, the Grand Narrative, the filler of vacuums, the dispeller of fears of the dark' (53).

The story Crick actually tells us and the 'Children' is one that is overtly fictive history, and we get to watch the fictionalizing process at work. At one point we are told: 'History does not record whether the day of Thomas's funeral was one of those dazzling mid-winter Fenland days' (Swift 1983: 70), but fourteen pages later, Thomas's funeral takes place under a definitely dazzling sky. Crick is aware of this creative, constructive process. At one point he stops: 'Children, you are right. There are times when we have to disentangle history from fairy-tale. . . . History, being an accredited sub-science, only wants to know facts. History, if it is to keep on constructing its road into the future, must do so on solid ground' (74) – something his slippery fen-country tale often seems to lack. Swift manages to raise the issue of narrative emplotment and its relation to both fictionality and historiography at the same time as he begins his problematization of the notion of historical knowledge. Crick tells his students: 'When you asked, as all history classes ask, as all history classes should ask, what is the point of history? Why history? Why the past?' he feels he can reply: 'Isn't this seeking of reasons itself inevitably an historical process, since it must always work backwards from what came after to what came before?' (92).

The study of history – that 'cumbersome but precious bag of clues' – involves inquiry that attempts to 'uncover the mysteries of cause and effect' (Swift 1983: 92), but most of all it teaches us 'to accept the burden of our need to ask why' (93). That process of asking becomes more important than the details of historiography: 'the attempt to give an account, with incomplete knowledge, of actions themselves undertaken with incomplete knowledge' (94). As he later says, 'History: a lucky dip of meanings. Events elude meaning, but we look for meanings' (122) and we create them.

Tom Crick is in some ways an allegorical representation of the postmodern historian who might well have read, not just Collingwood, with his view of the historian as storyteller and detective, but also Hayden White, Dominick LaCapra, Raymond Williams, Michel Foucault, and Jean-François Lyotard. The debates about the nature and status of narrative representation in historical discourse coincide and are inextricably intertwined with the challenges offered by historiographic metafiction. Yet we have seen that postmodern fiction is typically denounced as dehistoricized, if not ahistorical, especially by Marxist critics. In the light of fiction like *Waterland* or *Midnight's Children* or *Ragtime* this position would seem difficult to maintain. Of course, the problematized histories of postmodernism have little to do with the single totalizing History of Marxism, but they cannot be accused of neglecting or refusing engagement with the issues of historical representation and knowledge.

Among the consequences of the postmodern desire to denaturalize history is a new self-consciousness about the distinction between the brute *events* of the past and the historical *facts* we construct out of them. Facts are events to which we have given meaning. Different historical perspectives therefore derive different facts from the same events. Take Paul Veyne's example of Louis XIV's cold: even though the cold was a royal one, it was not a political event and therefore it would be of no interest to a history of politics, but it could be of considerable interest for a history of health and sanitation in France (Veyne 1971: 35). Postmodern fiction often thematizes this process of turning events into facts through the filtering and interpreting of archival documents. Roa Bastos's *I the Supreme* presents a narrator who admits to being a compiler of discourses and whose text is woven out of thousands of documents researched by the author. Of course, documents have always functioned in this way in historical fiction of any kind. But in historiographic metafiction the very process of turning events into facts through the interpretation of archival evidence is shown to be a process of turning the traces of the past (our only access to those events today) into historical representation. In so doing, such postmodern fiction underlines the realization that 'the past is not an "it" in the sense of an objectified entity that may either be neutrally represented in and for itself or projectively reprocessed in terms of our own narrowly "presentist" interests' (LaCapra 1987: 10). While these are the words of a historian writing about historical representation, they also describe well the postmodern lessons about fictionalized historical representation.

The issue of representation in both fiction and history has

usually been dealt with in epistemological terms, in terms of how we know the past. The past is not something to be escaped, avoided, or controlled – as various forms of modernist art suggest through their implicit view of the 'nightmare' of history. The past is something with which we must come to terms and such a confrontation involves an acknowledgement of limitation as well as power. We only have access to the past today through its traces – its documents, the testimony of witnesses, and other archival materials. In other words, we only have representations of the past from which to construct our narratives or explanations. In a very real sense, postmodernism reveals a desire to understand present culture as the product of previous representations. The representation of history becomes the history of representation. What this means is that postmodern art acknowledges and accepts the challenge of tradition: the history of representation cannot be escaped but it can be both exploited and commented on critically through irony and parody, as we shall see in more detail in chapter 4. The forms of representation used and abused by this paradoxical post-modern strategy can vary – from the parodic and historic architectural forms in Peter Ackroyd's *Hawksmoor* that mirror and structure the novel's intricate narrative representation (itself parodic and historic) to the strangely transcribed oral histories of the post-nuclear-holocaust world of Russell Hoban's *Riddley Walker*, where the narratives of the past exist but are, in the text's words, 'changet so much thru the years theyre all bits and blips and all mixt up' (Hoban 1980: 20).

As this kind of novel makes clear, there are important parallels between the processes of history-writing and fiction-writing and among the most problematic of these are their common assumptions about narrative and about the nature of mimetic representation. The postmodern situation is that a 'truth is being told, with "facts" to back it up, but a teller constructs that truth and chooses those facts' (Foley 1986: 67). In fact, that teller – of story or history – also constructs those very facts by giving a particular meaning to events. Facts do not speak for themselves in either form of narrative: the tellers speak for them, making these fragments of the past into a discursive whole. The 'true' story of the historical gangster, Jack Diamond, that we read in William Kennedy's *Legs* is shown to be a postmodern compromised one from its very title: 'Legs' is the protagonist's public label, the name the newspapers give him. In Jack's words: 'All the garbage they ever wrote about me is true to people who don't know me' (Kennedy 1975: 245) – that is to say, to people like us. Brian McHale calls this kind of work a 'revisionist historical novel' (McHale 1987: 90) because he feels it revises and reinterprets the official historical record and transforms the conventions of historical fiction. I would rather put this challenge in terms of a de-naturalizing of the conventions of representing the past in narrative – historical and fictional – that is done in such a way that the politics of the act of representing are made manifest.

One of the clearest examples of this process self-consciously at work is (ironically) a novel by a Marxist critic who has accused postmodern fiction of being ahistorical: Terry Eagleton's *Saints and Scholars*. The introductory note to the novel asserts that the story is 'not entirely fantasy.' Some of the characters are real, as are some of the events, but most of the rest is invented. This becomes evident in the first chapter, a fictionalized historical account of the last hours of Irish revolutionary James Connolly before he is executed in Kilmainham gaol on 12 May 1916. But the account ends with a remark that engenders the rest of the fiction to follow:

> But history does not always get the facts in the most significant order, or arrange them in the most aesthetically pleasing pattern. Napoleon survived the battle of Waterloo, but it would have been symbolically appropriate if he had been killed there. Florence Nightingale lingered on until 1910, but this was an oversight on history's part.
>
> (Eagleton 1987b: 10)

So the narrator arrests the bullets of the firing squad in mid-air in order to 'prise open a space in these close-packed events through which Jimmy may scamper, blast him out of the dreary continuum of history into a different place altogether' (10).

The plot action eventually comes to settle around a cottage on the west coast of Ireland where gather, thanks to irony and chance, a wondrous collection of historical and fictional excentrics: 'A Scottish Irishman [Connolly], an Irish Hungarian

[Leopold Bloom], an anglicized Austrian [Ludwig Wittgenstein], and a Russian [Nicolai Bakhtin, Mikhail's brother]' (Eagleton 1987b: 131–2). Though some are real and others fictional, all characters work to problematize the very distinction: Nicolai Bakhtin is said to be exceedingly extravagant but nevertheless historically real, and the others think he is 'an entirely fictional character, and the only real thing about him was that he knew it' (30). When he later tells the fictive Leopold Bloom that the notion of individuality is a 'supreme fiction,' Joyce's character replies: 'You might be a bleeding fiction. . . . You look pretty much like one to me. I happen to be real. I think I'm just about the only real person here' (135).

The novel's metafictionality operates through many such parodic intertextual echoes. To offer another instance: Bakhtin asks Connolly about the success of the Easter Rising because he is eager to know whether he is 'in the presence of a world-historical figure' (Eagleton 1987b: 94) – Lukács's term for the real personages found within historical fiction. The text's self-reflexivity also functions on the level of language and this is where Wittgenstein fits in. But what is also made clear is that Wittgenstein's famous linguistic theories are the direct product of his personal history, and particularly of his national history as a Viennese and his racial history as a Jew. When he (characteristically) tries to convince Connolly that the limits of his language are the limits of his world, the orator and man of action replies: 'What do you propose instead? That we should languish in the prison-house of language . . . ?' (114). The echo of the title of Jameson's book, *The Prison-House of Language*, is not just a clever move in some literary-critical recognition game: it invokes the entire context of Marxist criticism's (and Eagleton's own) stand against the reflexivity of language and narrative in the name of politics. This is important because *Saints and Scholars* attempts to reconcile these seemingly opposing positions – as indeed does much historiographic metafiction.

Eagleton's novel ends with another deferral of those firing-squad bullets heading for Connolly's body: 'When the bullets reached him he would disappear entirely into myth, his body nothing but a piece of language, the first cry of the new republic' (Eagleton 1987b: 145). Of course, we *do* only know Connolly today primarily from pieces of language, the traces and texts of the past. Eagleton wants to do more than problematize this epistemological reality, though. He offers as well a new way of representing history – not derived from the official accounts of the victors, but taken from the unofficial, usually unrecorded perspective of the victims of history. The novel's densely detailed descriptions of the life of the poor and the working class in Dublin are accompanied by analyses of the causes of the misery: the economic and political maneuverings of imperialist Britain. The plot contrasts a Viennese Jew's desire to be 'hiding from history' (84) with an Irish revolutionary leader's view that to be free 'you have to remember' (128), tell your own story, and represent yourself: 'A colonial territory was a land where nothing happened, where you reacted to the narrative of your rulers rather than created one of your own' (104). Talk is all that is left to 'a race bereft of its history' (104) but talk – 'discourse' – is a kind of action: 'Discourse was something you did. . . . The Irish had never fallen for the English myth that language was a second-hand reflection of reality' (105). Obviously, neither did the postmodern.

This is the kind of novel that works toward a critical return to history and politics *through* – not despite – metafictional self-consciousness and parodic intertextuality. This is the postmodernist paradox, a 'use and abuse' of history that Nietzsche, when considering that subject, never contemplated. In Roland Barthes's terms, we are shown that there is 'nothing natural anywhere, nothing but the historical' anywhere (Barthes 1977b: 139), and the consequences of this realization form the topic of the next chapter.

3
Re-presenting the past

'Total history' de-totalized

In the light of recent work in many theoretical areas, we have
seen that narrative has come to be acknowledged as, above all, a
human-made structure – never as 'natural' or given. Whether it
be in historical or fictional representation, the familiar narrative
form of beginning, middle, and end implies a structuring process that imparts meaning as well as order. The notion of its
'end' suggests both teleology and closure and, of course, both of
these are concepts that have come under considerable scrutiny
in recent years, in philosophical and literary circles alike. The
view of narrative that so much current theory challenges is not
new, but it has been given a new designation: it is considered a
mode of 'totalizing' representation.

The function of the term totalizing, as I understand it, is to
point to the *process* (hence the awkward 'ing' form) by which
writers of history, fiction, or even theory render their materials
coherent, continuous, unified – but always with an eye to the
control and mastery of those materials, even at the risk of doing
violence to them. It is this link to power, as well as process, that
the adjective 'totalizing' is meant to suggest, and it is as such
that the term has been used to characterize everything from
liberal humanist ideals to the aims of historiography. As
Dominick LaCapra has pointed out, the

dream of a 'total history' corroborating the historian's own desire for mastery of a documentary repertoire and furnishing the reader with a vicarious sense of – or perhaps a project for – control in a world out of joint has of course been a lodestar of historiography from Hegel to the Annales school.

(LaCapra 1985: 25)

Witness Annales historian Fernand Braudel's stated aim: 'Everything must be recaptured and relocated in the general framework of history, so that despite the difficulties, the fundamental paradoxes and contradictions, we may respect the unity of history which is also the unity of life' (Braudel 1980: 16). Totalizing narrative representation has also, of course, been considered by some critics as the defining characteristic of the novel as a genre, ever since its beginnings in the overt controlling and ordering (and fictionalizing) of Cervantes and Sterne.

In very general terms, the postmodern questioning of this totalizing impulse may well have its roots in some sort of 1960s' or late romantic need to privilege free, unconditioned experience. But this need seems to be countered these days by an equally strong terror that it is really someone else – rather than we ourselves – who is plotting, ordering, controlling our life for us. British-based critics tend to localize as a particularly American phenomenon a paradoxical desire for and suspicion of totalization, and the work of writers like Joseph Heller and Thomas Pynchon certainly explains why they do so. But there are equally powerful examples of the postmodern paradox of anti-totalizing totalization in resolutely non-American novels such as *Midnight's Children*, *The Name of the Rose*, or *The White Hotel*, novels which structurally both install and subvert the teleology, closure, and causality of narrative, both historical and fictive.

A similar and equally contradictory impulse can be seen in postmodern narrative photography – the same doubled urge, ironically playing with conventions in order to turn the apparent veracity of photography against itself. The overt self-reflexivity in the work of Duane Michaels, for example, points to his various series of photographs as self-consciously composed, fictionalized, and manipulated, but the images themselves nevertheless also function as seemingly transparent documentary representations within a temporal framework. This contradictory conjunction of the self-reflexive and the documentary is precisely what characterizes the postmodern return to story in poetry as well. Marjorie Perloff (1985: 158) has argued that much recent narrative poetry challenges the modernist or late romantic separation of lyric poetry and narrative prose by foregrounding both the narrative codes and their (and our) desire for closure as well as for the order usually implied by systematic plot structure. What this means is that – as in fiction – there is an opening up of poetry to material once excluded from the genre as impure: things political, ethical, historical, philosophical. This kind of verse can also work to contest representation and the traditional notion of the transparent referentiality of language in its problematizing of narrative form, and as such resembles, in its effect, historiographic metafiction.

In all these cases, there is an urge to foreground, by means of contradiction, the paradox of the desire for and the suspicion of narrative mastery – and master narratives. Historiography too is no longer considered the objective and disinterested recording of the past; it is more an attempt to comprehend and master it by means of some working (narrative/explanatory) model that, in fact, is precisely what grants a particular meaning to the past. What historiographic metafictions like *Waterland* or *I the Supreme* ask, as we have seen, is whether the historian *discovers* or *invents* the totalizing narrative form or model used. Of course, both discovery and invention would involve some recourse to artifice and imagination, but there is a significant difference in the epistemological value traditionally attached to the two acts. It is this distinction that postmodernism problematizes.

The totalizing impulse that postmodern art both inscribes and challenges should probably not be regarded either, on the one hand, as a naive kind of deliberately imperialistic desire for total control or, on the other, as utterly unavoidable and humanly inevitable, even necessary. The motivation and even existence of such totalization may certainly remain unconscious and repressed (or at least unspoken) or they may be completely overt, as in Fredric Jameson's deliberate totalizing in the name of Marxism as the only 'philosophically coherent and ideologically compelling resolution' to the dilemmas of historicism

(1981: 18). But Jameson's 'History' as 'uninterrupted narrative,' however repressed, is exactly what is contested by the plural, interrupted, unrepressed histories (in the plural) of novels like Rushdie's *Midnight's Children*.

That novel's postmodern narrating historian might be seen as indirectly suggesting that not even Marxism can fully subsume all other interpretive modes. In his postmodern storytelling there is no mediation that can act as a dialectical term for establishing relationships between narrative form and social ground. They both remain and they remain separate. The resulting contradictions are not dialectically resolved, but co-exist in a heterogeneous way: Rushdie's novel, in fact, works to prevent any interpretation of its contradictions as simply the outer discontinuous signs of some repressed unity – such as Marxist 'History' or 'the Real.' In fact, a novel like *Midnight's Children* works to foreground the totalizing impulse of western – imperialistic – modes of history-writing by confronting it with indigenous Indian models of history. Though Saleem Sinai narrates in English, in 'Anglepoised-lit writing,' his intertexts for both writing history and writing fiction are doubled: they are, on the one hand, from Indian legends, films, and literature and, on the other, from the west – *The Tin Drum*, *Tristram Shandy*, *One Hundred Years of Solitude*, and so on.

Rushdie's paradoxically anti-totalizing totalized image for his historiographic metafictive process is the 'chutnification of history' (Rushdie 1981: 459). Each chapter of the novel, we are told, is like a pickle jar that shapes its contents by its very form. The cliché with which Saleem is clearly playing is that to understand him and his nation, we 'have to swallow a world' and swallow too his literally preposterous story. But chutnification is also an image of preserving: 'my chutneys and kasaundies are, after all, connected to my nocturnal scribblings. . . . Memory, as well as fruit, is being saved from the corruption of the clocks' (38). In both processes, however, he acknowledges inevitable distortions: raw materials are transformed, given 'shape and form – that is to say, meaning' (461). This is as true of history-writing as it is of novel-writing. As Saleem himself acknowledges:

> Sometimes in the pickles' version of history, Saleem appears
> to have known too little; at other times, too much . . . yes, I
> should revise and revise, improve and improve; but there is
> neither the time nor the energy. I am obliged to offer no more
> than this stubborn sentence: It happened that way because
> that's how it happened.
>
> (Rushdie 1981: 560–1)

But does that opening 'It' of the last statement refer to the events
of the past or to the writing and preserving of them? In a novel
about a man writing his own and his country's history, a man
'desperate' for meaning, as he insists he is from the first
paragraph, the answer cannot be clear.

To challenge the impulse to totalize is to contest the entire
notion of *continuity* in history and its writing. In Foucault's terms
discontinuity, once the 'stigma of temporal dislocation' that it
was the historian's professional job to remove from history, has
become a new instrument of historical analysis and simultaneously a result of that analysis. Instead of seeking common
denominators and homogeneous networks of causality and
analogy, historians have been freed, Foucault argues, to note
the dispersing interplay of different, heterogeneous discourses
that acknowledge the undecidable in both the past and our
knowledge of the past. What has surfaced is something different
from the unitary, closed, evolutionary narratives of historiography as we have traditionally known it: as we have been
seeing in historiographic metafiction as well, we now get the
histories (in the plural) of the losers as well as the winners, of the
regional (and colonial) as well as the centrist, of the unsung
many as well as the much sung few, and I might add, of women
as well as men.

These are among the issues raised by postmodern fiction in its
paradoxical confrontation of self-consciously fictive and resolutely historical representation. The narrativization of past
events is not hidden; the events no longer seem to speak for
themselves, but are shown to be consciously composed into a
narrative, whose constructed – not found – order is imposed
upon them, often overtly by the narrating figure. The process of
making stories out of chronicles, of constructing plots out of
sequences, is what postmodern fiction underlines. This does not

in any way deny the existence of the past real, but it focuses attention on the act of imposing order on that past, of encoding strategies of meaning-making through representation.

Among the lessons taught by this didactic postmodern fiction is that of the importance of context, of discursive situation, in the narrativizing acts of both fiction and historiography: novels like Timothy Findley's *Famous Last Words* or Salman Rushdie's *Shame* teach us that both forms of narrative representation are, in fact, particularized uses of language (i.e. discourses) that inscribe social and ideological contexts. While both historians and novelists (not to mention literary critics) have a long tradition of trying to erase textual elements which would 'situate' them in their texts, postmodernism refuses such an obfuscation of the context of its enunciation. The particularizing and contextualizing that characterize the postmodern focus are, of course, direct responses to those strong (and very common) totalizing and universalizing impulses. But the resulting postmodern relativity and provisionality are not causes for despair; they are to be acknowledged as perhaps the very conditions of historical knowledge. Historical meaning may thus be seen today as unstable, contextual, relational, and provisional, but postmodernism argues that, in fact, it has always been so. And it uses novelistic representations to underline the narrative nature of much of that knowledge.

As Lyotard argued in *The Postmodern Condition*, narrative is still the quintessential way we represent knowledge and this explains why the denigration of narrative knowledge by positivistic science has provoked such a strong response from so many different domains and points of view. In many fields, narrative is, and always has been, a valid mode of explanation, and historians have always availed themselves of its ordering as well as its explanatory powers.

This is not unrelated to Collingwood's early notion that the historian's job is to tell plausible stories, made out of the mess of fragmentary and incomplete facts, facts which he or she processes and to which he or she thereby grants meaning through emplotment. Hayden White, of course, goes even further and points to how historians suppress, repeat, subordinate, highlight, and order those facts, but once again, the result is to endow the events of the past with a certain meaning. To call this act a literary act is, for White, in no way to detract from its significance. However, what contradictory postmodern fiction shows is how such meaning-granting can be undermined even as it is asserted. In Pynchon's *V.*, for instance, the writing of history is seen as an ultimately futile attempt to form experience into meaning. The multiple and peripheral perspectives offered in the fiction's eye-witness accounts resist any final meaningful closure. And despite the recognizable historical context (of the Cold War years and their paranoia or of German policies in southwest Africa), the past still resists complete human understanding. A plot, be it seen as a narrative structure or as a conspiracy, is always a totalizing representation that integrates multiple and scattered events into one unified story. But the simultaneous desire for and suspicion of such representations are both part of the postmodern contradictory response to emplotment.

In writing about historical events, both the emplotting historian and the novelist are usually considered as working within certain constraints – those of chronology, for instance. But what happens when postmodern fiction 'de-doxifies' even such obvious and 'natural' constraints, when *Midnight's Children*'s narrator notices an error in chronology in his narrative, but then decides, 'in my India, Gandhi will continue to die at the wrong time?' Later he also inverts the order of his own tenth birthday and the 1957 election, and keeps that order because his memory stubbornly refuses to alter the sequence of events. Rushdie offers no real answer to the questions Saleem poses, but the issues are raised in such an overt manner that we too are asked to confront them. Worried about that error in the date of Gandhi's death, Saleem asks us:

> Does one error invalidate the entire fabric? Am I so far gone, in my desperate need for meaning, that I'm prepared to distort everything – to re-write the whole history of my times purely in order to place myself in a central role? Today, in my confusion, I can't judge. I'll have to leave it to others.
>
> (Rushdie 1981: 166)

Well, others (like us) are indeed left to ask – but not only of this particular error within this particular novel – if one error would invalidate the entire fabric of representation in history or fiction?

A related question: in the drive to totalize and give unified meaning to historiography as well as fiction, are elisions (if not errors) not likely to occur which would condition the 'truth to fact' of any representation of the past? Related issues are certainly being discussed in Marxist and feminist theory today, but they also come up in a novel like John Berger's rather didactic *G*. Here, the narrator intervenes in the middle of a description of a fictive character caught up in a real historical event:

> I cannot continue this account of the eleven-year-old boy in Milan on 6 May 1898. From this point on everything I write will either converge upon a final full stop or else disperse so widely that it will become incoherent. Yet there was no such convergence and no incoherence. To stop here, despite all that I leave unsaid, is to admit more of the truth than will be possible if I bring the account to a conclusion. The writer's desire to finish is fatal to the truth. The End unifies. Unity must be established in another way.
>
> (Berger 1972b: 77)

The only other way offered here is the representation of the brute data of historical event (the number of dead workers in the Milan uprising) and their political consequences – 'the end of a phase of Italian history' and the initiation of a new one which meant that 'crude repression gave way to political manipulation' (77) which kept suppressed any revolutionary urges for at least twenty years.

While this is as much an 'End' and a 'Unity' as those of the fictive narrative would have been, it does act to foreground the postmodern suspicion of closure, of both its arbitrariness and its foreclosing interpretive power. Perhaps this explains the multiple endings of E.L. Doctorow's fictionalizing of the Rosenbergs' history in *The Book of Daniel*. Various plot and thematic threads are rather problematically tied up, but in such an overt way that they point to suspicious continuity as much as relativized finality. In one ending Daniel goes back to the site of past trauma, the house of his parents who have been executed for treason, only to find the quality of life there worse, perhaps, than that of his experience: in the life of the poor black inhabitants, however, he sees a continuity of suffering that forbids him to wallow in personal pain. Another ending presents his sister's funeral, complete with paid prayers, offering a Kaddish for all the dead, past and present, of Daniel's life and this novel. And in yet another ending, as he sits in the Columbia University library stacks in May 1968, writing the dissertation/novel/journal/confession we read, he is told to 'Close the book, man,' for the revolution has begun, and its locus is life, not books. As he writes the last pages we read, the book and this ending self-consciously self-destruct in a manner reminiscent of the final page of *One Hundred Years of Solitude*. And, of course, the very last words we actually read are those of yet another 'Book of Daniel' – the biblical one.

Postmodern fiction like this exploits and yet simultaneously calls into question notions of closure, totalization, and universality that are part of those challenged grand narratives. Rather than seeing this paradoxical use and abuse as a sign of decadence or as a cause for despair, it might be possible to postulate a less negative interpretation that would allow for at least the *potential* for radical critical possibilities. Perhaps we need a rethinking of the social and political (as well as the literary and historical) representations by which we understand our world. Maybe we need to stop trying to find totalizing narratives which dissolve difference and contradiction (into, for instance, either humanist eternal Truth or Marxist dialectic).

Knowing the past in the present

Among the unresolved contradictions of representation in postmodern fiction is that of the relation between the past and the present. In *The Book of Daniel*, various stands on this issue are thematized: the 1960s' revolutionary, Artie Sternlicht, rejects the past in the name of the present and future; Susan lives too much in the past and dies for it; Daniel tries to sort out the past in order to understand his present. This relationship is one that has preoccupied historiography since at least the last century. Historians are aware that they establish a relationship between the past they write about and the present in which they write. The past may have appeared as confused, plural, and unstructured as the present does *as it was lived*, but the historians' task is to order this fragmented experience into knowledge: 'For the whole point of history is *not* to know about actions as witnesses might, but as historians do, in connection with later events and as parts of temporal wholes' (Danto 1965: 185). In historiographic metafiction, it is this same realization that underlies the frequent use of anachronisms, where earlier historical characters speak the concepts and language clearly belonging to later figures (as in Banville's *Doctor Copernicus* or Doctorow's *Ragtime*).

For the most part historiographic metafiction, like much contemporary theory of history, does not fall into either 'presentism' or nostalgia in its relation to the past it represents. What it does is de-naturalize that temporal relationship. In both historiographic theory and postmodern fiction, there is an intense self-consciousness (both theoretical and textual) about the act of narrating in the present the events of the past, about the conjunction of present action and the past absent object of that agency. In both historical and literary postmodern representation, the doubleness remains; there is no sense of either historian or novelist reducing the strange past to verisimilar present. The contemporary resonances of the narration of a historical period piece like Natalie Zemon Davis's book (or film) of *The Return of Martin Guerre* coexist with their counter-expectation in the form of the challenge to our romantic clichéd conventions of love conquering all. This is deliberately doubly coded narrative, just as postmodern architecture is a doubly coded form: they are historical and contemporary. There is no dialectic resolution or recuperation in either case.

Works like Coover's *The Public Burning* or Doctorow's *The Book of Daniel* do not rewrite, refashion, or expropriate history merely to satisfy either some game-playing or some totalizing impulse; instead, they juxtapose what we think we know of the past (from official archival sources and personal memory) with an alternate representation that foregrounds the postmodern epistemological questioning of the nature of historical knowledge. Which 'facts' make it into history? And *whose* facts? The narrating 'historian' of Rushdie's *Shame* finds that he has trouble keeping his present knowledge of events from contaminating his representation of the past. This is the condition of all writing about the past, be it fictional ('it seems that the future cannot be restrained, and insists on seeping back into the past' (Rushdie 1983: 24)) or factual ('It is possible to see the subsequent history of Pakistan as a duel between two layers of time, the obscured world forcing its way back through what-had-been-imposed' (87)). The narrator knows that it 'is the true desire of every artist to impose his or her vision on the world' (87). He goes on to ponder this similarity of impulse between historical and fictional writing: 'I, too, face the problem of history: what to retain, what to dump, how to hold on to what memory insists on relinquishing, how to deal with change' (87–8). What he knows complicates his narrative task in that he is dealing with a past 'that refuses to be suppressed, that is daily doing battle with the present' (88), both in his novel and in the actual, present-day history of Pakistan. He even admits that the inspiration for his fictive investigation of the notion of shame came from a real newspaper account of a murder in London of a Pakistani girl by her own father (116) – or so he says. The present and the past, the fictive and the factual: the boundaries may frequently be transgressed in postmodern fiction, but there is never any resolution of the ensuing contradictions. In other words, the boundaries remain, even if they are challenged.

It is at this level that these epistemological questions of postmodern narrative representation are posed. How can the present know the past it tells? We constantly narrate the past, but what are the conditions of the knowledge implied by that totalizing act of narration? Must a historical account acknowledge where it does not know for sure or is it allowed to guess? Do we know the past only through the present? Or is it a matter of only being able to understand the present through the past? As we have seen, these confusing questions are those raised by postmodern novels like Graham Swift's *Waterland*. In the opposition between the history-teacher narrator and his present-oriented students are enacted the conflicts of contemporary historiographic debate. For the narrator, 'life is one-tenth Here and Now, nine-tenths a history lesson' (Swift 1983: 52), but it is that one-tenth that has taught him 'that history was no invention but indeed existed – and I had become part of it' (53). The novel's fens landscape opposes the flux of water (an image of both time and space) to the attempt at fixity by land reclamation – and also by the discipline of history (both as memory and as story-telling). The question is never whether the events of the past actually took place. The past did exist – independently of our capacity to know it. Historiographic metafiction accepts this philosophically realist view of the past and then proceeds to confront it with an anti-realist one that suggests that, however true that independence may be, nevertheless the past exists *for us – now –* only as traces on and in the present. The absent past can only be inferred from circumstantial evidence.

The tensions created by this realization that we can likely only know the past through our present do not absolve postmodern historians or novelists from trying to avoid dissolving those tensions, no matter how uncomfortable they might make them. This, of course, was one of the lessons of Brecht:

> we must drop our habit of taking the different social structures of past periods, then stripping them of everything that makes them different; so that they all look more or less like our own, which then acquires from this process a certain air of having been there all along, in other words, of permanence pure and simple. Instead we must leave them their distinguishing marks and keep their impermanence always before our eyes, so that our own period can be seen to be impermanent too.
>
> (Brecht 1964: 190)

Postmodern fiction stresses even more than this (if that is possible) the tensions that exist, on the one hand, between the pastness (and absence) of the past and the presentness (and presence) of the present, and on the other, between the actual events of the past and the historian's act of processing them into facts. The anachronistic intertextual references to modern works of science, philosophy, and aesthetics in Banville's *Doctor Copernicus* point to the contemporary relevance of the issues also raised in the sixteenth century: the relations between theory and praxis, words and things, science and the universe. But because the manner in which these questions are presented is self-consciously anachronistic, the text also points at the same time to the novelist's act of making past/present connections in such a way that there is still a radical discontinuity between then and now, between experiencing and knowing.

Knowing the past becomes a question of representing, that is, of constructing and interpreting, not of objective recording. Just as the Rankean objectivity theory of history-writing was challenged by Hegel, Droysen, Nietzsche, Croce, and so many others, so the metafictional aspects of historiographic metafiction also highlight the areas in which interpretation enters the domain of historiographic representation (in the choice of narrative strategy, explanatory paradigm, or ideological encoding) to condition any notion of history as objective presentation of past events, rather than as interpretive representation of those past events, which are given meaning (as historical facts) by the very discourse of the historian. What is foregrounded in postmodern theory and practice is the self-conscious inscription within history of the existing, but usually concealed, attitude of historians toward their material. Provisionality and undecidability, partisanship and even overt politics – these are what replace the pose of objectivity and disinterestedness that denies the interpretive and implicitly evaluative nature of historical representation.

The question of objectivity in historiography is not just one of methodology. As discussed in the last chapter, it is also related to what Jameson calls the 'crisis of representation' of our culture, 'in which an essentially realist epistemology, which conceives of representation as the reproduction, for subjectivity, of an objectivity that lies outside it – projects a mirror theory of knowledge and art, whose fundamental evaluative categories are those of adequacy, accuracy, and Truth itself' (Jameson 1984b: viii). The epistemological issues raised by representation in both historiography and fiction belong in the context of this crisis. The work of Hayden White has clearly been important in bringing these issues into the forefront of historical and literary critical discussions. He has asked the same kind of questions that novels like Berger's *G.* or Boyd's *The New Confessions* have asked:

What is the structure of a peculiarly historical consciousness? What is the epistemological status of historical explanations as compared with other kinds of explanations that might be offered to account for the materials with which historians ordinarily deal? What are the possible forms of historical representation and what are their bases? By what authority can historical accounts claim to be contributions to a secured knowledge of reality in general and to the human sciences in particular?

(White 1978a: 41)

The issue of representation and its epistemological claims leads directly to the problem introduced in the last chapter regarding the nature and status of the 'fact' in both history-writing and fiction-writing. All past 'events' are potential historical 'facts,' but the ones that become facts are those that are chosen to be narrated. We have seen that this distinction between brute event and meaning-granted fact is one with which postmodern fiction seems obsessed. At a certain moment in his relating of the contemporary history of India and Pakistan in *Midnight's Children*, Saleem Sinai addresses his reader: 'I am trying hard to stop being mystifying. Important to concentrate on good hard facts. But which facts?' (Rushdie 1981: 338). This is a serious problem because at one point he cannot tell, from 'accurate' accounts in documents (newspapers), whether Pakistani troops really did enter Kashmir or not. The 'Voice of Pakistan' and 'All-India Radio' give totally opposing reports. And if they did (or did not) enter, what were the motives? 'Again, a rash of possible explanations,' we are told (339). Saleem parodies the historiographical drive toward causality and motivation through his reductive, megalomaniacal exaggeration: 'This reason or that or the other? To simplify matters, I present two of my own: the war happened because I dreamed Kashmir into the fantasies of our rulers; furthermore, I remained impure, and the war was to separate me from my sins' (339).

Such a perspective may be the only possible response left to a world where '[n]othing was real; nothing certain' (Rushdie 1981: 340). Certainly the text's grammar here alters – from assertive sentences to a long list of interrogatives that ends with what might be the ultimate example of contradictory postmodern discourse: 'Aircraft, real or fictional, dropped actual or mythical bombs' (341). Compared to what the sources and documents of history offer him, Saleem himself is 'only the humblest of jugglers-with-facts' in a country 'where truth is what it is instructed to be' (326). The ideological as well as historiographic implications here are overt. The text's self-reflexivity points in two directions at once, toward the events being represented in the narrative and toward the act of narration itself. This is precisely the same doubleness that characterizes all historical narrative. Neither form of representation can separate 'facts' from the acts of interpretation and narration that constitute them, for facts (though not events) are created in and by those acts. And what actually becomes fact depends as much as anything else on the social and cultural context of the historian, as feminist theorists have shown with regard to women writers of history over the centuries.

Despite first appearances, the distinction between fact and event is actually quite different from that other opposition which is central to the criticism of the novel genre: that of fiction versus non-fiction. But because postmodern novels focus on the process of event becoming fact, they draw attention to the dubiousness of the positivist, empiricist hierarchy implied in the binary opposing of the real to the fictive, and they do so by suggesting that the non-fictional is as constructed and as narratively known as is fiction. For some critics, all novels are ambivalent in their attitude toward the separation of fact and fiction, but some historiographic metafictions do seem more overtly and problematically so. In his *Factual Fictions: The Origins of the English Novel* (1983), Lennard Davis argues convincingly for the coterminous discursive identity of fact and fiction in the mid-eighteenth-century novel of Defoe and others. But in the postmodern rewriting of *Robinson Crusoe* in J.M. Coetzee's *Foe*, it is necessary that we separate what we know of the history of the writing of Defoe's novel (its sources, its intertexts) from what Coetzee offers as the (fictionally) real – but absented and silenced – female origin of the story: the experience of castaway Susan Barton. This may not be 'true' of Defoe's particular story, but it does have something to say about the position of women and the politics of representation in both the fiction and the nonfiction of the eighteenth century.

When historiographic metafictions use the verifiable events and personages of history, like Defoe or Indira Gandhi, they are open to being attacked for inaccuracies, lying, slander, or simply bad taste. Fuentes's *Terra Nostra* deliberately and provocatively violates what is conventionally accepted as true about the events of the past: Elizabeth I gets married; Columbus is a century or so out in his discovery of America. But the facts of this warped history are no more – or less – fictionally constructed than are the overtly fictive and intertextual ones: characters from different Spanish-American novels all come together in one scene, with apt echoes of *At Swim-Two-Birds*, *Mulligan Stew*, and other experimental fiction. The realist notion of characters only being able to coexist legitimately if they belong to the same text is clearly challenged here in both historical and fictional terms. The facts of these fictional representations are as true – and false – as the facts of history-writing can be, for they always exist as facts, not events. In the representations of Coover's Nixon in *The Public Burning* and Bowering's George Vancouver in *Burning Water* this interpretive process is made overt.

It is interesting that, in his influential discussion of the historical novel, Georg Lukács did not demand correctness of individual facts as a condition of defining the historical faithfulness of situation. Historical data traditionally enter nineteenth-century historical fiction in order to reinforce the text's claim to verifiability or at least to a persuasive rendering into fact of its events. Of course, all realist fiction has always used historical events, duly transformed into facts, in order to grant to its fictive universe a sense of circumstantiality and specificity of detail, as well as verifiability. What postmodern fiction does is make overt the fact-making and meaning-granting processes. The narrator of Rushdie's *Shame* announces:

> The country in this story is not Pakistan, or not quite. There are two countries, real and fictional, occupying the same space. My story, my fictional country exist, like myself, at a slight angle to reality. I have found this off-centring to be necessary; but its value is, of course, open to debate. My view is that I am not writing only about Pakistan.
>
> (Rushdie 1983: 29)

The open mixing of the fictive with the historical in the narrator's story-telling is made into part of the very narrative:

In Delhi, in the days before partition, the authorities rounded up any Muslims . . . and locked them up in the red fortress . . . including members of my own family. It's easy to imagine that as my relatives moved through the Red Fort in the parallel universe of history, they might have felt some hint of the fictional presence of Bilquìs Kemal.

(Rushdie 1983: 64)

A few pages later, however, we are reminded: 'If this were a realistic novel about Pakistan, I would not be writing about Bilquìs and the wind; I would be talking about my youngest sister' (68) – about whom he then does indeed talk. The seeming *non sequitur* here points both to the arbitrariness of the process of deciding which events become facts and to the relationship between realist fiction and the writing of history. Although the narrator writes from England, he chooses to write about Pakistan, acknowledging that 'I am forced to reflect that world in fragments of broken mirrors. . . . I must reconcile myself to the inevitability of the missing bits' (69) – a warning meant for the reader of both fiction and history.

Historiographic metafiction like this is self-conscious about the paradox of the totalizing yet inevitably partial act of narrative representation. It overtly 'de-doxifies' received notions about the process of representing the actual in narrative – be it fictional or historical. It traces the processing of events into facts, exploiting and then undermining the conventions of both novelistic realism and historiographic reference. It implies that, like fiction, history constructs its object, that events named become facts and thus both do and do not retain their status outside language. This is the paradox of postmodernism. The past really did exist, but we can only know it today through its textual traces, its often complex and indirect representations in the present: documents, archives, but also photographs, paintings, architecture, films, and literature.

The archive as text

When critics write of the 'prior textualization' of history or suggest that events are really just abstractions from narratives, they directly echo the insights of historiographic metafiction. In theoretical debates, what has been emphasized is the specifically textual nature of the archival traces of those events, traces by which we infer meaning and grant factual status to those empirical data. We only know, for instance, that wars existed by the accounts of them in the documents and eye-witness reports of the time. And the point is, these archival traces are by no means unproblematic in their different possible interpretations. Historiographic metafiction's self-conscious thematizing of the processes of fact-producing also foregrounds this hermeneutic problem. In Christa Wolf's *Cassandra*, we are asked to imagine that the usually accepted 'fact' of Paris's abduction of Helen to Troy might actually have been a fiction created by the Trojan council and the priests. If so, in Cassandra's words: 'I saw how a news report was manufactured, hard, forged, polished like a spear' (Wolf 1984: 64). She watched as 'people ran through the streets cheering. I saw a news item turn into the truth' (65). What Wolf offers is the hypothesis that the war thought to have been fought over Helen was really fought over lying pride: Helen was, in fact, taken from Paris by the King of Egypt and never reached Troy. And, of course, according to the history books, if not Homer's epic, as she reminds us, the war was officially fought over sea trade routes. This is the postmodern problematizing of interpretive, selective fact in relation to actual event.

What novels such as this focus on are the discrepancies between the *res gestae* and the *historia rerum gestarum*. Needless to say, this has also become one of the fundamental issues of historiographic theory. Even an eye-witness account can only offer one limited interpretation of what happened; another could be different, because of many things, including background knowledge, circumstances, angle of vision, or what is at stake for that witness. Nevertheless, as Frank Kermode reminds us,

> although we are aware that a particular view of the world, about what must or ought to happen, affects accounts of what does or did happen, we tend to repress this knowledge in writing and reading history, and allow it free play only when firmly situated in the differently privileged ground of fiction.
>
> (Kermode 1979: 109)

Historiographic metafiction, however, also shakes up that privileged ground. The narrator of Gabriel García Márquez's *Chronicle of a Death Foretold* attempts to reconstruct a murder twenty-seven years after the event, from both his own memories and those of eye-witnesses. But, by the second page of the book, we are made aware of the radical unreliability of both sources: 'Many people coincided in recalling that it was a radiant morning. . . . But most agreed that the weather was funereal, with a cloudy, low sky' (García Márquez 1982: 2). He turns to the investigating judge's 500-page report of the crime, of which (significantly) he can only recover 322 pages. Again the documentary evidence turns out to be partial – in both senses of the word, for the judge, it seems, was 'a man burning with the fever of literature' (116) not history.

Texts like this suggest that among the issues about representation that have been subjected to 'de-doxification' are the concepts of truth of correspondence (to reality) and its relation to truth of coherence (within the narrative) (White 1976: 22). What is the relationship between the documentary and the formalizing impulses in historiographic representation? The source of this problematizing in postmodern fiction seems to lie in the *textual* nature of the archival traces of events which are then made into facts. Because those traces are already textualized, they can be 'buried, exhumed, deposed, contradicted, recanted' (Doctorow 1983: 23); they can be and indeed are inevitably *interpreted*. The same questioning of the status of the document and its interpretation that is being conducted in historiography can be found in postmodern novels like Berger's *G.* or Barnes's *Flaubert's Parrot*, or D.M. Thomas's *The White Hotel*. This sort of fiction has contributed to the now quite general reconsideration of the nature of documentary evidence. If the archive is composed of texts, it is open to all kinds of use and abuse. The archive has always been the site of a lot of activity, but rarely of such self-consciously totalizing activity as it is today. Even what is considered acceptable as documentary evidence has changed. And certainly the status of the document has altered: since it is acknowledged that it can offer no *direct* access to the past, then it must be a representation or a replacement through textual refiguring of the brute event.

In postmodern fiction, there is a contradictory turning to the archive and yet a contesting of its authority. In Maxine Hong Kingston's *China Men*, documents are shown to be extremely unstable sources of identity: American citizenship papers, visas, and passports are all bought and sold with ease. The historical archive may verify the existence of Harry Houdini, Sigmund Freud, Karl Jung, Emma Goldman, Stanford White, J.P. Morgan, Henry Ford, and other characters in Doctorow's *Ragtime*, but it remains stubbornly silent about the ride Freud and Jung are made to take through the Coney Island tunnel of love, though that fictive incident might be argued to be historically accurate as a metaphor of the two men's relationship. Is Doctorow's interpretation of the Rosenbergs' trial in *The Book of Daniel* somehow trivialized because he changes their name to Isaacson and makes their two sons into a son and daughter, and their incriminating witness not a family member, but a friend? Doctorow has not tried to solve the question of their historical innocence or guilt. What he has done, through his character Daniel's process of searching, is to investigate how we might begin to interrogate the documents in order to interpret them one way or the other.

If the past is only known to us today through its textualized traces (which, like all texts, are always open to interpretation), then the writing of both history and historiographic metafiction becomes a form of complex intertextual cross-referencing that operates within (and does not deny) its unavoidably discursive context. There can be little doubt of the impact of poststructuralist theories of textuality on this kind of writing, for this is writing that raises basic questions about the possibilities and limits of meaning in the representation of the past. The focus on textuality, in LaCapra's words, 'serves to render less dogmatic the concept of reality by pointing to the fact that one is "always already" implicated in problems of language use' (1983: 26) and discourse.

To say that the past is only *known* to us through textual traces is not, however, the same as saying that the past is only textual, as the semiotic idealism of some forms of poststructuralism seems to assert. This ontological reduction is not the point of postmodernism: past events existed empirically, but in epistemological terms we can only know them today through texts.

Past events are given *meaning*, not *existence*, by their representation in history. This is quite the opposite of Baudrillard's claim that they are reduced to simulacra; instead, they are made to signify. History is not 'what hurts' so much as 'what we say once hurt' – for we are both irremediably distanced by time and yet determined to grant meaning to that real pain of others (and ourselves).

What postmodern novels like Fowles's *A Maggot* or Findley's *Famous Last Words* do is to focus in a very self-reflexive way on the processes of both the production and the reception of paradoxically fictive historical writing. They raise the issue of how the intertexts of history, its documents or its traces, get incorporated into such an avowedly fictional context, while somehow also retaining their historical documentary value. The actual physical means of this particular incorporating representation are often, perhaps not surprisingly, those of history-writing, especially its 'paratextual' conventions: in particular, its footnotes and illustrations, but also its subtitles, prefaces, epilogues, epigraphs, and so on. The kind of paratextual practice found in postmodern fiction is not unique to it, of course. Think of the documentary function of newspaper accounts in Dreiser's *An American Tragedy*, for instance. Or we might also recall the use of history in the nonfictional novel, such as Norman Mailer's *Of a Fire on the Moon*. I mention this particular work only because, in it, Mailer made a factual error in describing the moon-landing lights on the Eagle. Though immediately corrected by a more knowledgeable reader, he never made the change textually, except to add a footnote in the paperback edition. He seems to have wanted to retain the dichotomy of its imaginative, if erroneous, fictionalizing and of the corrective paratext, as well, in order to signal to the reader the dual status of his representation of the Apollo mission: the events actually happened, but the facts that we read are those constituted by his narrativized account of them.

Similarly, the forewords and afterwords that frame many other nonfictional novels remind us that these works, despite their rooting in documentary reality, are still created forms, with a particular perspective that *transforms*. In these texts, the documentary is shown to be inevitably touched by the fictive, the shaped, the invented. In historiographic metafiction, however, this relationship is often more complex. In John Fowles's self-reflexively 'eighteenth-century' novel, *A Maggot*, the epilogue functions in two ways. On the one hand, it asserts the fictionalizing of a historical event that has gone on: the actual historical personages who appear in the novel are said to be 'almost all invention beyond their names.' But the epilogue also roots the fiction firmly in historical – and ideological – actuality: both that of the origins of the historical Shakers and that of the present metaphorical 'faith' of the writing narrator himself. In a statement which echoes the tone and sentiments of the fictive voice of Fowles's earlier (self-reflexively 'nineteenth-century') novel, *The French Lieutenant's Woman*, the contextualizing epilogist asserts: 'In much else we have developed immeasurably from the eighteenth century; with their central plain question – what morality justifies the flagrant injustice and inequality of human society? – we have not progressed one inch' (Fowles 1985: 454). Instead of the neat closure of the eighteenth-century narrative which he inscribes and then subverts, Fowles offers us an ending which is labelled as an 'epilogue' (that is, external to the narrative), but which (unlike the pre-textual 'prologue') is not signed 'John Fowles.' Whose voice addresses us, then, at the very end? Our inability to reply with any certainty points, not to any neatly completed plot structure, but to how it is we, as writers and readers, who desire and make closure.

Whatever the degree of complexity of the paratextuality, its presence is hard to ignore in this kind of postmodern writing. William Gass has pointed out that, from the first, the novel has been a 'fact-infested form' (Gass 1985: 86), and for him the novelistic battle for 'reality' has always been fought between 'data and design' (95). Therefore, the postmodern self-conscious use of paratexts to represent historical data within fictive narrative design might well be regarded as a highly artificial and un-organic mode of doing what novels have always done. And this would certainly be true. But perhaps it is deliberately awkward, as a means of directing our attention to the very processes by which we understand and interpret the past through its textual representations – be it in history or in fiction.

History-writing's paratexts (especially footnotes and the

textual incorporation of written documents) are conventions which historiographic metafiction both uses and abuses, perhaps parodically exacting revenge for some historians' tendency to read literature only as historical document. Although, as we have seen, the validity of the entire concept of objective and unproblematic documentation in the writing of history has been called into question, even today paratextuality remains the central mode of textually certifying historical events, and the footnote is still the main textual form by which this believability is procured. Although publishers hate footnotes (they are expensive and they disrupt the reader's attention), such paratexts have always been central to historiographic practice, to the writing of the doubled narrative of the past in the present.

Historiographic metafiction is, in a number of senses, even more overtly another example of doubled narrative, and even a brief look at the functions of footnotes in a novel like Fowles's *The French Lieutenant's Woman* shows the role paratextuality can play in the insertion of historical texts into metafiction. Here the specificity of Victorian social and literary history is evoked (in tandem with both the fictional narrative and the metafictional commentary) through footnotes which explain details of Victorian sexual habits, vocabulary, politics, or social practices. Sometimes a note is used to offer a translation for modern readers, who just might not be able to translate Latin quite as easily as their Victorian forebears could. This is in clear (and ironic) contrast to Laurence Sterne's assumption in *Tristram Shandy* that readers and commentators shared a certain educational background. Obviously, part of the function of these postmodern notes is extra-textual, referring us to a world outside the novel, but there is something else going on too: most of the notes refer us explicitly to other *texts*, other representations first, and to the external world only indirectly through them.

A second function of paratextuality, then, would be primarily a discursive one. The reader's linear reading is disrupted by the presence of a lower text on the same page, and this hermeneutic disruption calls attention to the footnote's own very doubled or dialogic form. In historical discourse, we know that footnotes are often the space where opposing views are dealt with (and textually marginalized), but we also know that they can offer a supplement to the upper text or can often provide an authority to support it. In historiographic metafiction these footnoting conventions are both inscribed and parodically inverted. They do indeed function here as self-reflexive signals to assure the reader as to the historical credibility of the particular witness or authority cited, while at the same time they also disrupt our reading – that is, our creating – of a coherent, totalizing fictive narrative. In other words, these notes operate centrifugally as well as centripetally. The roots of this kind of paradoxical practice predate postmodernism, of course. Think of the notes in *Finnegans Wake*.

The metafictional self-reflexivity induced by the postmodern footnote's paradox of represented yet resisted authority is made evident in novels such as Alasdair Gray's parodic *Lanark*, where the text incorporates self-commenting footnotes, which themselves also refer to a set of marginal notations (an 'Index of Plagiarisms,' in fact), which is in turn a parodic play on the marginal glosses of earlier literature, such as the same *Finnegans Wake* or 'The Rime of the Ancient Mariner.' Chinese-box-structured metafiction like this frequently upsets (and therefore foregrounds) the normal or conventional balance of the primary text and the traditionally secondary paratextual notes or commentary. Sometimes, too, the notes will even engulf the text, as in Puig's *Kiss of the Spider Woman*. In these particular overpowering footnotes, the irony of the seemingly authoritative documenting of psychoanalytic explanatory authorities is that they frequently do not at all explain the characters' behavior – either sexual or political. The conventionally presumed authority of the footnote form and content is rendered questionable, if not totally undermined. A similar paratextual de-naturalizing of the questions of precedence, origin, and authority can also be seen in those other, much discussed, paratextual classics: Nabokov's *Pale Fire* and Derrida's *Glas*.

A related, doubled use-and-abuse of conventional expectation accompanies other forms of metafictional paratextuality, such as chapter headings and epigraphs. As with footnotes, forewords, and epilogues, these devices in historiographic metafiction move in two directions at once: to remind us of the narrativity (and fictionality) of the primary text and to assert its factuality and historicity. In novels like John Barth's *LETTERS* the deliberately excessive kind of descriptive chapter headings points to the fictiveness and the organizational patterning that belie the realist representation conventionally suggested by the use of the epistolary form. On the other hand, there are novels, such as Audrey Thomas's *Intertidal Life* and Fowles's *The French Lieutenant's Woman* once again, which use epigraphs to direct the reader to a specific, real historical context within (or against) which the fictive universe operates, however problematically. These paratexts prevent any tendency on the part of the reader to universalize and eternalize – that is, to dehistoricize. In Fowles's novel, the historical particularity of both the Victorian and the contemporary is asserted. This is yet another way in which postmodern literature works to contest (from within) any totalizing narrative impulse. Recalling Lyotard's definition of the postmodern condition as that which is characterized by an active distrust of the master narratives that we have used to make sense of our world, the aggressive assertion of the historical and the social particularity of the fictive worlds of these novels ends up calling attention, not to what *fits* the master narrative, but instead, to the ex-centric, the marginal, the borderline – all those things that threaten the (illusory but comforting) security of the centered, totalizing, masterly discourses of our culture.

Whatever the paratextual *form* – footnote, epigraph, title – the *function* is to make space for the intertexts of history within the texts of fiction. To the historian, though, such 'intertexts' are usually thought of in quite different terms: as documentary evidence. But, as we have seen, historians have increasingly had to face challenges to their traditional trust in documentary authenticity as the repository of truth, as what allows them to reconstitute brute experiential events into historical facts in an unproblematic way. There has always been an implicit or explicit hierarchy among documentary sources for historians: the farther we get from the actual event, the less trustworthy is the document. But whether historians deal with seemingly direct informational reports and registers or with eye-witness accounts, the problem is that historians deal with representations, with texts, which they then process. The denial of this act of processing can lead to a kind of fetishizing of the archive, making it into a substitute for the past. In postmodern novels like Chris Scott's *Antichthon* or Rushdie's *Midnight's Children*, the stress is on the act of de-naturalizing documents in both historical and fictional writing. The document can no longer pretend to be a transparent means to a past event; it is instead the textually transformed trace of that past. D.M. Thomas used the text of Dina Pronicheva's eye-witness account of Babi Yar in his *The White Hotel*, but this account was already doubly distanced from the historical event: it was her later recounting of her experience, as told by Anatoli Kuznetsov in his book, *Babi Yar*. Historians never seize the event directly and entirely, only incompletely and laterally – through documents, that is, through texts like this. History does not so much say what the past was; rather, it says what it is still possible to know – and thus represent – of it.

Historians are readers of fragmentary documents and, like readers of fiction, they fill in the gaps and create ordering structures which may be further disrupted by new textual inconsistencies that will force the formation of new totalizing patterns. In Lionel Gossman's terms: 'The historian's narrative is constructed not upon reality itself or upon transparent images of it, but on signifiers which the historian's own action transforms into signs. It is not historical reality itself but the present signs of the historian that limit and order the historical narrative' (Gossman 1978: 32). And Gossman points to paratextuality as the very sign of this ontological split: 'The division of the historiographical page [by footnotes] is a testimony to the discontinuity between past "reality" and the historical narrative' (32). But even that past 'reality' is a textualized one – at least, for us today. What historiographic metafiction suggests is a recognition of a central responsibility of the historian and the novelist alike: their responsibility as makers of meaning through representation.

Postmodern texts consistently use and abuse actual historical documents and documentation in such a way as to stress both the discursive nature of those representations of the past and the narrativized form in which we read them. In Cortázar's *Libro de Manuel*, suggestively translated as *A Manual for Manuel*, the physical intrusion of newspaper clippings in the text that we read constitutes a formal and hermeneutic disruption. Their typographical reproduction (in a typeface different from that of the text's body) asserts their paratextual, authenticating role. They act as a kind of collage, but only ironically, because what they incorporate is not any actual fragment of the real referent, but – once again – its textualized representation. It has been argued that the collage form is one that remains representational while still breaking with realism through its fragmentation and discontinuity. Cortázar's paratextual use of a collage of newsclippings inserted into the fictional text points not only to the actual social and political background of the novel's action, but also to the fact that our knowledge of that background is always already a discursive one: we know past (and present?) reality mostly through texts that recount it through representations, just as we pass on our historical knowledge through other representations. The book is (as its title suggests) a manual for the revolutionaries' child, Manuel. Newspapers and magazines are the recording texts and the representations of contemporary history. In Coover's *The Public Burning, Time* magazine and the *New York Times* are revealed as the documents – or docu-fictions – of twentieth-century America, the very creators and manipulators of ideology.

Another function of the paratextual insertion of actual historical documents into historiographic metafictions can be related to Brecht's alienation effect: like the songs in his plays, the historical documents dropped into the fictions have the potential effect of interrupting any illusion, of making the reader into an aware collaborator, not a passive consumer. The potential for Brechtian ideological challenge is perhaps present in those modes of art that incorporate history's texts very self-consciously and materially. In Maxine Hong Kingston's *China Men* the documents of American law regarding Chinese citizens as immigrants are juxtaposed with the fictionalized narrative of the actual realities of the American treatment of Chinese railway workers. One chapter begins with the representation of this document:

> The United States of America and the Emperor of China cordially recognize the inherent and inalienable right of man to change his home and allegiance, and also the mutual advantage of the free migration and emigration of their citizens and subjects respectively from the one country to the

other for purposes of curiosity, of trade, or as permanent residents. ARTICLE V OF THE BURLINGAME TREATY, SIGNED IN WASHINGTON, D.C., JULY 28, 1868, AND IN PEKING, NOVEMBER 23, 1869.

(Kingston 1980: 150)

By 1878, however, only Chinese fishermen in California were being required to pay fishing taxes; by 1882, the first Chinese Exclusion Act had been passed, preventing immigration for ten years; and by 1893, the Supreme Court of the United States had decreed that Congress had 'the right to expel members of a race who "continued to be aliens, having taken no steps toward becoming citizens, and *incapable of becoming such* under the naturalization laws"' (153, emphasis mine). The Supreme Court seemed unaware of the heavy irony of the 'Catch-22' of Chinese immigrants not becoming citizens when, in fact, prevented from doing so by law. The ideological impact here is a strong one.

It is worth noting, however, that in fiction like this, despite the metafictional self-reflexivity, the general apparatus of novelistic realism is in a sense retained. For example, the reproduction of pages from the *Gentleman's Magazine* for 1736 in *A Maggot* does offer other – external, but still textualized – contexts for the fiction. These documents do have a self-verifying place in the narrative, but this is always a paradoxical place: there is both the assertion of external reference and the contradictory reminder that we only know that external world through other texts. This postmodern use of paratextuality as a formal mode of overt intertextuality both works within and subverts that apparatus of realism still typical of the novel genre, even in its more metafictional forms. Parodic play with what we might call the trappings of realist representation has increased lately, perhaps because of the new trappings that technology has offered us. The popular device of the tape recorder, for instance, has brought us the 'talked book' (taped interviews, transcribed and edited) and the nonfictional novel based on tape-recorded 'documents' which may appear to filter out the narrator and allow some direct access to actuality – though only if we ignore the distorting effect that the taping process itself can have upon speakers. Metafictional parody of this pretence of objectivity sometimes takes the form of an intense textual awareness of the process of oral recording (as in Julio Cortázar's *Hopscotch* or Jack Hodgins's *The Invention of the World*).

In one sense, however, what such postmodern parody points to is the acknowledgement that these are only technological updatings of those earlier trappings of realism: the written, clerical transcriptions of oral statements. These are metafictively ironized in *A Maggot*, with an air of authenticity but with more avowed room for error (or fictionalizing gap-filling). The clerk who takes down in shorthand the testimonies of witnesses being interrogated admits: 'where I cannot read when I copy in the long hand, why, I make it up. So I may hang a man, or pardon him, and none the wiser' (Fowles 1985: 343). Historiographic metafiction also uses some of the newer trappings, however, in order to mimic an electronically reproduced oral culture, while always aware that the reader only has access to that orality in written form. As novelist Ronald Sukenick puts it: 'Fiction, finally, involves print on a page, and that is not an incidental convenience of production and distribution, but an essential of the medium' (1985: 46).

While the oral tradition has traditionally been directly connected with the cultural handing down of the past and of our knowledge of the past, its particular role in postmodern fiction is tied up with that of the trappings of realism upon which paratextuality relies. The desire for self-authenticating oral presence is matched by a need for permanence through writing. In *The Temptations of Big Bear*, Rudy Wiebe has attempted, in a very self-reflexive manner, to capture in print and in fiction a historical character whose essence was his voice. He also had to convey the rhetorical and ritualistic power of oral Indian speech in written English. This attempt to present the historical fact of Big Bear's oral presence was further complicated for Wiebe by the lack of records (much less recordings) of the great Cree orator's speeches. But the novel's textual self-consciousness about this oral/written dichotomy points to the text's triple ironic realization: that Big Bear's dynamic oral presence in the past can be conveyed to us today only in static print; that the oratorical power that went *beyond* words can be expressed only *in* words; and that, maybe, the truth of historical fact can be represented most powerfully today in self-consciously novelistic fiction.

Illustrations, especially photographs, function in much the same manner as other paratexts in relation to the apparatus of novelistic realism. That this is especially true in historiographic metafiction should not be surprising. As we have seen, the photograph presents both the past as presence and the present as inescapably historical. All photographs are by definition representations of the past. In *Coming Through Slaughter*, Michael Ondaatje paratextually reproduces the one known photograph of the early jazz musician, Buddy Bolden, the one taken by E. J. Bellocq. In this biographical metafiction, Bellocq's presence in the narrative and the narrator's own entrance as photographer (as well as writer) are used to juxtapose the fluid, dynamic, but unrecorded music of the mad, and finally silent, Bolden with the static, reductive, but enduring recording on paper – by both photography and biography. But both forms of recording or representing in a way mark only the absence of the recorded. Both do record yet in a very real sense they also falsify the real they represent. This is the paradox of the postmodern.

In *Camera Lucida* Roland Barthes offers another way of look-ing at photography and history, one that might seem to explain even better the paratextual attraction to photos within post-modern fiction. Photographs are said to carry their referent within themselves: there is a necessarily real thing which was once placed before the lens and which, while happening only once, can be repeated on paper. As Barthes says, '*the thing has been there*' (1981: 76) in the past. The photo ratifies what was there, what it represents, and does so in a way that language can never do. It is not odd that the historiographic metafictionist, grappling with the same issue of representation of the past, might want to turn, for analogies and inspiration, to this other medium, this 'certificate of presence' (87), this paradoxically undermining yet authentifying representation of the past real. As we have already seen, it was Walter Benjamin's insight that photography also subverts romantic uniqueness and authorial authenticity, and it is this subversion that postmodern fiction foregrounds too in the constant contradiction at the heart of its use of photographic paratextual representation: photos are still presences of absences. They both verify the past and void it of its historicity. Like writing, photography is as much transformation as recording; representation is always alteration, be it in language or in images, and it always has its politics.

Postmodern paratextual insertions of these different kinds of historical traces of events, what historians call documents – be they newspaper clippings, legal statements, or photographic illustrations – de-naturalize the archive, foregrounding above all the textuality of its representations. These documentary texts appear in footnotes, epigraphs, prefaces, and epilogues; sometimes they are parachuted directly into the fictive discourse, as if in a collage. What they all do, however, is pose once again that important postmodern question: how exactly is it that we come to know the past? In these novels, we literally see the paratextual traces of history, the discourses or texts of the past, its documents and its narrativized representations. But the final result of all this self-consciousness is not to offer us any answers to that question, but only to suggest even more problematizing queries. How can historiography (much less fiction) begin to deal with what Coover's Uncle Sam calls 'the fatal slantindicular futility of Fact?'

4

The politics of parody

Parodic postmodern representation

Parody – often called ironic quotation, pastiche, appropriation, or intertextuality – is usually considered central to postmodernism, both by its detractors and its defenders. For artists, the postmodern is said to involve a rummaging through the image reserves of the past in such a way as to show the history of the representations their parody calls to our attention. In Abigail Solomon-Godeau's (1984a: 76) felicitous terms, Duchamp's modernist 'ready made' has become postmodernism's 'already made.' But this parodic reprise of the past of art is not nostalgic; it is always critical. It is also not ahistorical or de-historicizing; it does not wrest past art from its original historical context and reassemble it into some sort of presentist spectacle. Instead, through a double process of installing and ironizing, parody signals how present representations come from past ones and what ideological consequences derive from both continuity and difference.

Parody also contests our humanist assumptions about artistic originality and uniqueness and our capitalist notions of ownership and property. With parody – as with any form of reproduction – the notion of the original as rare, single, and valuable (in aesthetic or commercial terms) is called into question. This does not mean that art has lost its meaning and purpose, but that it

will inevitably have a new and different significance. In other
words, parody works to foreground the *politics* of representation.
Needless to say, this is not the accepted view of postmodernist
parody. The prevailing interpretation is that postmodernism
offers a value-free, decorative, de-historicized quotation of past
forms and that this is a most apt mode for a culture like our own
that is oversaturated with images. Instead, I would want to
argue that postmodernist parody is a value-problematizing,
de-naturalizing form of acknowledging the history (and
through irony, the politics) of representations.

It is interesting that few commentators on postmodernism
actually use the word 'parody.' I think the reason is that it is still
tainted with eighteenth-century notions of wit and ridicule. But
there is an argument to be made that we should not be restricted
to such period-limited definitions of parody and that twentieth-
century art forms teach that parody has a wide range of forms
and intents – from that witty ridicule to the playfully ludic to the
seriously respectful. Many critics, including Jameson, call postmodern ironic citation 'pastiche' or empty parody, assuming
that only unique styles can be parodied and that such novelty
and individuality are impossible today. In the light of the
parodic yet individual voices of Salman Rushdie and Angela
Carter, to mention only two, such a stand seems hard to defend.
In fact it could be ignored – if it had not proved to have such a
strong following.

For instance pastiche has been offered as the 'official sign' of
neoconservative postmodernism (Foster 1985: 127), for it is said
to disregard the context of and continuum with the past and yet
falsely to resolve 'conflictual forms of art and modes of production' (16). But as I see it, postmodern parody does not disregard
the context of the past representations it cites, but uses irony to
acknowledge the fact that we are inevitably separated from that
past today – by time and by the subsequent history of those
representations. There is continuum, but there is also ironic
difference, difference induced by that very history. Not only is
there no resolution (false or otherwise) of contradictory forms in
postmodern parody, but there is a foregrounding of those very
contradictions. Think of the variety of parodied texts in Eco's
The Name of the Rose: Jan Potocki's *Manuscrit trouvé à Saragosse* and
the work of Borges, the writings of Conan Doyle and Wittgen-

stein, the *Coena Cypriani*, and conventions as diverse as those of the detective novel and theological argument. Irony makes these intertextual references into something more than simply academic play or some infinite regress into textuality: what is called to our attention is the entire representational process – in a wide range of forms and modes of production – and the impossibility of finding any totalizing model to resolve the resulting postmodern contradictions.

By way of contrast, it could be argued that a relatively unproblematized view of historical continuity and the context of representation offers a stable plot structure to Dos Passos's *USA* trilogy. But this very stability is called into question in Doctorow's postmodern ironic reworking of the same historical material in his historiographic metafiction, *Ragtime*. Parodying Dos Passos's very historicity, Doctorow both uses and abuses it. He counts on our knowledge that a historical Freud or Jung or Goldman existed in order to challenge our perhaps unexamined notions about what might constitute historical truth. Postmodern parody is a kind of contesting revision or rereading of the past that both confirms and subverts the power of the representations of history. This paradoxical conviction of the remoteness of the past and the need to deal with it in the present has been called the 'allegorical impulse' of postmodernism (Owens 1980a: 67). I would simply call it parody.

Peter Ackroyd's *Chatterton* offers a good example of a postmodern novel whose form and content de-naturalize representation in both visual and verbal media in such a way as to illustrate well the deconstructive potential of parody – in other words, its politics. *Chatterton* is a novel about history and representation and about parody and plagiarism. As the title suggests, here the focus of representation (in history, biography, and art) is Thomas Chatterton, eighteenth-century poet and 'forger' – that is, author of poems said to be by a medieval monk. The novel posits that, contrary to official biographical history, Chatterton did not die by suicide in 1770 at the age of 18 (thus becoming the stereotypical representation of the gifted and doomed youthful genius). Instead, two alternate versions are offered: that he died, not by suicide, but from an accident produced by his inept and inexpert self-medication for VD; and that he did not die at 18 at all, but faked his death to avoid being exposed as a fraud and lived on to compose other great forgeries, such as the ones we know today as the works of William Blake.

The official historical record is given on the first page of the novel, so we are always aware of deviations from it, including the actual historical ones of Henry Wallis's famous nineteenth-century painting of the death of Chatterton, in which the image of the poet's corpse was painted from a model: the writer George Meredith. The production of this painting provides a second line of plot action. The eighteenth- and nineteenth-century stories are then played off against a contemporary one, also involving a poet (Charles Wychwood) who finds a painting which he believes to represent the aged Chatterton. To add to this already parodically complicated plot, Charles sometimes works for a writer who is a plagiarizer. She in turn has a friend who is writing a history of beautiful representations of death in English painting – such as Wallis's of Chatterton. Charles's wife is employed in an art gallery that deals in forgeries. From the start, then, this is a novel self-consciously, even excessively, *about* representation – its illusions and its powers, its possibilities and its politics. In the nineteenth-century plot line, Meredith poses as the dead Chatterton for Wallis, calling himself 'the model poet' because 'I am pretending to be someone else' (Ackroyd 1987: 2). Nevertheless, he is uneasy portraying a dead poet: 'I can endure death. It is the representation of death I *cannot* bear' (2 and 138).

In this novel all visual and verbal representations are important, from the paintings described to the fiction's obsession with names as representing people. Wallis's painted representation of Chatterton's death is important to the various plots and to the theme of the novel, but so is the writer who was the model: as Wallis paints Meredith they talk about the real versus the ideal in representation – in words or paint. Both forms are said to create 'true fictions' which paradoxically fix and falsify reality. A final irony lies in the fact that the representations remain and live on; their creators and models do not. Wallis's realist belief that the real exists and 'you have only to depict it' is countered by Meredith partly because the real (Chatterton) being painted is in fact Meredith, who remarks:

I said that the words were real, Henry, I did not say that what
they depicted was real. Our dear dead poet created the monk
Rowley out of thin air, and yet he has more life in him than
any medieval priest who actually existed. . . . But Chatterton
did not create an individual simply. He invented an entire
period and made its imagination his own. . . . The poet does
not merely recreate or describe the world. He actually creates
it.

(Ackroyd 1987: 157)

Similarly, Wallis's painting of Meredith *creates* the death of
Chatterton for posterity through its representation: 'this will
always be remembered as the true death of Chatterton' (157).
And so it is. Even the dying Charles Wychwood identifies with
his obsession, Chatterton, and feels he is living out – in dying –
Wallis's representation of his death. But Charles knows he
should resist: 'This is not real. I am not meant to be here. I have
seen this before, and it is an illusion' (169) – in more than one
sense.

The plots of this novel are heavy with such self-reflexive
moments and with unresolved suspicious coincidences that
center on plagiarism, faking, forging, and parody. Chapter 6 is
even narrated by Chatterton, telling us how he 'reproduc'd the
Past' by mixing the real and the fictive in a way reminiscent of
the technique of *Chatterton*: 'Thus do we see in every Line an
Echo, for the truest Plagiarism is the truest Poetry' (Ackroyd
1987: 87). In a similarly self-conscious way, the historical
record is shown to be no guarantee of veracity. As Charles reads
the various historical representations of the life of Chatterton,
he discovers that 'each biography described a quite different
poet: even the simplest observation by one was contradicted by
another, so that nothing seemed certain' (127) – neither the
subject nor the possibility of knowing the past in the present.
The postmodern condition with respect to history might well be
described as one of the acceptance of radical uncertainty: 'Why
should historical research not . . . remain incomplete, existing
as a possibility and not fading into knowledge?' (213). Supposedly real documents – paintings, manuscripts – turn out to
be forgeries; the beautiful representations of death turn out to be
lies. The novel ends with a powerful representation in words of

the actual reality of death by arsenic poisoning – a death rather different from that 'depicted' so beautifully by Wallis from his (very living) model.

Many other novels today similarly challenge the concealed or unacknowledged politics and evasions of aesthetic representation by using parody as a means to connect the present to the past without positing the transparency of representation, verbal or visual. For instance, in a feminist parody of Leda and the Swan, the protagonist of Angela Carter's *Nights at the Circus* (known as Fevvers) becomes 'no longer an imagined fiction but a plain fact' (Carter 1984: 286) – 'the female paradigm,' 'the pure child of the century that just now is waiting in the wings, the New Age in which no woman will be bound to the ground' (25). The novel's parodic echoes of *Pericles, Hamlet,* and *Gulliver's Travels* all function as do those of Yeats's poetry when describing a whorehouse full of bizarre women as 'this lumber room of femininity, this rag-and-bone shop of the heart' (69): they are all ironic feminizations of traditional or canonic male representations of the so-called generic human – 'Man.' This is the kind of politics of representation that parody calls to our attention.

In objecting, as I have, to the relegation of the postmodern parodic to the ahistorical and empty realm of pastiche, I do not want to suggest that there is not a nostalgic, neoconservative recovery of past meaning going on in a lot of contemporary culture; I just want to draw a distinction between that practice and postmodernist parody. The latter is fundamentally ironic and critical, not nostalgic or antiquarian in its relation to the past. It 'de-doxifies' our assumptions about our representations of that past. Postmodern parody is both deconstructively critical and constructively creative, paradoxically making us aware of both the limits and the powers of representation – in any medium. Sherrie Levine, whose name keeps recurring here as the parodic Pierre Menard of the art world today, has stated her reasons why parody is unavoidable for postmodernism:

Every word, every image, is leased and mortgaged. We know that a picture is but a space in which a variety of images, none of them original, blend and clash. A picture is a tissue of quotations drawn from the innumerable centers of culture. . . . The viewer is the tablet on which all the quotations that make up a painting are inscribed without any of them being lost.

(Levine 1987: 92)

When she photographs Egon Schiele's self-portraits, she parodically cites not just the work of a specific artist, but the conventions and myths of art-as-expression and points to the politics of that particular view of representation.

Mark Tansey's parodic painting called *The Innocent Eye Test* takes on another canonical form of representation. It presents the unveiling of Paulus Potter's 1647 painting of a *Young Bull*, once accepted as the paradigm of realist art. But Tansey's parodically realist reproduction of this work is depicted as being judged – by a cow, for who better to adjudicate the success of such 'bullish' realism and who better to symbolize ironically the 'innocent eye' assumed by mimetic theories of the transparency of representation. (A mop is depicted at the ready, lest she 'voice' her opinion in material terms.) This is postmodern ironic parody, using the conventions of realism against themselves in order to foreground the complexity of representation and its implied politics.

Of course, parody was also a dominant mode of much modernist art, especially in the writing of T.S. Eliot, Thomas Mann, and James Joyce and the painting of Picasso, Manet, and Magritte. In this art, too, parody at once inscribed convention and history and yet distanced itself from both. The continuity between the postmodernist and the modernist use of parody as a strategy of appropriating the past is to be found on the level of their shared (compromised) challenges to the conventions of representation. There are significant differences, however, in the final impact of the two uses of parody. It is not that modernism was serious and significant and postmodernism is ironic and parodic, as some have claimed; it is more that postmodernism's irony is one that rejects the resolving urge of modernism toward closure or at least distance. Complicity always attends its critique.

Unacknowledged modernist assumptions about closure, distance, artistic autonomy, and the apolitical nature of representation are what postmodernism sets out to uncover and deconstruct. In postmodernist parody:

modernist pretensions to artistic independence have been further subverted by the demonstration of the necessarily 'intertextual' nature of the production of meaning; we can no longer unproblematically assume that '*Art*' is somehow 'outside' of the complex of other representational practices and institutions with which it is contemporary – particularly, today, those which constitute what we so problematically call the 'mass-media.'

(Burgin 1986a: 204)

The complexity of these parodic representational strategies can be seen in the photography of Barbara Kruger or Silvia Kolbowski with its parodic appropriation of mass-media images. The 1988 show entitled *Photographs Beget Photographs* (curated by the Minneapolis Institute of Art) gave a good sense of the parodic postmodern play with the history of photography – both as scientifically accurate documentary recording and as formalist art. Marion Faller and Hollis Frampton presented 'Sixteen studies from "vegetable locomotion"' which (in title and form) parodied Muybridge's famous human and animal scientific locomotion studies by using (normally inert) vegetables and fruit as the subjects. Other artists in the show chose to parody icons of photography-as-high-art by Ansel Adams (John Pfahl, Jim Stone) or Weston (Pfahl again, Kenneth Josephson), always pointing with irony to how modernism contributed to the mystification and canonization of photographic representation. Contrary to the prevailing view of parody as a kind of ahistorical and apolitical pastiche, postmodern art like this uses parody and irony to engage the history of art and the memory of the viewer in a re-evaluation of aesthetic forms and contents through a reconsideration of their usually unacknowledged politics of representation. As Dominick LaCapra has so forcefully put it:

irony and parody are themselves not unequivocal signs of disengagement on the part of an apolitical, transcendental ego that floats above historical reality or founders in the abysmal pull of aporia. Rather a certain use of irony and parody may play a role both in the critique of ideology and in the anticipation of a polity wherein commitment does not exclude but accompanies an ability to achieve critical distance on one's deepest commitments and desires.

(LaCapra 1987: 128)

Postmodernism offers precisely that 'certain use of irony and parody.'

Double-coded politics

As form of ironic representation, parody is doubly coded in political terms: it both legitimizes and subverts that which it parodies. This kind of authorized transgression is what makes it a ready vehicle for the political contradictions of postmodernism at large. Parody can be used as a self-reflexive technique that points to art as art, but also to art as inescapably bound to its aesthetic and even social past. Its ironic reprise also offers an internalized sign of a certain self-consciousness about our culture's means of ideological legitimation. How do some representations get legitimized and authorized? And at the expense of which others? Parody can offer a way of investigating the history of that process. In her feminist pacifist work Cassandra, we have seen that Christa Wolf parodically rewrites Homer's tale of men and war, offering economic and political rather than romantic reasons for the Trojan war (trade access to the Bosporus and sexual one-up-man-ship, not Helen) and telling the silenced story of the everyday life of the Trojan women omitted by the historical and epic narratives written by the conquering foreigners, the Greeks. Other texts are parodied too – Aeschylus's Oresteia, the writings of Herodotus and Aristotle, Goethe's Faust and Schiller's 'Cassandra' – and frequently it is the male representation of the female (or the lack thereof) that is the focus of the rewriting. As Wolf claims in the essay 'Conditions of a narrative' (which accompanies Cassandra in its English translation): 'How quickly does lack of speech turn into lack of identity?' (Wolf 1984: 161). This is especially true of Cassandra who, though she had speech, was not believed. Furthermore, as Wolf asks: 'Who was Cassandra before people wrote about her? (For she is a creation of the poets, she speaks only through them, we have only their view of her)' (287). Because we only know Cassandra through male representations of her, Wolf adds her own feminist representation, one that is equally the 'creation' of a writer, of course.

In feminist art, written or visual, the politics of representation are inevitably the politics of gender:

> The way women appear to themselves, the way men look at women, the way women are pictured in the media, the way women look at themselves, the way male sexuality becomes fetishism, the criteria for physical beauty – most of these are cultural representations and therefore not immutable but conditioned.
>
> (Malen 1988: 7)

Postmodern parodic strategies are often used by feminist artists to point to the history and historical power of those cultural representations, while ironically contextualizing both in such a way as to deconstruct them. When Sylvia Sleigh parodies Velásquez's *Rokeby Venus* in her descriptively entitled *Philip Golub Reclining*, she de-naturalizes the iconographic tradition of the female erotic nude intended for male viewing through her obvious gender reversal: the male is here represented as reclining, languorous, and passive. The title alone, though, parodically contests the representation of specific yet anonymous women models as generic mythic figures of male desire. The postmodern version has the historical specificity of a portrait. But it is not just the history of high-art representation that gets 'de-doxified' in postmodern parody: the 1988 *Media Post Media* show (at the Scott Hanson Gallery in New York) presented mixed media works that did parody the representational practices of high art (David Salle's) but also those of the mass media (videos, ads). All nineteen artists were women, perhaps underlining the fact that women have more to win, not lose, by a critique of the politics of representation.

Some male artists have used parody to investigate their own complicity in such apparatuses of representation, while still trying to find a space for a criticism, however compromised. Victor Burgin's photography is one example of this very postmodern form of complicitous critique. In one photo, from the series *The Bridge*, he parodies John Everett Millais's *Ophelia* through a 'transcoding' of its female subject into a representation of a model in Ophelia's pose but portraying Kim Novak's representation of the character, Madeleine in Hitchcock's *Vertigo*. This is no transparent realist representation: the water is obviously cellophane (a parodic echo of Cecil Beaton's use of cellophane in his fashion photography) and the model is obviously posed in a period-piece wig and dress. But this Ophelia/Madeleine/(fashion) model figure is still represented as dead or dying and, given the context, also as an enigma to be investigated obsessively by male voyeuristic curiosity. Burgin admits to being a modernist-trained artist who wants to milk the density and richness of art history in his photography, but he also wants to do two other things: first, to use parody to throw off the 'dead hand' of that art history and its beliefs in eternal values and spontaneous genius; and second, to use the history of representation (here, in painting and in film) to comment critically on the politics of the representation of women by men – including himself.

The intersection of gender with class politics is a particular interest of Burgin's. In a series of photographs parodying Edward Hopper's painting *Office at Night*, he reinterprets this canonical icon in terms of the organization of sexuality within and for capitalism (Burgin 1986b: 183). Hopper's depicted secretary and her boss working late at the office come to represent all couples within a capitalist patriarchal system of values: the man ignores the woman, whose clinging dress and full figure and yet downcast eyes manage to make her both seductive and modest. Burgin says that the representation of the man ignoring the woman allows male viewers to look at and enjoy the pictured woman while safely identifying with the man who does not. Burgin's *Preparatory Work for Office at Night* self-reflexively updates to the present these representations and their now problematized politics – in both gender and class terms – by absenting the (safe) male.

When parody and its politics are discussed, it is not only this kind of visual art that should be considered. Latin American fiction, for instance, has consistently underlined the intrinsically political character of parody and its challenges to the conventional and the authoritative. The politics of representation and the representation of politics frequently go hand in hand in parodic postmodern historiographic metafiction. Parody becomes a way of ironically revisiting the past – of both art and history – in a novel like Salman Rushdie's *Midnight's Children* with its double parodic intertexts: Grass's *The Tin Drum* and Sterne's *Tristram Shandy*. Both parodies politicize representation, but in very different ways. *Midnight's Children* translates all the German social, cultural, and historical detail of Grass's novel into Indian terms. In addition, Saleem Sinai shares everything from little Oskar's physical strangeness to his withdrawn alienated position with regard to his society. Both tell their stories to someone else and both offer literally self-begetting novels, *Bildungsromanen* which show how they are 'handcuffed to history,' to use Saleem's phrase. The representation of politics is here achieved through the overt politicizing and historicizing of the act of representing.

Both Saleem's and Oskar's stories have Shandian openings – or non-openings – and both narrators echo Sterne's much earlier parody of narrative conventions. In Rushdie's text, however, the intertextual presence of *Tristram Shandy* does more than simply work to undercut Saleem's megalomaniac attempts at ordering and systematizing by reminding us of the inevitability of contingency; it also points to the Empire, the imperialist British past, that is literally a part of India's self-representation as much as of Saleem's. The structure of the parody enables that past to be admitted as inscribed, but also subverted at the same time. The literary inheritance of an Indian writing in English is inescapably double, as Omar Khayyám in *Shame* comes to see so clearly. Similar political paradoxes underlie the use of parody in black American writing as well. Ishmael Reed has parodied the historical novel (*Flight to Canada*), the western (*Yellow Back Radio Broke-Down*), the detective story (*Mumbo Jumbo*), Dickens (*The Terrible Twos*), and *Uncle Tom's Cabin* (*Flight to Canada*), but always within a political context that points to what the dominant white traditions silence: the representations both of blacks and by blacks – the entire Afro-American literary tradition of the past and the present.

A similar critical contextualizing and appropriating of the past and its representational practices can be seen in the visual arts too, for instance, in the San Francisco Museum of Modern Art's *Second Sight* show where Mark Tansey showed his painting entitled *The Triumph of the New York School*. The parodies operating here are multiple. The title refers to Irving Sandler's well-known textbook, *The Triumph of American Painting*. But the work itself ironically literalizes this title: members of the French army (looking like Picasso, Duchamp, Apollinaire, and Léger) surrender their outdated arms to the technically superior American forces (whose officers represented include Jackson Pollock, Clement Greenberg, and Barnett Newman). Tansey's overall composition is a parody of Velásquez's *Surrender of Breda* (1634) which represents both a specific act of chivalry in the Thirty Years' War and a more general glorification of art through war (see Beal 1986: 9). Here all that is ironically inverted and placed in an entirely different context.

Is there a problem of accessibility here, however? What if we do not recognize the represented figures or the parodied composition? The title, I suppose, does alert us to the place to look for a means of access – Sandler's textbook. This functions much as do the acknowledgement pages of postmodern parodic fiction (such as Berger's *G.*, Thomas's *The White Hotel*, Banville's *Doctor Copernicus*). These may not provide all the parodic allusions, but they teach us the rules of the game and make us alert to other possibilities. This is not to deny, however, that there exists a very real threat of elitism or lack of access in the use of parody in any art. This question of accessibility is undeniably part of the politics of postmodern representation. But it is the complicity of postmodern parody – its inscribing as well as undermining of that which it parodies – that is central to its ability to be understood. This may explain the frequent parodic reappropriation of mass-media images in particular by many postmodern photographers: there is no need to know the entire history of art to understand the critique of these representations. All you have to do is look around you. But some artists want to use parody to recover that high-art history too, to reconnect the representational strategies of the present with those of the past, in order to critique both. As Martha Rosler puts it:

At certain historical junctures, quotation [or what I have called parody] allows a *defeat* of alienation, an asserted reconnection with obscured traditions. Yet the elevation of an unknown or disused past emphasizes a rupture with the immediate past, a revolutionary break in the supposed

stream of history, intended to destroy the credibility of the
reigning historical accounts – in favor of the point of view of
history's designated losers. The homage of quotation is capable of signalling not self-effacement but rather a strengthen-
ing or consolidating resolve.

(Rosler 1981: 81)

As we shall see in the next chapter, Rosler's challenge to social
and economic history through a parody of the history of photography does indeed offer a new way to represent 'history's
designated losers.' The financial and artistic success of the
American documentary art of the 1930s in contrast to its
subjects' continuing conditions of poverty and misery is part of
the historical context that formal parody calls up in Rosler's
series, *The Bowery in Two Inadequate Descriptive Systems*.

Barbara Kruger chooses to appropriate mass-media images
and use their formal complicity with capitalist and patriarchal
representational strategies to foreground conflictual elements
through ironic contradictions. Parody, she asserts, allows for
some distance and critique, especially of notions such as 'competence, originality, authorship and property' (Kruger 1982:
90). Certain of Vincent Leo's works may look like derivative
variations or pastiches of the work of Robert Frank – and they
are. They are cut-up collages of reproductions from Frank's
canonical book of photographs *The Americans*. It has been
argued that this kind of parodic play has its own complex
politics of representation: it points to the legions of contemporary photographers who unreflectively copy the canonical icons
and their techniques; it undercuts the myth and mystique of
originality in art; it works to recall the history of photography by
literally using the past as the building blocks of the present; and
it comments critically on the canonical status of photographers
like Frank within the art institution (Solomon-Godeau 1984a:
83).

Parody in postmodern art is more than just a sign of the
attention artists pay to each others' work and to the art of the
past. It may indeed be complicitous with the values it inscribes
as well as subverts, but the subversion is still there: the politics
of postmodern parodic representation is not the same as that of
most rock videos' use of allusions to standard film genres or

texts. This is what should be called pastiche, according to Jameson's definition. In postmodern parody, the doubleness of the politics of authorized transgression remains intact: there is no dialectic resolution or recuperative evasion of contradiction in narrative fiction, painting, photography, or film.

Postmodern film?

In his article, 'Metacinema: a modern necessity,' William Siska characterizes 'modernist' cinema in terms of a new kind of self-reflexivity, one that challenges the traditional Hollywood variety of movies about movie-making that retain the orthodox realist notion of the transparency of narrative structures and representations: *Sunset Boulevard, Day for Night, Singin' in the Rain* (Siska 1979: 285). The 'modernist' contesting of this, he argues, takes the form of an insistence on formal intransitivity by such techniques as the rupturing of the chain of causation upon which character and plot motivation depend, spatial or temporal fragmentation, or the introduction of 'alien forms and information' (286). Examples would include *W.R.*, *Persona*, and *8½*. But what happens when the 'alien' form introduced is parody? And what if it is that very self-conscious introduction of the 'alien' that is itself being parodied? What happens when we get Woody Allen's *Stardust Memories* parodying and challenging, however respectfully, Fellini's modernist *8½*?

What happens, perhaps, is something we should label as postmodern, something that has the same relation to its modernist past as can be seen in postmodern architecture today: both a respectful – if problematized – awareness of cultural continuity and a need to adapt to changing formal demands and social conditions through an ironic contesting of the authority of that same continuity. The postmodernist is in this sense less radical than the modernist; it is more willfully compromised, more ideologically ambivalent or contradictory. It at once exploits and subverts that which went before, that is, both the modernist and the traditionally realist.

Parody, of course, is omnipresent in contemporary film and it is not always challenging in mode. Parody can work to signal continuity with (though today it is usually with some ironic difference from) a tradition of film-making: *Witness* rewrites *High Noon*'s characterization structure (law officer male/pacifist woman) and even echoes individual shots (villains on the high road), but adds the distancing irony of the increased (not, as might be expected, decreased) ruralization of the modern world, at least in terms of the Amish community. Similarly, *Crossroads* reworks *Leadbelly*'s thematic and formal structure in fictionalized terms, with differences that foreground the relation of race to the blues. While both music films operate within the same historical framework (Allan Lomax and Folkway recordings figure prominently in both plots), the new climactic contest scene has significant ironic differences: it pits the electric guitar versus the acoustic (in the original it was six- versus twelve-string) and adds a heavy dose of Faustian challenge.

Another way of talking about the political paradoxes of parody would be to see it as self-consciously intransitive representation (film recalls film) which also milks the power of transitivity to create the spectator's identification. In other words, it simultaneously destabilizes and inscribes the dominant ideology through its (almost overly obvious) interpellation of the spectator as subject in and of ideology (Althusser 1971; Belsey 1980: 56–84). In other chapters, too, I have argued that the question of ideology's relation to subjectivity is central to postmodernism. The challenges to the humanist concept of a coherent, continuous, autonomous individual (who paradoxically also shares in some generalized universal human essence) have come from all sides today: from poststructuralist philosophical and literary theory, Marxist political philosophy, Freudian/Lacanian psychoanalysis, sociology, and many other domains. We have also seen that photography and fiction – two art forms with a certain relevance for film – have shared in this questioning of the nature and formation of subjectivity. Where modernism investigated the grounding of experience in the self, its focus was on the self seeking integration amid fragmentation. In other words, its (for many, defining) focus on subjectivity was still within the dominant humanist framework, though the obsessive search for wholeness itself suggests the beginnings of what would be a more radical postmodern questioning, a challenging brought about by the doubleness of postmodern discourse. In other words, postmodernism works both to

underline and to undermine the notion of the coherent
self-sufficient subject as the source of meaning or action.

Think of films like Woody Allen's *Zelig*, with its many parodic
intertexts, including actual historical film footage and the conventions of documentary as well as other specific films from
Citizen Kane to *Reds*. Parody points at once to and beyond
cinematic textuality to the ideological formation of the subject
by our various cultural representations. *Zelig* is centrally concerned with the history and politics of the prewar years for
which the chameleon Zelig becomes the ironic symbol. Real
historical personages (Susan Sontag, Saul Bellow) 'document'
and 'authenticate' Zelig in this symbolic role: his freakishness
becomes his typicality. But what does it mean to be a symbol of
something when that something only wants to be other than
what it is? The implied historical intertexts give us the answer to
this contradiction: as a Jew, Zelig has a special (and historically
ironic) interest in fitting in, in being other than what he is – as
we know from subsequent history. In other words, this is more
than just the typical Allen assimilation anxiety: the history of
the Holocaust cannot be forgotten by the contemporary viewer
of this film. Nor can the history of the representation of the
subject in cinema. The story of a self that changes constantly,
that is unstable, decentered, and discontinuous, is a parody
both of the traditional filmic subject of realist cinema and also of
the modernist searching for integration and wholeness of per-
sonality. Here the only wholeness attained is that of the media
monster the public makes of the protean protagonist. *Zelig* is
'about' the formation of subjectivity, both the subjectivity of the
spectator and that created by the spectator – the Star.

This critique from within the institution and history of film
production is part of what is postmodern about Allen's work: its
insider–outsider doubled position. Through parody, it uses and
abuses dominant conventions in order to emphasize both the
process of subject-formation and the temptations of easy accom-
modation to the power of interpellation. It questions the nature
of the 'real' and its relation to the 'reel' through its parody and
metacinematic play. This questioning becomes even more overt
in *The Purple Rose of Cairo*, where real and reel life mingle with
self-conscious irony. This kind of postmodern film never loses
sight of the appeal of that humanist-modernist wholeness;

indeed, it exploits it. But the exploitation is done in the name of contesting the values and beliefs upon which that wholeness is constructed – with the emphasis on the act of construction – through representations.

Showing the formation process not just of subjectivity but also of narrativity and visual representation has become a staple of metacinema today. The postmodern variant of this kind of self-reflexivity calls attention to the very acts of production and reception of the film itself. In Richard Rush's *The Stunt Man*, the audience is placed in the same (hermeneutic) position as the protagonist, as the conventions of movie-making are both employed (and employed effectively – to dramatic and suspenseful ends) and undercut, that is, bared *as conventions* in a self-conscious way. This focus on what we might call the enunciation is typical of postmodern art in general, with its overt awareness that art is produced and received within a social and political, as well as aesthetic, context.

Suzanne Osten's *The Mozart Brothers* gives a good sense of the complexity of parody's politics of representation. Walter, an opera director who wants to do Mozart's opera *Don Giovanni* as a series of flashbacks set in a graveyard, is played by co-writer Etienne Glaser who, in fact, is also an opera director who has done precisely such a production. Within this film about rehearsing an opera, we also watch a female director make a documentary film about Walter. Her camera and her feminist perspective are periodically brought to our attention, problematizing the gender politics of all representation – filmic, operatic, documentary.

This is a movie about a Swedish opera company's production of an utterly unconventional version of Mozart's famous opera. The outrage that greets Walter's anti-canonical directorial decisions comes from singers, orchestra, theater managers, voice trainers, stage crew, in short, everyone who has worked within certain Mozartian conventions and sees them as fixed 'doxa' – 'what Mozart intended.' However, the ghostly apparition of the composer himself keeps assuring Walter that it is convention – not opera itself – that is boring and that even if people hate his production, at least they will be responding emotionally to it. The opposite of love is not hate, but indifference. In a scene which parodically recalls the Volksoper parody of *Don Giovanni* in the film of *Amadeus*, the ghost of Mozart appears in the mirror, as Walter eats and drinks with the cleaners and theater workers who lustily sing in falsetto voices Zerlina's interactions with Masetto. Mozart smiles in delight at their true joyous pleasure in his music, even if it is not sung in any traditional manner or place.

The most intricate example of how parodic representation functions in this film is in the structural parallels between the opera and the movie: the members of the opera company live out the opera's emotions and even its plot details. The womanizing Walter is clearly the modern Don Giovanni; the vengeful Donna Elvira is to be sung in this production by Walter's ex-wife, a strong and forceful woman who loves him still – despite herself. Walter's musical assistant calls himself Leporello and at one point even changes shirts, if not cloaks and hats, with Giovanni/Walter. Walter insults the singer who plays Donna Anna, but she has no father to avenge her slighted (singing) honor. She does, however, have a mother-figure, her teacher, who attacks Walter with her sword-like umbrella. Similarly, it is not Leporello who tells Donna Elvira of the Don's many female conquests; it is the office receptionist who tells the singer portraying Donna Elvira of Walter's other wives and conquests. This ex-wife herself then warns the female film director of Walter's perfidy, but this is no innocent Zerlina, warned and protected by Donna Elvira: the woman directing is as much seducer as seduced.

The Mozart Brothers inevitably suggests other parodic contexts: as a Swedish film about a Mozart opera, it probably cannot avoid recalling Bergman's *The Magic Flute*, with which it shares similarities of self-reflexivity in terms of staging and also in its play with the usual transparent conventions of realist representation. And its unconventional stage setting in mud and water is a comment, perhaps, on Joseph Losey's famous Venetian film of the opera, with its beautiful watery sets. The final irony of all this parody and self-reflexivity is that we never get to hear or see the planned production. Or do we? Through the rehearsal action and the singers' interactions, we actually have seen a full, if ironically transcoded, version of *Don Giovanni* that is at least as untraditional as that envisaged by Walter.

Films made from postmodern novels seem to be particularly

open to the referential complexities of parody. While all filming of novelistic narrative involves the clash of two very different representational systems, in the postmodern form there are added levels of intricacy. John Fowles's *The French Lieutenant's Woman*, with its intense self-reflexivity of narration and its dense parodic intertextuality (of both specific Victorian novels and generic conventions), had to be cinematically transcoded in order to change its insistently novelistic focus into a filmic one.

Another example would be Manuel Puig's novel, *Kiss of the Spider Woman*, where the ironies of Molina's parodic verbal representations of films had to be visually inscribed for the spectator, while remaining narrated for Molina's cell companion, Valentin. The number of narrated films in the novel had to be drastically reduced in the film without losing the function and significance of the representational process itself. In addition, as we have already seen, the irony of the novel's extended paratextual parody in the form of long footnotes full of authenticating psychoanalytic sources of information (which explain nothing of the subjectivity they presume to illuminate) has to be played out solely through character interaction.

In these and other films, parody is not a form of self-regarding narcissism or in-joke elitist allusions by film-school trained directors. The complex transcoding in Carlos Saura's *Carmen* of French high art (Bizet's opera and Mérimée's literary text) into the conventions of Spanish flamenco offers a good example of the kind of political critique of which parodic representation is indeed capable. Flamenco is historically not the music and dance of high art; it is the regional and popular art of the poor and the socially marginalized. Saura's film is about the relation of the present to the past traditions of both Spanish folk art and European high-art culture (with its fascination for the stereotypically exotic).

Like *The French Lieutenant's Woman*, however, this is a very postmodern film in its dialogic doublings. It is textually aware of – and challenges – the boundaries between genres and ultimately between art and life. The wall-size studio window onto the outside world is curtained, and the performance goes on *behind* those curtains. Somewhat reminiscent of the one in Fellini's *The Orchestra Rehearsal*, the performance is both a documentary on a form of music and a rehearsal of a fiction.

Added to this is the plot structure's reflexivity, wherein the dancers begin to enact – in their private lives – the jealousy and passion of the fiction. The fact that as viewers we often cannot tell whether we are watching the fiction or the dancers' 'real'-life action underlines the doubling boundary play of the film. The self-reflexivity of *Carmen* also raises another issue of ideological import: this is a film about the production of art, about art as representation derived from the words and music of others, but as filtered through the imagination of the artist figure, the male Pygmalion who wills reality – a woman and a dancer – to take the form of art and become his Carmen. The overt process of subject-formation here underlines the cognate relationship between subject and subjection.

The dominant view of postmodern parody as trivial and trivializing that we saw earlier is also to be found in the field of film criticism. Jameson (1983, 1984a) argues that parody in films like *Body Heat* or *Star Wars* is a sign of nostalgic escapism, 'the imprisonment of the past' through pastiche that prevents confronting the present. However, at the same time, we have seen that Jameson laments a loss of a sense of history in today's art. He sees parodic art as simply narcissistic, as 'a terrible indictment of consumer capitalism itself – or at the very least, an alarming and pathological symptom of a society that has become incapable of dealing with time and history' (Jameson 1983: 117). However, *Zelig*, *Carmen*, *The French Lieutenant's Woman*, and other postmodern films do indeed deal with history and they do so in ironic, but not at all un-serious, ways. The problem for Jameson may simply be that they do not deal with Marxist *H*istory: in these films there is little of the positive utopian notion of History and no unproblematic faith in the accessibility of the 'real referent' of historical discourse.

What they suggest instead is that there is no directly and naturally accessible past 'real' for us today: we can only know – and construct – the past through its traces, its representations. As we have repeatedly seen, whether these be documents, eye-witness accounts, documentary film footage, or other works of art, they are still representations and they are our only means of access to the past. Jameson laments the loss of a sense of his particular definition of history, then, while dismissing as nostalgia the only kind of history we may be able to acknowledge: a contingent and inescapably intertextual history. To write this off as pastiche and nostalgia and then to lament that our contemporary social system has 'begun to lose its capacity to retain its own past, has begun to live in a perpetual present' (Jameson 1983: 125) seems of questionable validity. Postmodernist film (and fiction) is, if anything, obsessed with history and with how we can know the past today. How can this be an 'enfeeblement of historicity' (Jameson 1986: 303)?

Writing as I do in an Anglo-American context, I think that Jameson's blanket condemnation of Hollywood for its wholesale implication in capitalism (made from within an academy that is just as implicated) is what is behind his distrust of irony and ambiguity, a distrust that blinds him to the possibilities of the potentially positive oppositional and contestatory nature of parody. Postmodern film does not deny that it is implicated in capitalist modes of production, because it knows it cannot. Instead it exploits its 'insider' position in order to begin a subversion from within, to talk to consumers in a capitalist society in a way that will get us where we live, so to speak. The difference between postmodern parody and nostalgia – which once again I do not deny is part of our culture today – lies in the role of this double-voiced irony. Compare the ponderousness of *Dune* (which takes itself most seriously) with *Star Wars*' irony and play with cultural conventions of narrative and visual representation or with *Tampopo*'s cultural inversion of both the traditional western (e.g. *Shane* with its lone hero helping needy widow) and the Italian 'spaghetti western' into what might literally be called a 'noodle eastern.' What postmodern parody does is to evoke what reception theorists call the horizon of expectation of the spectator, a horizon formed by recognizable conventions of genre, style, or form of representation. This is then destabilized and dismantled step by step. It is not accidental, of course, that irony has often been the rhetorical vehicle of satire. Even a relatively 'light' parody such as De Palma's *Phantom of the Paradise* offers irony working with satire, ranging in target from the sexism of Hugh Hefner-like harems (Swan's – with ironic echoes perhaps of *Du côté de chez Swann*) to the interpellation of the Star by the public and its taste for extremes. The vehicle of this satire is multiple parody: of *The Bird Man of Alcatraz* (transported to Sing Sing – a more

appropriate site for a singer-composer), *Psycho* (the knife replaced by a plunger; the female victim by a male), *The Picture of
Dorian Gray* (the painting updated to video tape). Despite the
obvious fun, this is also a film about the politics of representation, specifically the representation of the original and origin-
ating subject as artist: its dangers, its victims, its consequences.
The major intertexts are *Faust* and the earlier film, *The Phantom
of the Opera*, here transcoded into rock music terms. This
particular parodied text and only this can explain such otherwise unmotivated details as the organ overtones to the protagonist's opening piano playing. The *Faust* parody is overt as
well, since the phantom writes a rock cantata based on it. And of
course his pact with the demonic Swan is signed in blood.

Multiple and obvious parody like this can paradoxically
bring out the politics of representation by baring and thus
challenging convention, just as the Russian formalists had
suggested it could. Metacinematic devices work in much the
same way. The mixing of the fictive and the historical in
Coppola's *Cotton Club* warns the spectator to beware of institutionalized boundaries, to refuse to let life and art get either too
separated or totally merged, so that when the club's stage acts
echo and foreshadow the action of the main plot, we do not miss
the implications. For instance, the dance of the light-skinned
Lila Rose and the darker Sandman Williams prefigures on stage
their tortured relationship for she, but only she, can pass in a
white world. Genre boundaries are structurally analogous to
social borders (here racially defined) and both are called to
account.

This parodic genre-crossing between the discourses of fiction
and history may well reflect a general and increasing interest in
non-fictional forms since the 1960s. In film, popular works such
as *The Return of Martin Guerre* and (somewhat more problematically) *Amadeus* would support such an interpretation of the
orientation of much current culture. But a film like Maximilian
Schell's *Marlene* can also parody the documentary genre in a
postmodern cinematic way. It opens asking 'Who is Dietrich?'
and the question is revealed as unanswerable. The postmodernist investigation of subject-formation combines here
with one of the forms that the postmodern challenge to historical knowledge has taken: the one that operates in the realm of

private history, that is, biography. Novels like Banville's *Kepler* or Wiebe's *The Temptations of Big Bear* or Kennedy's *Legs* all work to present a portrait of an individual and yet to subvert any stability in or certainty of ever knowing – or representing – that subject. This is what *Marlene* is also about. The much photographed Dietrich remains off-stage, never represented visually. She is only a querulous voice, a cantankerous absent presence.

Schell turns this to postmodern advantage by making this into a film about trying to make a documentary about a willfully absent subject, one who refuses to be subjected to the discourses and representations of others any longer. Dietrich has her own version of her life, one which, as the metacinematic frame makes clear, is itself a fictionalized one. She claims at one point that she wants a documentary without criticism: what Schell should do is show archival pictures of, for instance, the boat on which she arrived in America. Schell then immediately offers us these very pictures and the effect is both humorous and revelatory: the archive may be real but it tells us little about the subject. The portrait of Dietrich that emerges here is of a woman of contradictions, business-like yet sentimental, self-denigrating yet proud, rejecting almost all her work as rubbish yet moved to enthusiasm by watching Schell in *Judgment at Nuremburg*. The suggestion is that all subjectivity would be as radically split as this if we were to examine it this closely, that the humanist ideal representation of a whole, integrated individual is a fiction – a fiction that not even the subject (or her biographer) can ever successfully construct. Schell's despair is as much at this as at Dietrich's stubborn inaccessibility to his camera. He can edit her films all he likes (and we watch him do so), but she remains elusive and for ever contradictory.

Marlene is the kind of film I would label as postmodern: parodic, metacinematic, questioning. Its constantly contradictory, doubled discourse calls to our attention the issue of the ideological construction – through representation – of subjectivity and of the way we know history, both personal and public. Very few films have managed to raise these particular issues as obsessively as has Peter Greenaway's *A Zed and Two Noughts*. Everything in this movie is doubled, from the characters to the parodies. The master intertext is the ('photographic') realist representation of Vermeer's paintings (the lighting techniques of which are echoed directly in the filming). But even this overt intertext becomes problematic. Within the film's narrative there is a surgeon named Van Meegeren. This is also the name of Vermeer's principal forger, the man who successfully convinced Goebbels (and the rest of the world) that there existed more than the once accepted twenty-six authenticated Vermeer paintings. As in Ackroyd's *Chatterton*, the real and the fictive or the authentic and the fake cannot be separated. And, by means of one character's personal sense of loss, the entire history of the human species is placed in the context of evolution and devolution: Charles Darwin becomes both a biological historian and an ingenious storyteller.

A Zed and Two Noughts seems to me to be a borderline case, however, a *cas limite* of the postmodern film. Its challenges to the spectator's expectations are more radical than those of any of the other films I have mentioned. While its contradictions are not really resolved, they are certainly stylized in the extreme. Postmodern film, as I see it, would be more compromised than this. Its tensions would be more deliberately left unresolved, its contradictions more deliberately left manifest. This constant double encoding – inscribing and subverting prevailing conventions – is what causes some critics to reject such films utterly, while others acclaim them enthusiastically. This discrepancy may be caused by the fact that if only one side – either – of the postmodern contradiction is seen (or valued), then the ambivalent doubleness of the parodic encoding can easily be resolved into a single decoding. Postmodern film is that which paradoxically wants to challenge the outer borders of cinema and wants to ask questions (though rarely offer answers) about ideology's role in subject-formation and in historical knowledge. Perhaps parody is a particularly apt representational strategy for postmodernism, a strategy once described (Said 1983: 135) as the use of parallel script rather than original inscription. Were we to heed the implications of such a model, we might have to reconsider the operations by which we both create and give meaning to our culture through representation. And that is not bad for a so-called nostalgic escapist tendency.

5
Text/image border tensions

The paradoxes of photography

Postmodern photographic theorists and practitioners are fond of using the image of 'fringe interference' to describe their work. By this, they mean to signal what happens when the aesthetic equivalent of different wave forms encounter each other: two stones thrown into a pond make ripples which meet and, at the point of meeting, something new happens – something that is based on the individual forms that preceded it, but is neverthe-less different. Today, photographic artists like Victor Burgin, Barbara Kruger, Martha Rosler, and Hans Haacke are all working across various 'wave' forms: high art, advertising, documentary, theory. The ripples emanate from each, intersect, and changes occur that can be called postmodern.

Burgin has argued that 'fringe' is better than 'margin' as a term to describe the postmodernist site of operations: it is more dynamic and decentered (Burgin 1986b: 56). But whatever the word chosen for it, that site is clearly on the borders of what have traditionally been thought of as discrete forms of discourse, not to say disciplines. My particular interest in this chapter is in those photographic 'fringe' constructions that combine the visual and the verbal, mass media and high art, artistic practice and aesthetic theory, and, in particular, in the spots where these apparent opposites overlap and interfere both with each other and with mainstream notions of 'art.' This postmodern photographic practice interrogates and problematizes, leaving the viewer no comfortable viewing position. It upsets learned notions of the relations between text/image, non-art/art, theory/practice – by installing the conventions of both (which are often taken for granted) and then by investigating the borders along which each can be opened, subverted, altered by the other in new ways. This typically postmodern border tension between inscription and subversion, construction and deconstruction – within the art itself – also places new demands upon critics and their means of approaching such works. And, one of the most insistent of these demands involves a coming to terms with the theoretical and political implications of what has too often been seen as an empty, formal play of codes.

Since I have been defining postmodernism from a model based on architecture, I have argued that postmodern art in other forms is art that is fundamentally paradoxical in its relation to history: it is both critical of and complicitous with that which precedes it. Its relationship with the aesthetic and social past out of which it openly acknowledges it has come is one characterized by irony, though not necessarily disrespect. Basic contradictions mark its contact with artistic conventions of both production and reception: it seeks accessibility, without surrendering its right to criticize the consequences of that access. Postmodernism's relation to late capitalism, patriarchy, and the other forms of those (now suspect) master narratives is paradoxical: the postmodern does not deny its inevitable implication in them, but it also wants to use that 'insider' position to 'de-doxify' the 'givens' that 'go without saying' in those grand systems. Thus, it is neither neoconservatively nostalgic nor radically revolutionary; it is unavoidably compromised – and it knows it.

I have summarized my argument in order to show why the typical postmodern site of operations might well be *between* traditional art forms, even if its manifestations can still be seen ensconced in major museums, as well as in the alternative spaces. Just as postmodernist novels by Umberto Eco or Peter Ackroyd can make the best-seller lists, so too the work of Barbara Kruger or Victor Burgin appears as well both in commercial galleries and in national museums. This is not to say that their work is not controversial and deliberately contest-ing. It clearly aims to de-naturalize the entire notion of rep-resentation in high art as well as mass media, and it succeeds in so doing; but it has consistently done so from within the conventions it seeks to dismantle and destabilize. Therefore, it remains accessible to quite a wide public; it has to, if its political message is to be effective. And its combining of the verbal and the visual has been an important key to this accessibility and effectiveness.

The formation, in 1983, of a journal called *Representations*, co-edited by an art historian and a literary critic, signalled less the merging of disciplines than the recognition, on the one hand, that theory and art or the verbal and the visual are not as discrete discourses as their historical institutionalization would suggest (at least when considered as signifying practices) and, on the other, that modes of analysis are having to change as a result: how art represents (in various discourses) cannot be separated from the historical, cultural, and social contexts in which that representing occurs – and is interpreted. Photo-graphy has been seen as important to this de-naturalizing process since the early 1970s, because of its own interrogation of its traditional role in documentation and also because of painting's use of photo-realist techniques. The postmodern photographic art that interests me here, though, is important for other reasons too. It is self-consciously *theoretical*; it is 'factographic' art in 'its insistence on the necessity to explore and clarify the construction and operation of representation within present day reality' (Buchloh 1984b: 10) – be that in the ubiquitous mass media or in the high art of museums.

I have been suggesting that photography may be the perfect postmodern vehicle in many ways, for it is based on a set of paradoxes inherent in its medium, general paradoxes which make it ripe for the particular paradoxes of postmodernism. For example, photography could be seen as Baudrillard's perfect industrial simulacrum: it is, by definition, open to copy, to infinite duplication. Yet, since its canonization by New York's Museum of Modern Art (or, more specifically, by its Director of Photography, John Szarkowski), photography has also become high art: that is, singular, authentic, complete with Benja-minian 'aura.' However, as we saw in chapter 2, this (historically

modernist) view of photography-as-high-art must daily confront the fact that photographs are also everywhere in mass
culture, from advertising and magazines to family vacation
snapshots. And its very instrumentality (be it in terms of either
documentary testimony or consumerist persuasion) would
seem to contest the formalist view of the photograph as autonomous work of art. There are still other paradoxes at the heart of
the photographic medium: the subject-framing eye of the photographer is difficult to reconcile with the objectivity of the
camera's technology, its seemingly transparent realism of recording. Nevertheless, the trend in the last decade or so has been
toward a suspicion of the scientific neutrality of that technology:
the 'photograph has ceased to be a window on the world,
through which we see things as they are. It is rather a highly
selective filter, placed there by a specific hand and mind'
(D. Davis 1977: 62). Postmodern photographic work, in
particular, exploits and challenges both the objective and the
subjective, the technological and the creative.

Postmodern photographic art, which often mixes the verbal
with the visual, is also implicated in another debate that has
developed around the definition of the process of 'reading'
photographs, for it suggests that what representational images
and language share is a reliance upon *culturally determined codes*
which are learned. This is where (and why) the ideological
cannot be separated from the aesthetic in postmodernism, why
representation always has its politics. If images, like words, are
seen as signs, then it is possible to look beyond what W.J.T.
Mitchell calls the 'deceptive appearance of naturalness and
transparence concealing an opaque, distorting, arbitrary
mechanism of representation, a process of ideological mystification' (1986: 8). Though this particular formulation is
deliberately provocative, it does serve to point to the need to
deal with the paradoxes of a form of art that both plays on and
subverts its presumed naturalness and transparency, and does
so to overt political ends.

Many take Baudrillard's view that television, not photography, is the paradigmatic form of postmodern signification
because its transparency seems to offer direct access to reality.
But since I am here defining postmodernism in terms of its
contradictions, the inherently paradoxical medium of photo-

graphy seems even more apt than television to act as the paradigm of the postmodern. As Susan Sontag has argued at length, photography both records and justifies, yet also imprisons, arrests, and falsifies time; it at once certifies and refuses experience; it is a submission to and an assault upon reality; it is 'a means of appropriating reality and a means of making it obsolete' (1977: 179). Postmodern photographic art is both aware of and willing to exploit all of these paradoxes in order to effect its own paradoxical use and abuse of conventions – and always with the aim of disabuse. Barbara Kruger's confronting of the visual with the verbal in her cut-up works returns to art what many have seen as having been eclipsed by modernist photographic formalism: its materiality, its status as signifying sign, and thus its inevitable, if usually unacknowledged, politics of representation. A fragmented photo of a woman (likely a model) stares out at the viewer, amid a series of white dots, equally reminiscent of pills, jewellery beads, or even studio lights. Superimposed over these shattered (and repeated) images – with their multiple possible readings – are the words: 'We are your circumstantial evidence.' This is material, as well as circumstantial, evidence – of a subject deliberately fragmented, never whole. The contradictions of ideology are literally materialized.

In his work, too, Victor Burgin manages both to exploit and to undercut the idea of photography as mimetic reduplication, a view which leads to that sense of the familiar, natural, self-effacing quality of the image as image. These photographic/textual works also deliberately challenge the concept of the transhistorical universality of visual experience. Here the address to the viewer (both implicit and explicit) is specific and historical, pointing directly to the different cultural restraints on interpretation – depending on time, place, gender, race, creed, class, sexual orientation. In *Possession* (also 'exhibited' as a poster in the streets of Newcastle upon Tyne), a photo of a man and woman embracing is topped with the words: 'What does possession mean to you?' The visual and verbal sexual politics then gets quickly re-coded in economic terms by the bottom line of text: '7% of our population own 84% of our wealth.'

The desire to contextualize, to 'situate' the particularities of both reception and production in opposition to humanist universals, is common to all the art and theory I shall be considering here. They show how the danger of photography lies in its apparent transparency, but also in the pleasure it arouses in viewers without creating any awareness of its act of ideological constructing. The photographic semblance of eternal, universal Truth and innocent, uncomplicated pleasure is what always potentially links the medium to institutional power; it seems to reproduce so easily those grand narratives of our culture. Perhaps this is why so many of the postmodernists have turned to the addition of verbal texts, both within and alongside their visual images. It is not that Roland Barthes was right – that photography is a message without a code – but, rather, that it is usually viewed as such in this image-saturated society.

These postmodern text/image combinations consciously work to point to the *coded* nature of all cultural messages. They do so by overtly being re-visions: they offer a second seeing, through double vision, wearing the spectacles of irony. Thus, they can be subtly critical of received notions of art and artistic production: there is nothing eternal or universal or natural about representation here. The conjunction of text and image raises new questions, but these are also questions that what is called the New Photography has been asking since the 1960s:

> Why is such and such an image significant? How does it manage to signify? Why does a society require certain images at particular times? Why do genres arise in photography? How and why do particular images become judged aesthetically worthy? Why do photographers produce pictures which, above and beyond their technical wizardry or creative acumen, say something about the social world? What are the political meanings of photography? Who controls the machinery of photography in contemporary society?
>
> (Webster 1980: 4–5)

Postmodern artists and their art are implicated in a very particular historical and ideological context – which they are more than willing to signal.

Of course, such a stand marks one of the major distinctions we have seen between modernism and postmodernism. While, obviously, neither can be said to be apolitical, in postmodernism there is an acceptance, even embracing, of the paradox of the inevitability of both art's implication in Jameson's 'cultural logic of late capitalism' and the possibility of internal challenge to it. Because photography today is the medium of advertising, of magazines, and of news reporting – that is, the medium of commercial and informational practices – it cannot be seen only in modernist terms as an autonomous form but rather must be accepted as implicated in an inevitably politicized social arena.

Postmodern photographic art uses this arena, uses its viewers' cultural knowledge (and expectations), and then turns it all against itself – and against the viewers as well. Barbara Kruger, for instance, disrupts notions of proper high-art codes by presenting the same text/image combinations in forms that vary in size and mode from billboards to postcards, from huge enlargements (often 6 feet by 10 feet) hanging on gallery walls to much smaller scale reproductions in art books or on T-shirts. In appropriating images from both high art and clichéd mass media and then 'violating' them by severe cropping and by the superimposition of verbal one-liners, she uses 'fringe interference' to new and openly political ends.

I should add that my interest here is not in magazine 'photo texts' or in books which bring texts and photographic images together. Postmodern photographic art is also different from the photo-essays of photojournalism. Each work (or series of works) is in itself both *photo* and *graphic*; any critical approach to it must therefore be literally iconological: it must concern itself with both the art's *icon* and its *logos*, as well as with their interactions. This is literally *photo-graphic* art.

The ideological arena of photo-graphy

In *Ideology and the Image* Bill Nichols argues that the visual image is a mute object, in a way; its meaning 'though rich, may be profoundly imprecise, ambiguous, even deceiving' (1981: 57). The addition of a verbal text to the visual in photo-graphy, then, might be seen as a possible tactic used to secure visual meaning. In this kind of postmodern art, however, while the relation of the text to the image is never one of pure redundancy, emphasis, or repetition, the text also never guarantees any one single, already apparent meaning. Roland Barthes (1977a: 39–41) argued that the addition of a linguistic message to an iconic one (in advertising or in press photos) could act as either an anchorage or a relay. By anchorage, he meant that the text can name and fix the many possible signifieds of the image, and thereby guide identification and interpretation. This repressive (or at least controlling) function of the verbal component is consciously problematized in photo-graphy, however: though the very presence of a text might suggest this function, the actual words, when read in relation to the picture, turn it against itself – as in the double-meaning play in *Possession*. Is the relationship between the linguistic and the pictorial in photo-graphy therefore one of relay, where the text and image complement each other? Not really. In Kruger's *We are your circumstantial evidence*, the text does not elucidate the image; it adds no obvious information not evident in the image. It is more Derridean supplement than substitution. What it does above all, though, is de-naturalize the relation between the visual and the verbal and also any evaluative privileging of one over the other.

One theorist has suggested a reciprocity between the visual (as a script to be deciphered) and the verbal (as a visual phenomenon) (Owens 1980a: 74–5). What results from such reciprocity, however, is often a kind of riddling quality in the visual/verbal interaction, as with a rebus or hieroglyph. Of course, riddles or enigmas are perfect postmodern analogues, since they offer the attractions and pleasures of deciphering: they demand active participation and self-conscious work in creating the meaning of the text. In photo-graphy these riddles foreground the fact that meaning may be conditioned by context, yet is never fixed. What does the text 'Your comfort is my silence' mean when superimposed upon Kruger's reproduced picture of a (floating) male face with its finger to its lips? Clearly, silence is being invoked by the clichéd gesture, but whose silence? And what has comfort to do with it? And whose comfort – the artist's, the viewer's, the pictured male's?

The forms this kind of 'fringe' riddling can take vary considerably, but there are two basic intersections of the visual and the verbal in postmodern photo-graphy: the text as distinct from (though linked to) the image, and the text actually incorporated physically into or onto the image. The first form (the text separate from the image) is a very common one that surrounds us daily and has already received considerable critical attention. It exists in news photos with their captions, in the complex relations of mutual illustration and supplementarity of the verbal and visual in illustrated books and magazines, not to mention in more banal examples like art books and catalogues and even the identification labels on works of visual art in galleries. Obviously titles alone constitute its most simple form. This use of an image with an accompanying text has a long history in high-art culture too, from the illuminated manuscripts to the work of William Blake.

Another common and even more directly relevant use of a text alongside an image would be in didactic photo-installations used for educational or even propagandistic purposes. These rely on their potential for both verbal and visual argumentation. Postmodern photo-graphy often plays on this potential – and, in fact, often enacts it in interesting ways. Martha Rosler's *The Bowery in Two Inadequate Descriptive Systems* offers an extended set of texts and images. The first three panels or pieces consist of verbal texts only, offering isolated printed words from the 'descriptive system' of language. These describe drinking in positive terms ('aglow glowing'); this is the view of bourgeois comfort, a view from outside skid row. But then the visual 'system' begins and we visually enter skid row and literally watch how our linguistic system also changes. The words become progressively more negative: 'groggy boozy.' The second 'descriptive system' of visual images offers a series of empty doorways of shabby shops in the Bowery. The subjects (the drunks being referred to in the language) are absent, though their empty bottles often remain. The accompanying words of the text become more and more derogatory: 'lush wino rubbydub inebriate alcoholic barrelhouse bum.'

I should mention too that these photos themselves are postmodernly parodic – and paradoxical. They are presented in the bare style of documentary realism, inevitably recalling the 1930s American liberal ('social conscience') documentary photography, which, however, represented – rather than absented – its subject without hesitation. In the essay entitled 'In, around and afterthoughts (on documentary photography),' which was published in the same volume as the *Bowery* work, Rosler explains how she sees herself as part of that earlier tradition of revelation in the name of the rectification of wrongs, but that she also cannot avoid seeing the limits of that tradition's ideological aims (to awaken the privileged to pity and charity). Nor can she condone its arrogance in speaking *for* the poor (through representation), without urging them to change their own conditions. (The famous documentary photography of the 1930s was, of course, commissioned by the American Government through the Farm Securities Administration.) Similarly, in the liberal 'victim photography' of the Bowery that sells so well, the inhabitants are made to fall prey to photography as well as poverty.

Rosler refuses this kind of documentary, which she sees as carrying 'information about a group of powerless people to another group addressed as socially powerful' (Rosler 1981: 73). She rejects the 1930s aestheticizing and formalizing of the meaning of poverty; she contests the 'impoverishment of representational strategies' too – both the verbal and the visual – in dealing with real poverty (79). But she does so by actualizing this social *theory* through two (albeit inadequate) 'descriptive systems' or representational strategies within her work. In her actualizing of each of them, their conventionality is foregrounded, and with it, a political message: drunkenness is not so much described or depicted as shown to be *constructed* by these systems. All photography, she suggests, works in ideological ways, and she wants her art to reveal the choices made by the artist, choices like those of event, camera angle, and formal composition which represent ideologically significant acts even in seemingly transparent documentary, and certainly in her own work.

German artist Hans Haacke uses the separation of text and image in still different ways in his photo-graphy. The pieces themselves are usually mixtures of the verbal and the visual, but he also often places, either on the wall or in a pamphlet given to viewers, additional textual information about how he came to choose the subject in hand, and what he discovered in researching it. While he often uses a riddle-relation of text to image, he is still considerably more didactic than Burgin, for instance, for his commentary about the subject matter of his art (often multinational corporations such as Mobil or Exxon) cannot help conditioning the viewers' interpretation of what they see before them, especially since the gallery in which they stand is often shown to be directly implicated (through funding or administration) in those same corporations. Like Brecht, Haacke wants to address his viewers directly – and challenge them. He wants them to acknowledge their active role in making meaning in a specifically capitalist system. His use of text alongside image is one way of making room for what modernist, formalist art tried to squeeze out: that is, what Jameson calls 'the issue of the possibilities of representation against the whole new framework of a global multinational system, whose coordinates can as yet not enter the content of any of our older representational systems' (Jameson 1986–7: 43). Haacke's act of offering – within his art works – what may at first seem aesthetically irrelevant facts about Mobil's economic involvement in South Africa, for instance, sets up a riddle or puzzle that involves the viewers as interpreters, asking them to investigate with him certain factual information that is inextricably connected to the images he presents.

The second kind of combination of the linguistic and the pictorial – that of a text used right within an image – is equally common today. Maps; charts; magazine, book, and record jacket covers; posters and advertising in general all superimpose texts upon images in almost as complex a manner as did cubist collage, though we may have come to take that complexity as transparent and natural through familiarity. As, in some ways, print equivalents of film (which also obviously superimposes the verbal on the visual in another way), comic books, or comic strips are particularly interesting from a postmodern perspective. Their insertion of verbal dialogue into the image and their sequential narrative form have both been used and abused by postmodern photo-graphy (as they had been by Roy Lichtenstein's paintings earlier). The frequent use of a *series* of pieces by Duane Michals, Victor Burgin, or Hans Haacke introduces an implied notion of narrative sequence which is both exploited and yet undermined.

But even within single works, the relations between image and superimposed text are often complex. For instance, one of Kruger's works consists of a photograph of a page of a book, upon which rests a pair of glasses and over which are superimposed the words, 'You are giving us the evil eye.' Complex things are going on in this work. It is clearly a parody of

Kértész's famous photo, *Mondrian's Glasses*, a parody that points to what Kértész and Mondrian, despite their differences (as formalist photographer and abstract painter), share: their status as creators of modernist high art. The glasses here sit on a page of text and their lenses magnify certain words – 'legitimacy,' 'picture', 'mere effect'; 'of my eye,' 'come back,' 'when I do this.' Now, none of these words is innocent in an ambiguously addressed work with the words 'You are giving us the evil eye' superimposed over it, words which by contiguity then make other words in the text also suddenly stand out (though not magnified): 'spectator,' 'beauty.' Again, these are hardly innocent words in postmodern art. The power of Kruger's work lies in the interpretive gap it allows between 'illusioned object' and 'assaultive, contradictory voice' (Linker 1984: 414), between representation and address.

But it is not usually echoes of high art like this that Kruger turns to in order to effect her kind of complicitous postmodern critique of representation. The most common visual images in her work are those borrowed (stolen?) from the mass media: pictorial equivalents of the clichés and colloquialisms of the superimposed verbal texts. The deliberate banality of both codes signals her rejection of the notion of art as original and authoritative, while it also calls to our attention the pervasive – and persuasive – mixing of the verbal and visual in mass culture. She uses the commonplaces of both systems *because of* their pre-existing meanings, that is, *because* they are loaded with cultural meanings. In this, they are exemplary of what surrounds everyone daily, at least in Europe and North America. Therefore they are also culturally understandable and accessible, part of the vernacular of pictorial and linguistic life in the west in the twentieth century and of the representations by which men – and especially women – *construct* their notions of self. As Kruger says, the spectators who view her work do not have to understand the language of art history: they 'just have to consider the pictures that bombard their lives and tell them who they are to some extent' (in Squiers 1987: 85). This is not a denial of the theoretical complexity of the processes involved in the *production* of her visual/verbal confrontations: she was trained in the didactic captioning of the print media, and she both recalls and undoes all its forms and implications through formal interplay that suggests, if anything, the complexity of constructivist political posters.

Hans Haacke is even more explicitly political in his work that unites image with text, for he consciously plays with the logo and advertising format of different multinational companies which he then targets: their corporate advertising semiotics are both adopted and made to implode in works like *The Chase Advantage* (Chase Manhattan Bank) or *The Road to Profits is Paved with Culture* (which inverts the motto of an Allied Chemical ad.). But this is clearly not empty play with verbal and visual form. In *A Breed Apart*, Haacke takes on the ad. style and logo of British Leyland, and then combines either (a) the company's statements about its products (Jaguar, Land Rover) with photos of repression in South Africa, or (b) a company advertising photo of its product with a contesting text about British Leyland's involvement in South Africa.

In another obvious attack, this time on American Cyanamid, Haacke photographically reproduces a 'Breck girl' picture (from the ad. of the shampoo made by the corporation) and ironically re-contextualizes it (though in a way that retains the visual coding of Breck ads) with a long text that states: 'those of its employees of child-bearing age who are exposed to toxic substances are now given a choice.' The choice is: 'They can be reassigned to a possibly lower paying job within the company. They can leave if there is no opening. Or they can have themselves sterilized and stay in their old jobs.' The text then adds: 'Four West Virginia women chose sterilization,' before its final, heavily ironic, bottom line: 'American Cyanamid. Where Women Have a Choice.' As with Rosler's separation of the verbal and the visual, their conjunction here within the work of art is no empty ludic play. Postmodern photo-graphy is political art of the first order. It is also very 'theoretical' – and often demanding – art.

If photography is, as a visual medium, inherently paradoxical, it is also semiotically hybrid. In Peirce's terms, it is both *indexical* (its representation is based on some physical connection) and *iconic* (it is a representation of likeness) in its relation to the real. This complex hybrid nature is another reason why photography has become particularly important in a time of challenge to modes of representation. Photo-graphic postmodern art contributes yet another complication and another level of challenge: in Peirce's terminology, the addition of language is the addition of the *symbolic* to the *indexical* and the *iconic*. The process of 'reading' the conventions of both the verbal and the visual can now be seen as related, though different: both involve hermeneutic work by the viewer, but this work includes the interpretation of three types of signs, as well as their combinations. This semiotic 'fringe interference' contests at once two related assumptions: that the visual and the verbal are always totally independent sign systems, and that meaning is universal. The image in these works does not derive its semantic properties from conditions within the visual itself; information here is the outcome of a culturally determined mediation which is inscribed in two different systems.

This is why Victor Burgin has called his book of photography and interviews *Between*. There are other reasons too, of course: it is 'between' the gallery and the book, the single image and narrative, the reader and the text, high art and popular/mass media. But the way in which each work mixes the verbal with the visual in fact mirrors in miniature the entire book's liminal space: this is also the site where the discourse of theory meets that of art – with important results for the politics of representation. For Burgin, as a (British) teacher as well as practitioner of photo-graphy, this meeting signifies something quite specific: 'My work is produced out of and into an extant discursive community based in politics, semiotics, and psychoanalysis' (Burgin 1986b: 86). When critics analyze Burgin's work, they too must come to terms with the (literally) inherent theoretical nature of his art, for his 'project entails an extended analysis, constructed across the signifying practice of photography, of the role of psychic structures in the formation of daily reality, and of the particular part played by photography as a central ideological apparatus' (Linker 1984: 405). This 'project' includes both theoretical writings and actual artistic practice, but his photo-graphy itself incorporates theoretical texts, either superimposed upon or alongside the images. The theory and the theoretical art argue equally powerfully for a view of language as difference (Saussure), as deferral (Derrida), as the Symbolic (Lacan). The relation between the verbal and the visual is here both literalized and theorized within the art itself.

While it is true that images are always *interpreted* through language, there exists a particularly complex and explicit interaction in this kind of photo-graphy between our verbal and visual modes of thought. Language may always shape and even delimit the interpretation of images, but in postmodern photographs, such an assumption is paradoxically both accepted and problematized. The mixing of visual and verbal codes certainly aims at making overt a doubled-pronged attack. Much fine work today is being done by literarily trained critics of the visual arts. That 'fringe interference' has had fruitful results in criticism and theory as well as art. The photo-graphers I have been discussing have clearly also been influenced by contemporary literary, psychoanalytic, and philosophical theories, and their work similarly suggests the importance of working on the 'fringes' of traditional institutionalized disciplines in the study of postmodernism.

Photo-graphy today is also very self-consciously aware of the fact that both language and photography are *signifying practices*, that is, that both contribute to the production and dissemination of meaning – in terms of both the producer and receiver, the artist and viewer. And 'meaning' in these terms is never separable from the social. Never was this clearer, perhaps, than now, when the conjunction of language and images together is constantly bombarding all western eyes through the mass media. In postmodern art, those very borders between the pictorial and the linguistic are simultaneously being asserted and denied – in short, radically de-naturalized. More than ever, the question must be asked: what interests and powers does the traditional separation of the visual and the verbal serve in both consumer mass culture and high art? Postmodern photo-graphy is one articulation of that question, even if it offers no final answer to it.

The ideological dimension implied here is inextricably a part of the theoretical dimension that is literally built into photographic art. By 'theoretical dimension,' I do not just mean that theory *is* an art, though it likely is. Nor do I only mean that the artists I am dealing with are also important theorists, though they are. I mean that the works themselves are literally informed by and constructed with theory: their verbal components are often theoretical statements against (or with) which the visual images must be read. Or sometimes the interplay of the two codes has explicitly theoretical implications that the context demands be addressed. This goes beyond most conceptual art's self-referential mixing of photo-document and text; here, through the interaction of text and image, there is, instead, an internalized theoretical exposition of cultural, sociopolitical, and economic conditions of production and reception. In postmodern photo-graphy, theory and art are not separable.

For the last decade, the most important theoretical conjuncture seems to have been that of Marxist and feminist politics, psychoanalytic and deconstructive theory. This has meant that what photo-graphy foregrounds is the representation of difference (class, gender, race, sexual preference), the sexual politics of representation, and photography's lost innocence (its concealed compromises with the social system it cannot escape). As one commentator puts it: '[t]heory forced a rupture with the established aesthetic conventions of the autonomous image but it also provided a framework for an alternate aesthetic' (Mulvey 1986: 7). The photo-graphic art of postmodernism also reveals other internalized theoretical contexts as well. For example, many of the theories of Roland Barthes are clearly influential – from his early de-mythologizing semiology to his later work on both pleasure in general and photography in particular. Similarly, as we have seen, Althusser's reworking of Marx's notion of base and superstructure has offered a more complex notion of ideological practices that has been welcomed by these postmodernists in their challenges to the concealed politics of representation.

But it was probably the feminist rethinking of Lacan's rereading of Freud through Saussure that had the greatest impact, maybe because it provided a psycho-sexual context for all those other destabilizing theoretical strategies. In the work of Burgin, Kruger, or Silvia Kolbowski, the focus is also on sexual differentiation and on the constructing of gender positions within patriarchy. Gender difference is here both theorized and actualized through a self-conscious, textualized awareness of the implications of Lacan's notion of the construction of the subject in and through language: in postmodern photo-graphs (such as those shown in New York at the 1985 New Museum of Contemporary Art's show, *Difference: On Representation and Sexuality*) the subject is seen to be known only as represented, that is, only in terms of social and cultural Symbolic formations which are clearly patriarchal.

Verbal and visual interaction is often what is used to illustrate and even to enact this kind of theoretical concern. For example, Marie Yates's *The Missing Woman* offers twenty-one photographic images of 'documentary' texts (telegrams, letters, diaries, newspapers) which explicitly represent the Lacanian identification of the subject in language. In other words, viewers are made to construct the notion of a woman through this sequence of text/images which act as the literal traces of the social discourses which construct womanhood. But the female herself is always the permanent Lacanian lack, the absent 'missing woman' of the title. Similarly, Victor Burgin's more recent works have integrated his early Marxist and Althusserian theoretical interests within a psychoanalytic framework, and it is verbal/visual interaction, as well as the explicitly theoretical texts accompanying the images in *Gradiva* or *Olympia*, that foreground the inextricability of theory and art in postmodernism. The work of Mary Kelly or David Askevold could also be studied from this point of view, since (in their different ways) their incorporation of verbal texts within the visual also offers an explicit theory of meaning and reference in relation to difference. Of course, it might be said that this kind of mix was radicalized much earlier by Dada, but postmodernism's mutually effective interferences on the 'fringes' of both the linguistic and the pictorial cannot be separated from the theoretical – and also political – contexts that they inevitably evoke in photo-graphy.

The politics of address

What could be called the rhetoric of postmodern apostrophe or, better perhaps, its semiotics of address cannot but be of importance in postmodern art and theory which self-consciously work to 'situate' their production and reception and to contextualize the acts of perception and interpretation. The addition of verbal texts to photographic images in photo-graphy makes explicit what is usually left implicit in the visual: the implication of an addressed viewer. It is likely that certain earlier forms of context-dependent and context-problematizing art that foregrounded the role of the viewer have been influential here: I am thinking of the video art of the 1970s which often required the physical presence of the spectator just to become activated, or the mixed media installations of Don Jean-Louis (where mirrors reflected not only his paintings but also the viewers interacting with them) or Laurie Anderson (such as her *Handphone Table (When You We're Hear) (sic)*). When viewers stepped into the room at *Documenta 7* in which Hans Haacke's *Oelgemelde, Hommage à Marcel Broodthaers* was placed, they entered the archetypally liminal and politically unstable 'fringe' space of postmodernism. On one side of the room was hung a gold-framed, brass-labelled oil painting of Ronald Reagan (though the label read, not 'Ronald Reagan,' as viewers might expect, but, in translation, 'Oil Painting, Homage to Marcel Broodthaers'). In front of this were two brass stanchions with a red velvet rope between them, such as are used in galleries to signal important art pieces that must not be approached too closely. A red carpet led from the stanchions to the opposite wall on which appeared a giant photo-enlargement, direct from a contact sheet (complete with borders), of a crowd scene from a recent German anti-Reagan rally. The space of the viewers here was made self-conscious and also unavoidably politicized – in an allegory, perhaps, of the implicit politics of all art viewing and address.

In a consumer society, where the verbal and visual most frequently come together in the form of advertising, this kind of rendering both self-conscious and political of the position of the viewer is an obvious form that a compromised but still effective postmodern critique can take. In the work of Burgin and Kruger, the poster and the billboard (known mostly for their commercial uses) are deployed against themselves, becoming the forms of political and formal self-reflexivity. These formats also emphasize the daily instrumentality of photography as a social fact. But what the *mixing* of the text and image often does is to underline, through the use of direct verbal address to a viewer, the fact that, as a signifying system, pictures too represent both a scene and the look of a viewer, both an object and a subject.

Photo-graphy highlights what Burgin calls the 'seeing subject' (1982b: 211) with its investment in looking (narcissistic

identification or voyeuristic surveillance). Its means of addressing that subject are several. Burgin favors the more enigmatic
mode of text/image interaction which invokes an implied
riddle-solving, active viewer, while Kruger is more direct or
at least more directive. She has argued that most of the mass-
media and high-art representations that surround viewers are
really 'undifferentiated addresses to a male audience' (in
Squiers 1987: 80) and so she wants to introduce *difference* into
her act of addressing, in both visual and verbal codes. The piece
Surveillance is your busywork offers a complex inscription of power
and its relation to address, for instance. These four words sit
atop a picture of a male face, shot from below (a cinematic
commonplace by which camera angle signifies power structure), holding a loupe in his eye. Through text and image, the
Foucauldian discourses on power and the Panopticon meet the
cliché of Big Brother, who is watching 'you.'

But the text's own addressed 'you' puts viewers in a problematic position: either they can deny its implicating deictics or
they can recognize themselves in them. While the male-figured
image tends to suggest a limitation of the gender of the 'you'
addressed here, in many of Kruger's works, the addressee is
neither always male nor always even representative of the forces
that marginalize and commodify and oppress (though that is
the most common designation). A photo of a male holding his
head in his hand in distress is placed below the line 'Your life is a
perpetual insomnia,' for instance. Or a picture of a woman,
reflected in a shattered mirror, has the words 'You are not
yourself' superimposed upon it. The 'you' can change in gender, but its position is always clear in context, and it always has
to do with a power situation.

Kruger's use of the first- and second-person pronouns in her
art reveals her self-conscious awareness of the linguistic theory
of 'shifters' as empty signs that are filled with meaning only by
their context. When the tone of the text is particularly accusatory, this works to disrupt (traditionally male) pleasures of
visual voyeurism. The 'you' is most often explicitly associated
with power (and often capital): *You make history when you do
business* (with a photo of men's legs and feet). The plural first
person is also often present, usually in opposition, as in *Our time
is your money*. Most frequently (though not always), when taken

in conjunction with the images, this first-person pronoun is gendered female: a silhouette of a woman pinned down like an entomological specimen offers the superimposed caption, 'We have received orders not to move.' By using pronominal shifters to signify, on a theoretical level, the shifting nature of subject and object identities and their construction in and by language, Kruger also achieves her other goal: 'to ruin certain representations, to displace the subject and to welcome a female spectator into the audience of men' (in Gauss 1985: 93). For instance, the work *We are being made spectacles of* uses these words literally to disrupt the visual continuity of a conventional cinematic image of a male embracing (and also towering over) a woman. Of course, that second person, the 'you' addressed by Kruger's photo-graphs, is not limited to the male (or female) represented within the works; the artist is often a possible referent and, of course, viewers are also implicated and addressed, usually in a very confrontational and accusatory tone.

Kruger's use of direct (verbal) address with visual images, often from movies or advertising, is particularly designed to confront any such lapse on the viewers' part that would conceal the (usually unacknowledged) ideological apparatuses of either the mass media or high art. Her kind of stealing or appropriating of these forms of representation is clearly both complicitous and critical. It wants to speak to a consumer society from within its recognizable set of representations, while still challenging its power. And, for her, verbal (and by implication visual) address is one of the most effective and direct means of challenge. For Rosler and Haacke, photo-graphic address is specifically aimed at awakening the viewer to an awareness of class relations; for Kruger and Burgin, it is both class and gender that are at stake.

Somewhat more problematically, Hannah Wilke's photographic poster (in her *So Help Me Hannah* installation) called *What Does This Represent? What Do You Represent?* aims directly at contemporary theories of both representation and address and it does so in such a manner as to upset any of our complacent assumptions about word/image relations – or their politics. The photo of the artist herself – nude, sitting despondently in the corner of the room, surrounded by pieces of phallic weaponry scattered like toys around a naughty child – rebounds off the superimposed questions: 'What Does This Represent? What Do

You Represent?' If there is an answer to either question, it is not an obvious (or unproblematic) one, I suspect. But it certainly has something to do with the politics of representation.

Photography may well be a particularly politicizable form of representation. It has often been granted special status by Marxist critics because of its seeming transparency and its didactically useful instrumentality. But postmodern photography, I think, works to link art to the social formation in more specifically direct and explicit ways than the medium in general does. It offers two discourses, visual and verbal, interacting to produce meaning in such a way that the viewer becomes aware of the theoretical implications of the differences between, on the one hand, meaning-producing within the two separate and differing discourses and, on the other, any meaning created through their interaction.

I am aware that my use of the very word 'discourse' here – and elsewhere in this book – is what has been called an 'ideological flag' (McCabe 1978–9: 41), signaling that I am unwilling to analyze form without considering political and ideological address. But I think this is precisely what postmodern photo-graphy itself self-consciously demands of its critics today. Both discourses, visual and verbal, 'hail' (in the Althusserian sense) their 'reader' in this postmodern art, and the direct address of the verbal text works to unmask what I have been referring to as the more hidden but no less real assumption of a certain viewer position in the visual. Our act of recognizing – or refusing to recognize – ourselves in the address of Barbara Kruger's work is a production of meaning, as well as a making conscious of the fact that meaning is made out of the interaction of the addressee and the text in perception as much as interpretation. The codes that permit recognition or rebuttal are produced by ideology, at least in the sense that ideology uses the fabrication of images to invite us to occupy fixed places within the dominant social order.

This is what postmodern photo-graphy works to 'de-doxify' by making both the visual and the verbal into overt sites of signifying activity and communication. It also contests the glossing over of the contradictions that make representations (linguistic or pictorial) serve ideology by seeming harmonious, ordered, universal. Its paradoxes of complicity and critique, of use and abuse of both verbal and visual conventions, point to contradiction and, thereby, to the possible workings of ideology. A series of works like Burgin's *Olympia* or Kolbowski's *Model Pleasure* may indeed, as Hal Foster claims, elicit 'our desire for an image of woman, truth, certainty, closure' but it does so 'only to draw it out from its conventional captures (e.g. voyeurism, narcissism, scopophilia, fetishism), to reflect back the (masculine) gaze to the point of self-consciousness' (Foster 1985: 8).

Photo-graphy today is neither iconoclastic nor iconophilic. The addition of the verbal within a visual discourse could be seen as a limiting gesture (Barthes's anchorage, once again) or as a liberating one, as Benjamin foresaw when he asked that photographers put such a caption beneath their pictures as would rescue them from stylishness and confer on them a revolutionary use value. Martha Rosler acknowledges that her political decision to absent the 'victims' of the Bowery from her visual 'inadequate descriptive system' is no final statement, that postmodern compromised contestation is not revolutionary in itself:

> If photos are to be populated, though, they ought to be made with a clarity that neither sell short the lives of the people shown nor pretend not to notice the built-up meanings of photographic discourses. Eventually the photography of the real has to give up the fear of engagement in favor of the clearest analysis that can be brought.
>
> (Rosler 1981: 82)

In uniting theory and practice within their art, photographers like Rosler and Haacke may reject the liberal social reformism of earlier documentary photography, but they also know that they too induce no collective struggle of the oppressed. They can only be critical and analytic of the power and privilege that have created the social conditions that make the Bowery or South African apartheid possible.

In Haacke's work, the ideological engagement of the artist is even more explicit and direct than in that of most of the other photo-graphers I have been discussing here. His parodic play with the documentary points not to that form's assumption of general, human constants, but to real, political differences. It is never empty play; it reveals – and names – the network of largely concealed or at least unacknowledged corporate sponsorships that directly connect art to the world of economic and indeed political power. His particular targets are those corporations which support the arts and want to be seen as liberal and generous, but whose economic power is central to the maintenance of white power in South Africa, for instance. There are at least three forms of protest going on in Haacke's work: (a) there is a 'moral protest against the enlistment of "pure" art as an ally by late capitalism' in general (Bois 1986: 129); (b) there is a more specific 'washing away the mask of culture' which multinational power uses both to hide behind and as a major marketing strategy; (c) there is the offer of an antidote, a counter-text, within the work of art itself. This is institutional critique in its most context-specific form. Corporate sponsorship may be a reality of the late-twentieth-century art world, but it can still be challenged, argues Haacke, by 'stealth, intelligence, determination – and some luck' (1986–7: 72).

Postmodern photo-graphy is for me one of the art forms that best exemplifies the heritage of the politicized 1960s and 1970s, of Vietnam protest and feminism, of civil rights and gay activism. It is not disconnected from the social and the political. The 'fringe interferences' of photo-graphy are multiple; they play with the border tensions of theory, politics, and art as well as those of high art and mass media, and they do so while de-naturalizing the borders between text and image. The conventions of the discourses of both the verbal and the visual, however, are at once inscribed and challenged, used and abused. This is the art of complicity as well as critique, even in its most radically polemical political forms. This does not invalidate its critique; rather, it can be seen as both an important means of access and an avoidance of the kind of bad faith that believes art (or criticism) can ever be outside ideology. In Barbara Kruger's postmodern terms: 'I don't think there's a blameless place where work can function. One has to work within the confines of a system' (in Schreiber 1987: 268).

6

Postmodernism and feminisms

(A note on the plural 'feminisms' in my title: the designation is as awkward as it is accurate. While there are almost as many feminisms as there are feminists, there is also a very real sense in which there is today no clear cultural consensus in feminist thinking about representation. As Catherine Stimpson has argued, the history of feminist thought on this topic includes the confrontation of dominant representations of women as misrepresentations, the restoration of the past of women's own self-representation, the generation of accurate representations of women, and the acknowledgement of the need to represent differences among women (of sexuality, age, race, class, ethnicity, nationality), including their diverse political orientations (Stimpson 1988: 223). As a verbal sign of difference and plurality, 'feminisms' would appear to be the best term to use to designate, not a consensus, but a multiplicity of points of view which nevertheless do possess at least some common denominators when it comes to the notion of the *politics* of representation.)

Politicizing desire

If, in the postmodern age, we do live in what has been called a recessionary erotic economy brought about by fear of disease and a fetishization of fitness, the erotic cannot but be part of that *eroto* = *part 1* general problematizing of the body and its sexuality. And this is one of the sites of the conjunction of interest of both postmodernism and feminisms as they both zero in on the representation of and reference to that body and its subject positions. The body cannot escape representation and these days this means it cannot escape the feminist challenge to the patriarchal and masculinist underpinnings of the cultural practices that subtend those representations. But, without those feminisms, the story would be a rather different one, for I would want to argue for the powerful impact of feminist practices on postmodernism – though not for the conflation of the two.

With the rise of performance and 'body art' in the last decade have come unavoidably gender-specific representations of the body in art. Because of these and other specifically feminist practices, postmodernism's 'de-doxifying' work on the construction of the individual bourgeois subject has had to make room for the consideration of the construction of the *gendered* subject. I say this in full awareness that some of the major theorists of the postmodern have not yet noticed this. While it is certainly demonstrable that both feminisms and postmodernism are part of the same general crisis of cultural authority (Owens 1983: 57) as well as part of a more specific challenge to the notion of representation and its address, there is a major difference of orientation between the two that cannot be ignored: we have seen that postmodernism is politically ambivalent for it is doubly coded – both complicitous with and contesting of the cultural dominants within which it operates; but on the other side, feminisms have distinct, unambiguous political agendas of resistance. Feminisms are not really either compatible with or even an example of postmodern thought, as a few critics have tried to argue; if anything, together they form the single most powerful force in changing the direction in which (male) postmodernism was heading but, I think, no longer is. It radicalized the postmodern sense of difference and de-naturalized the traditional historiographic separation of the private and the public – and the personal and the political – as the last section of this chapter will investigate.

The reason for the none the less quite common conflation of the feminist and the postmodern may well lie in their common interest in representation, that purportedly neutral process that is now being deconstructed in terms of ideology. In shows like *Difference: On Representation and Sexuality*, held at the New Museum of Contemporary Art in New York in 1985, sexual difference was shown to be something that is continuously reproduced by cultural representations normally taken for granted as natural or given. Few would disagree today that feminisms have transformed art practice: through new forms, new self-consciousness about representation, and new awareness of both contexts and particularities of gendered experience. They have certainly made women artists more aware of themselves as women and as artists; they are even changing men's sense of themselves as gendered artists. They have rendered inseparable feminisms as socio-political movements and feminisms as a (plural) phenomenon of art history. Temporally, it is no accident that they have coincided with the revival of figurative painting and the rise of conceptual art, of what I have called photo-graphy as a high-art form, of video, alternative film practices, performance art – all of which have worked to challenge both the humanist notion of the artist as romantic individual 'genius' (and therefore of art as the expression of universal meaning by a transcendent human subject) and the modernist domination of two particular art forms, painting and sculpture. But feminisms have also refocused attention on the politics of representation and knowledge – and therefore also on power. They have *made* postmodernism think, not just about the body, but about the female body; not just about the female body, but about its desires – and about both as socially and historically constructed through representation.

Whether the medium be linguistic or visual, we are always dealing with systems of meaning operating within certain codes and conventions that are socially produced and historically conditioned. This is the postmodern focus that has replaced the modernist/romantic one of individual expression. And it is not hard to see why suddenly the politics of representation becomes an issue: what systems of power authorize some representations while suppressing others? Or, even more specifically, how is desire instilled through representation by the management of the pleasure of reading or looking? Many feminist theorists have been arguing for the need to de-naturalize our common-sense understanding of the body in art, the need to reveal the semiotic mechanisms of gender positioning which produce both that body image and the desires (male and female) it evokes.

This mixing of the political with the sexual has proved bothersome to some critics, especially to those for whom notions of pleasure and desire are key terms of aesthetic experience. Both feminist and postmodern theory and practice have worked to 'de-doxify' any notion of desire as simply individual fulfill-ment, somehow independent of the pleasures created *by* and *in* culture. The political impulse of postmodern and feminist art challenges the conditions of desire: desire as satisfaction end-lessly deferred, that is, as an anticipatory activity in the future tense; desire as fueled by the inaccessibility of the object and dissatisfaction with the real. This is the realm of displaced desire – of advertising and pornography – and of Baudrillard's simulacrum. While the very notion of desire would seem to presuppose a coherent subjectivity, we have seen that much feminist and postmodern theory has worked to question and problematize this concept. But such theory has itself been divided, between those for whom desire is something beyond culture and politics, and those who see the desiring subject as inscribed in and by certain ideologically determined subject-positions.

Desire is clearly problematic: is there a difference between desire as textual play, say, and desire as foregrounding the political economy of the image in a patriarchal and capitalist society? Desire is not just a value of poststructuralist ideology; it is also a norm in consumer society, one that Marxist critics have been working to deconstruct. But so too have feminists: Carol Squiers's critical thematic exhibits, such as her 1984 *Design for Living*, bring together magazine images of women with an aim to unmask and challenge, through ordering and positioning, the capitalist and patriarchal politics of mass-media presentations of woman's body and desire.

In her book, *Female Desire*, Rosalind Coward argues from a feminist poststructuralist perspective that women's pleasures are constructed within a range of signifying practices; in other words, they are not natural or innate. Produced by discourses which often sustain male privilege, feminine desire – its satisfac-tions, its objects – may need rethinking, especially to consider what Catherine Stimpson calls its 'herterogeneity' (1988: 241).

But first, those male discourses need confronting, challenging, debunking. This is where the work of feminist artists is so important. For instance, in a short story called 'Black Venus' by Angela Carter, two discourses meet – and clash: the poetic language of male sublimated desire for woman (as both muse and object of erotic fantasy) and the language of the political and contextualizing discourses of female experience. This is one of those texts that almost demands to be read as the site for the discursive construction of the meaning of gender, but in a problematic sense: there are two conflicting discourses which work to foreground and contest the history of desire, male desire.

This is the story of Baudelaire and his mulatto mistress, Jeanne Duval. In his journal, Baudelaire once wrote: 'Eternal Venus, caprice, hysteria, fantasy, is one of the seductive forms [assumed] by the Devil,' a devil he both courted and despised. His biographers have been rather kind to him, patiently explaining to us the sublimatory advantages of his preference for desire over consummation, anticipatory imagination over the actual sexual act – for us, if not for Duval. We get the poems; she seems to have ended up with very little. But the same biographers have been considerably less kind to Duval: as painted by Manet, she is usually described as a sensuous beauty, a melancholic if exotic shrew, whom Baudelaire treated as a goddess but who never understood his poetry and who repaid his generosity and kindness with nagging and ill temper. (What they seem to want to avoid mentioning, by the way, is that he was also rather generous with his syphilis.) The woman to whom history denied a voice is the *subject* of Carter's 'Black Venus' – as she was the *object* of Baudelaire's 'Black Venus' poems.

Carter's text consistently contrasts the language of Baudelairean decadent male eroticism with the stark social reality of Jeanne Duval's position as a colonial, a black, and a kept woman. Male erotic iconography of women seems to have two poles: the romantic/decadent fantasist (like Baudelaire's) and the realist (the woman as sexual partner), but in neither case is the woman anything but a mediating sign for the male (Tickner 1987: 264). Carter's verbal text attempts to code and then re-code the 'colonized territory' of the female body; it is coded as erotic masculine fantasy, and then re-coded in terms of female experience. The text is a complex interweaving of the discourses of desire and politics, of the erotic and the analytic, of the male and the female.

The story opens with an overt echo of the evening descriptions of Baudelaire's poems, 'Harmonie du soir' and 'Crépuscule du soir.' But the woman described in Carter's text as a 'forlorn Eve' is represented in a language different from that of the male poet: she 'never experienced her experience *as* experience, life never added to the sum of her knowledge; rather subtracted from it' (Carter 1985: 9). In contrast, the male (identified at this point only by the pronoun 'he') offers to her his fantasy, a fantasy that makes him into a parody of 'le pauvre amoureux des pays chimériques,' the Baudelairean inventor of Americas in 'Le Voyage.' The details of his fantasy parody those of the poems 'Voyage à Cythère' and 'La Chevelure' in that they offer the same topoi but vulgarized as bourgeois tourist escapism ('Baby, baby, let me take you back where you belong'). This is mixed with Yeatsian Byzantian parody ('back to your lovely, lazy island where the jewelled parrot rocks on the enamel tree') (10). The woman's reply assaults this fantasy: 'No! . . . Not the bloody parrot forest! Don't take me on the slavers' route back to the West Indies' (11). Erotic reverie meets political and historical reality, perhaps reminding us that even Cythera, the island of Venus, is no paradise: the Baudelairean poet hangs from its gallows. For the West Indian woman, the island paradise he imagines is one of 'glaring yellow shore and harsh blue skies,' of 'fly-blown towns' that are not Paris. Those thousand sonnets that Baudelaire's 'Dame Créole' was to have inspired in the heart of the poet are here used to roll her cheroots. This dream literally goes up in smoke.

Then, the language of male eroticism again takes over. Aroused from her 'féconde paresse,' this particular 'Dame Créole' dances naked for him, lets down her fleece-like 'chevelure,' clothes herself only in the bangles described in the poem, 'Les Bijoux.' The 'brune enchanteresse' 'grande et svelte' dances, but in Carter's story she does so in 'slumbrous resentment' against her lover, in a room that 'tugged at its moorings, longing to take off on an aerial quest for that Cythera beloved of poets' (Carter 1985: 12). The text points us directly to Baudelaire here and then makes the intertext problematic. As he dreamily watches, we are told that 'she wondered what the distinction was between dancing naked in front of *one* man who paid and dancing naked in front of a group of men who paid' (12). He dreams erotic dreams; she ponders what is called her 'use value' and her syphilis: 'was pox not the emblematic fate of a creature made for pleasure and the price you paid for the atrocious mixture of corruption and innocence this child of the sun brought with her from the Antilles?' (13). The pox is called America's, 'the raped continent's revenge' against European imperialism, but the revenge has backfired here. The text then returns to the Baudelairean erotic discourse: her hair, the cat. He thinks of her as a 'vase of darkness . . . not Eve, but herself, the forbidden fruit, and he has eaten her!' (15). We are then offered four lines (in translation) from Baudelaire's poem, 'Sed non satiata' – an ironic intertextual comment on his desire but also on hers, unsatiated as it is.

With a break in the text, what begins (seven and a half pages into the story) is yet another discourse. 'He' is identified as Baudelaire; 'she' as Jeanne Duval, also known as Jeanne Prosper or Lemer 'as if her name were of no consequence' (Carter 1985: 16). Her origins are equally vague. In parentheses we read: '(Her *pays d'origine* of less importance than it would have been had she been a wine.)' (16). Perhaps she came from the Dominican Republic where, as we are pointedly told, Toussaint L'Ouverture had led a slave revolt. The racial, economic, and gender politics of French colonial imperialism are brought to our attention. Yet the text immediately returns to the Baudelairean erotic discourse to describe Jeanne to us. That it should do so is not surprising. After all, besides a portrait by Manet, today that is all we have to know her by. Through both the literary and the historical references, the text attempts to give back to Jeanne the history of which she was deprived as 'the pure child of the colony' – the 'white, imperious' colony (17). She has also been deprived of her language. We are told that she spoke Créole badly, that she tried to speak 'good' French when she arrived in Paris. But herein lies the true irony of those erotic literary representations by which we know her today:

you could say, not so much that Jeanne did not understand
the lapidary, troubled serenity of her lover's poetry, but that
it was a perpetual affront to her. He recited it to her by the
hour and she ached, raged and chafed under it because his
eloquence denied her language.

(Carter 1985: 18)

She cannot hear his tributes to herself outside of her colonial –
racial and linguistic – context.

The text then adds yet another context, the obvious one of
gender: 'The goddess of his heart, the ideal of the poet, lay
resplendently on the bed . . . ; he liked to have her make a
spectacle of herself, to provide a sumptuous feast for his bright
eyes that were always bigger than his belly. Venus lies on the
bed, waiting for a wind to rise: the sooty albatross hankers for
the storm' (Carter 1985: 18). But, for the reader of Baudelaire's
poetry, there is a curious reversal here – not only of color ('sooty
albatross'), but of roles. In the poem called 'L'Albatros,' it is the
poet who flies on the wings of poesy, though clumsy on earth. In
Carter's parodic version, the woman is the graceful albatross;
the poet is instead that great dandy of birds (from Poe's
Adventures of Arthur Gordon Pym), the one who always builds its
nest near that of the albatross: the penguin – flightless,
bourgeois, inescapably comic. We are told: 'Wind is the element
of the albatross just as domesticity is that of the penguin' (19).
The poet is demystified, as is the lover.

The erotic encounters of these two strange birds are carefully
and sharply coded and the text situates the code historically and
culturally for us:

It is essential to their connection that, if she should put on the
private garments of nudity, its non-sartorial regalia of jewellery and rouge, then he himself must retain the public
nineteenth-century masculine impedimenta of frock coat
(exquisitely cut); white shirt (pure silk, London tailored);
oxblood cravat; and impeccable trousers.

(Carter 1985: 19)

That Manet's work might come to mind here is no accident:

There's more to 'Le Déjeuner sur l'Herbe' than meets the eye.
(Manet, another friend of his.) Man does and is dressed to do

so; his skin is his own business. He is artful, the creation of culture. Woman is; and is, therefore, fully dressed in no clothes at all, her skin is common property.

(Carter 1985: 20)

Together Baudelaire and Duval untangle 'the history of transgression' (21) but his customary erotic rhetoric keeps giving way to her reality. The statement that 'Jeanne stoically laboured over her lover's pleasure, as if he were her vineyard' (21) recalls (though ironically) his poem 'Les Bijoux' where her breasts are the 'grappes de ma vigne' – that is, the poet's. In that revisionist version, she does not have to labor over his pleasure; she is passive: 'elle se laissait aimer.'

The text breaks here. He dies 'deaf, dumb and paralysed'; she loses her beauty and then her life. But Carter offers a second fate for her Jeanne Duval. She buys new teeth, a wig, and restores some of her ravaged beauty. She returns to the Caribbean using the money from the sale of Baudelaire's manuscripts and from what he could sneak to her before his death. ('She was surprised to find out how much she was worth.') She reverses the associations of this trip's direction – it is the 'slavers' route,' after all. She dies, in extreme old age, after a life as a madam. The text then betrays its fantasy status through its future tense: from her grave, 'she will continue to dispense, to the most privileged of the colonial administration, at a not excessive price, the veritable, the authentic, the true Baudelairean syphilis' (Carter 1985: 23). This is Angela Carter's parodic voicing of a doubled discourse of complicity and challenge, of the feminist politicization of desire.

But I said earlier that it was the *postmodern* that was characterized by complicity and critique, not the feminist. Yet perhaps this is another point of overlap that might be theorized: in other words, it is not just a matter of feminisms having had a major impact on postmodernism, but perhaps postmodern strategies can be deployed by feminist artists to deconstructive ends – that is, in order to *begin* the move towards change (a move that is not, in itself, part of the postmodern). Carter's text is not alone in suggesting that the erotic is an apt focus for this kind of critique, since it raises the question of desire and its gendered politics and also the issue of representation and its politics. The exploring of the role of our cultural and social discourses in constructing both pleasure and sexual representations is what results from the clash of two discursive practices across which conflicting notions of gender and sexual identity are produced in Carter's story. A similar, even more direct politicizing of male desire can be seen in Margaret Harrison's collage/painting *Rape*. In this work, a frieze across the top presents reproductions of high-art male erotic images of women as available, passive, offering themselves to the male gaze: familiar canonical paintings by Ingres, Rubens, Rossetti, Manet, and so on. Underneath is a strip of press cuttings about rape trials where the legal profession is shown to condone violence against women. Beneath that is a series of painted representations of instruments of rape: knives, scissors, broken bottles. Like Carter's text, *Rape* presents a parodic clashing of discourses: high-art nudes, judicial reports, representations of violence. Yet what all the discourses are shown to share is the objectification of the female body.

The parodic use (even if also abuse) of male representations of women in both Carter's and Harrison's work is a postmodernist strategy at least in so far as it implies a paradoxically complicitous critique. But even the more generally accepted articulations of specifically female and feminist contestation, such as Mary Kelly's *Post-Partum Document*, could be seen as an implicitly parodic challenge to the patriarchal madonna and child tradition of western high art: as I suggested earlier, it politicizes and de-naturalizes what has been seen as the most 'natural' of relationships by articulating it through the everyday discourse of the actual female experience of mothering. But it is this change of discourse that makes Kelly's work less problematic as a feminist work than that of some others. When artists like Cindy Sherman or Hannah Wilke parodically use the female nude tradition, for example, different issues arise, for the femaleness of the nude tradition – like that of the Baudelairean erotic – makes it an art form in which the male viewer is explicit and the notion of masculine desire is constitutive. Yet, this very femaleness is what has been ignored in art historical accounts of the nude genre.

Feminist postmodernist parody

When Ann Kaplan asks of cinema 'Is the gaze male?' (1983), she problematizes to some extent what feminisms have accepted (at least since Laura Mulvey's important article on 'Visual pleasure and narrative cinema') as the maleness of the camera eye that makes women into exhibitionists to be observed and displayed, 'coded for strong visual and erotic impact so that they can be said to connote *to-be-looked-at-ness*' (Mulvey 1975: 11). This leaves the female as spectator in the position of either narcissistic identification or some kind of psychic cross-dressing.

But do we have here a very basic problem for the very existence of feminist visual arts (as opposed to feminist critique of male art)? If the mastering gaze which separates the subject from the object of the gaze, projecting desire onto that object, is inherently masculine, as many feminists argue, could there ever be such a thing as women's *visual* art? I think this may potentially be a very real impasse, but nevertheless one which postmodernist parody has offered at least one possible exit strategy – a compromised one, but one with some possible political efficacy. By using postmodern parodic modes of installing and then subverting conventions, such as the maleness of the gaze, representation of woman can be 'de-doxified.' The postmodern position is one articulated best, perhaps, by Derrida when he writes: 'the authority of representation constrains us, imposing itself on our thought through a whole dense, enigmatic, and heavily stratified history. It programs us and precedes us' (Derrida 1982: 304). This does not mean, though, that it cannot be challenged and subverted – but just that the subversion will be from within. The critique will be complicitous.

An example would be Gail Geltner's parodic play with Ingres's canonical nude, the *Grande Odalisque*, in her *Closed System*, shown at the 1984 Toronto *Alter Eros Festival*. This collage is clearly parodically inscribing, but the changes are as important as the similarities: Ingres's female figure is reproduced, but the implicit male gaze is now literally made part of the work in the form of a group of Magrittian men who are inserted into a background window, looking inside at the nude. But, given where the male gaze is now placed (that is, at the back), Ingres's female is seen to turn away from it, suggesting that the viewer to whom she does turn might be gendered otherwise. The difference between this and Mel Ramos's *Plenti-grande Odalisque* illustrates for me the difference between the feminist and the postmodernist. Ramos's postmodern complicity is much clearer, though his critique is also evident: by recoding that classic nude in pornographic code (of *Playboy*'s naked women), he deconstructs the alibi of this particular convention of high art, pointing to male desire, but offering no specifically gendered response to it.

What both feminist and postmodern art like this show, however, is that desire and pleasure are socially validated and normalized. While postmodern art does seek to disrupt – while exploiting – these expected pleasures, feminist art wants to disrupt but also change our allowable pleasures as women viewers and artists. As we have seen, the work of Silvia Kolbowski, Barbara Kruger, and also Alexis Hunter deploys the postmodern strategy of parodic use and abuse of mass-culture representations of women, subverting them by excess, irony, and fragmented recontextualization – all of which work to disrupt any passive consumption of such images. Complicity is perhaps necessary (or at least unavoidable) in deconstructive critique (you have to signal – and thereby install – that which you want to subvert), though it also inevitably conditions both the radicality of the kind of critique it can offer and the possibility of suggesting change. The feminist use of postmodern strategies, therefore, is a little problematic, but it may also be one of the only ways for feminist *visual* arts to exist.

Many commentators have recently pointed to the maleness of the modernist tradition, and therefore to the implied maleness of any postmodernism that is either in reaction to or even a conscious break from that modernism. Feminisms have resisted incorporation into the postmodern camp, and with good reason: their political agendas would be endangered, or at least obscured by the double coding of postmodernism's complicitous critique; their historical particularities and relative positionalities would risk being subsumed. Both enterprises clearly work toward an awareness of the social nature of cultural activity, but feminisms are not content with exposition: art forms cannot change unless social practices do. Exposition may be the first step; but it cannot be the last. Nevertheless feminist and postmodern artists do share a view of art as a social sign inevitably and unavoidably enmeshed in other signs in systems of meaning and value. But I would argue that feminisms want to go beyond this to work to *change* those systems, not just to 'de-doxify' them.

But there is another difference between the two enterprises. Barbara Creed puts it this way:

> Whereas feminism would attempt to explain that crisis [of legitimation that Lyotard has described] in terms of the workings of patriarchal ideology and the oppression of women and other minority groups, postmodernism looks to other possible causes – particularly the West's reliance on ideologies which posit universal truths – Humanism, History, Religion, Progress, etc. While feminism would argue that the common ideological position of all these 'truths' is that they are patriarchal, postmodern theory . . . would be reluctant to isolate a single major determining factor.
>
> (Creed 1987: 52)

'Reluctant to' because it cannot – not without falling into the trap of which it implicitly accuses other ideologies: that of totalization. Creed is right that postmodernism offers no privileged, unproblematic position from which to speak. Therefore, she notes, the 'paradox in which we feminists find ourselves is that while we regard patriarchal discourses as fictions, we nevertheless proceed as if our position, based on a belief in the oppression of women, were somewhat closer to the truth' (67). But postmodernism's rejection of a privileged position is as much an ideological stand as this feminist taking of a position. By ideology here – as throughout this book – I mean to imply that all-informing complex of social practices and systems of representation. The political confusion surrounding postmodernism is not accidental, as we have been seeing, but is a direct result of its double encoding as both complicity and critique. While feminisms may use postmodern parodic strategies of deconstruction, they never suffer from this confusion of political agenda, partly because they have a position and a 'truth' that offer ways of understanding aesthetic and social practices in the light of the production of – and challenge to – gender relations. This is their strength and, in some people's eyes, their necessary limitation.

While feminisms and postmodernism have both worked to help us understand the dominant representational modes at work in our society, feminisms have focused on the specifically female subject of representation and have begun to suggest ways of challenging and changing those dominants in both mass culture and high art. Traditionally representations of the female body have been the province of men. Except in advertising, perhaps, women are not usually the intended addressees of pictures of women. So, if they do view them, they can either look – as surrogate males – or identify with the woman and be passive, be watched. But postmodern parodic strategies at least allow artists like Kolbowski or Kruger to contest these options, to suggest female positions of spectatorship that might go beyond narcissism, masochism, or even voyeurism. Their Brechtian challenges to the representations of women in mass culture demand critique, not identification or objectification. This art parodically inscribes the conventions of feminine representation, provokes our conditioned response and then subverts that response, making us aware of how it was induced in us. To work it must be complicitous with the values it challenges: we have to feel the seduction in order to question it and then to theorize the site of that contradiction. Such feminist uses of postmodern tactics politicize desire in their play with the revealed and the hidden, the offered and the deferred.

So-called high art is no more innocent than mass culture, of course. Perhaps what we call eroticism is only the pornography of the elite, as Angela Carter (1979: 17) has suggested. In feminist hands, parody becomes one of the ways of 'rereading against the grain of the "master works" of Western culture' (de Lauretis 1986b: 10). Commenting on Eugène Delacroix's numerous, obsessional sketches of women, one of his fictional mistresses (in Susan Daitch's overtly feminist novel, *L.C.*) comments: 'Art in league with seduction, two halves in constant dialogue' (Daitch 1986: 72). Gender is obviously a division of power here too, and the female body is the locus of power politics. When writers like Maxine Hong Kingston, Margaret Atwood, or Audrey Thomas represent women's bodies as vulnerable, diseased, injured, or as experiencing their own pleasure – from the inside – they implicitly protest the male erotic gazing at their external form. In *Ways of Seeing*, John Berger suggests that women are split, that they both watch themselves and watch men watch them as objects (while experiencing themselves as female subjects). Can postmodern strategies offer women a way out of the impasse implied here, and still remain within the conventions of visual art? When Kolbowski presents parodically re-positioned media images of the fashion model (traditionally, the idealized image of either the male gaze or female narcissistic identification), she does so in such a way as to articulate the confrontation of the passive objectified image with the power of representations to construct identity. The female body here is neither neutral nor natural; it is clearly inscribed in a system of differences in which the male and his gaze hold power. In her *Model Pleasure* series, she fragments the fetishized female body to show that all the represented images are invested with the same ideologically 'natural' status.

Barbara Kruger and Victor Burgin have also used postmodern tactics in their art to point to the spot where the erotic usually overlaps with the discourse of power and possession – traditionally the realm of the pornographic. As we saw earlier, works like Burgin's *Possession* foreground how sexuality is 'the construction of something called "sexuality" through a set of representations' (Heath 1982: 3). The meaning of that construction is not in the representations themselves, but in the relation between spectator, representation, and the entire social context. The sexual play of the words 'What does possession mean to you?' and of the photo of that embracing couple is played off against the lower caption: '7% of our population own 84% of our wealth.' This kind of linking of the critiques of capitalism and patriarchy has been undertaken by feminists and postmodernists and by feminist postmodernists.

As John Berger (1972a: 47) pithily put it: '*Men act* and *women appear*.' There is a long tradition of instructional literature whose purpose is to tell women how to 'appear' – to make themselves desirable – to men: from Renaissance coterie poetry to contemporary fashion magazines. Even fairy tales work to pass on the received collective 'wisdom' of the past and therein reflect the myths of sexuality under patriarchy. Angela Carter's feminist use of postmodernist parody in her rewritings of 'Bluebeard' and 'Beauty and the Beast' in *The Bloody Chamber* exposes the inherited sexist psychology of the erotic. Parody, rewriting, re-presenting woman is one option which postmodernism offers feminist artists in general, but especially those who want to work within the visual arts, overtly contesting the male gaze.

When Sherrie Levine literally takes those photos of famous art photos by men, she is doing more than appropriating the images of high art in order to contest the cult of originality (which is a postmodernist aim). She is doing something else too. She is quoted as saying: 'Where as a woman artist could I situate myself? What I was doing was making this explicit: how this Oedipal relationship artists have with artists of the past gets repressed; and how I, as a woman, was only allowed to represent male desire' (in Marzorati 1986: 97). Cindy Sherman has found another way to contest that maleness of the gaze: her many self-portraits which offer her own body in the guise of social or media stereotypes are so self-consciously posed that the social construction of the female self, fixed by the masculine gaze, is both presented and ironized, for she herself is the gaze behind the camera, the active absent presence, the subject and object of her representation of woman as sign, of woman as positioned by gender – but also by race and class.

What postmodern tactics have allowed feminist artists is a way to foreground the politics of the representation of the body through parody and counter-expectation, while remaining within the conventions of visual art. Barbara Kruger's contestatory problematizing of the erotic in *Give me all you've got* is a good example of this. One of her few works which is not in black and white, with a signature red frame, this one is framed in ironically feminine pink: it is the articulation of female desire. This is a photo of a mass of *petits fours* and the little cakes are made to look rather phallic: their tilting has been said to suggest more than just aroused male members – they are also somewhat reminiscent of heavy artillery. In either case, they offer images of male power, but reduced to a literalization of the 'sweet-talk' of male seduction. But that verbal demand – 'Give me all you've got' – is aggressively imperative in tone and not at all the traditional articulation of female desire.

In this work, Kruger goes beyond dismantling male phallic identity and female masochistic identity as modes of erotic behavior; in it, I think, she makes the step from deconstructive postmodernism to feminism. To use the title of Mary Kelly's 1983 show, she goes 'beyond the purloined image.' Kruger's work is usually seen as part of a postmodern focus on representation, on the decentering of the unitary, autonomous subject of humanist discourse. And so it is; but it is also feminist in that it reinjects the assumed but concealed maleness of that humanist subject into the discussion. Her image/text combinations may use already existing mass-media images of women, but this is not simply a case of what Harold Rosenberg wittily called 'dejavunik' art, art which presents the already assimilated dressed in new clothes. Mass culture is the site of her contestation, partly because that is where desire is really produced for most women – not only in art museums, though it operates there too.

Barbara Kruger's work has become commercially successful, and this too has been used as a criticism of her feminist politics. But we should ask: if her photography *has* negotiated a relationship between existing art institutions and feminist practices, is this a matter of complicity on its part, or of recuperation by those institutions? Or, more positively, is this an example of the kind of active intervention in the discourses and institutions of art that makes feminist practices the site of political action? Can that (postmodern) complicity enable a feminist subversion from within? Part of the problem, perhaps, might stem from what I would see as a limitation of postmodernism – in itself and in its use by feminist artists: the postmodern may offer art as the site of political struggle by its posing of multiple and deconstructing questions, but it does not seem able to make the move into political agency. It asks questions that reveal art as the place where values, norms, beliefs, actions are produced; it deconstructs the processes of signification. But it never escapes its double encoding: it is always aware of the mutual interdependence of the dominant and the contestatory. As feminists have shown in their appropriation of its parodic modalities, postmodernism has at least the potential to be political in effect. As we saw in the last chapter, Kruger achieves this effect by the most overt means possible, perhaps: by direct address to the viewer. The print text of her works always addresses that gender-specific viewer by means of those linguistic shifters, 'you' and 'we.' While the gender of each also shifts (thereby underlining the instability of viewer positions and subjectivities), it is always clear.

I have mentioned a number of times Cindy Sherman's portraits of herself and their challenges to the fiction behind photography's purportedly transparent representation of reality. Many critics have noted her obvious and very postmodern contesting of the unitary and autonomous subject, but what needs reviewing again is the gender of that subject. This is less problematic in Sherman's work than it is in, for instance, that of Hannah Wilke. In a piece like *Marxism and Art*, Wilke's address, while as direct and polemical as Kruger's, is also a problem for me, precisely because of its manipulation of the nude tradition and the notion of desire. Writing about body art, Lucy Lippard has argued that it is 'a subtle abyss that separates men's use of women for sexual titillation from women's use of women to expose that insult' (Lippard 1976: 125), but in Wilke's work, the subtlety of that abyss of difference is problematic. Some feminist theory argues that the body of woman, when used by men, is colonized, appropriated, even mystified; when used by women, that body reveals its fertility and self-sufficient sexuality, even if it parodically uses the conventions of the masculinist nude tradition in order to do so.

In this work Wilke offers herself in what is known as a frontal nudity pose from the waist up. Above her portrait are the words: 'Marxism and Art' and below it: 'Beware of Fascist Feminism.' There is potential in women's self-portrayal for radical critique but also much inherent ambivalence:

> The depiction of women *by* women (sometimes themselves) in this quasi-sexist manner as a political statement grows potentially more powerful as it approaches actual exploitation but then, within an ace of it, collapses into ambiguity and confusion. The more attractive the women, the higher the risk, since the more closely they approach conventional stereotypes in the first place.
>
> (Tickner 1987: 273)

While Cindy Sherman may 'uglify' some of her self-portraits, Wilke does not really (despite her pasting on of chewing-gum 'scars'). She bares her body to the camera, as do Carolee Schneeman and Lynda Benglis – all good-looking women who have been accused of political ambiguity and narcissism. Wilke's work has been defended as both a satire and a defense of the pin-up girl or even the fashion-model conventions, because she poses herself, albeit provocatively. She flaunts her own pride and pleasure in her sexuality and sexual power. Is this how we are to interpret 'Beware of Fascist Feminism' – the feminism that might find this a little too complicitous, or the feminism whose ideology permits no such (maybe male-determined) figuration of female desire?

But this photo does not really represent the sexploitational posing of the beautiful woman as tease: this is the pose of a self-assertive woman wearing the semiotic signs of masculinity atop her nude body – a tie, low-slung jeans. If 'fascist feminism' meant prudish feminism, then the commodification of the female body in male art (is this how to link Marxism and Art?) might be what such feminism underwrites by refusing woman the use of her own body and its pleasures. But what about the position of the addressed viewer: is it voyeuristic, narcissistic, critical? Can we even tell? Does this work problematize or confirm the maleness of the gaze? I really cannot tell. In the face of the manifest contradictions of this work, it is tempting to say that, while Wilke is clearly playing with the conventions of pornographic address (her eyes meet and engage the viewer's), she is also juxtaposing this with the discourse of feminist protest – but turned against itself in some way. She does not make her own position clear and thus risks reinforcing what she might well be intending to contest, that is, patriarchal notions of female sexuality and male desire.

I wonder if what we have here (to borrow a wonderful term from Marguerite Waller) is a case of the 'Tootsie trope' – 'a work's failure to allow its feminist intentions to alter its male-centered mode of signification.' Male desire, while supposedly discredited, is in fact inscribed without even the contestation that postmodern complicitous critique would offer. I really do not know what to do with this. At times I wonder if, in order to represent herself, woman must assume a masculine position;

yet, Kruger and others have shown that this positioning can be done parodically, through postmodern strategies that still allow for serious contestation.

I suppose this leaves a final question: what would the full rejection of that male position look like? Feminist film provides the most obvious and important examples and Nancy Spero's 'peinture féminine,' while still implicitly deconstructing the male sexuality underlying the erotic conventions of female representations, offers a female gaze in which women are protagonists and subjects, not the traditional erotic objects of desire. Her refigurations of the female body may be one answer, suggesting a move beyond that potential impasse of the (perhaps inevitable) maleness of the gaze. So too are the works of Mira Schor, Nancy Fried, Louise Bourgeois, and the other women in the 1988 *Politics of Gender* show at the QCC Gallery in New York.

However, I also think postmodernist parody would be among the 'practical strategies' that have become 'strategic practices' (Parker and Pollock 1987b) in feminist art's attempt to present new kinds of female pleasure, new articulations of female desire, by offering tactics for deconstruction – for inscribing in order to subvert the patriarchal visual traditions. But I also think feminisms have pushed postmodern theory and art in directions they might not otherwise have headed. One of these directions involves a return to a topic treated in some detail earlier in this study: that of history.

The private and the public

In granting new and emphatic value to the notion of 'experience,' feminisms have also raised an issue of great importance to postmodern representation: what constitutes a valid historical narrative? And who decides? This has led to the re-evaluation of personal or life narratives – journals, letters, confessions, biographies, autobiographies, self-portraits. In Catherine Stimpson's terms: 'Experience generated more than art; it was a source of political engagement as well' (1988: 226). If the personal is the political, then the traditional separation between private and public history must be rethought. This feminist rethinking has coincided with a general renegotiation of the separation of high art from the culture of everyday life – popular and mass culture – and the combined result has been a reconsideration of both the context of historical narrative and the politics of representation and self-representation.

In postmodern writing this particular impact of feminisms can be seen in a number of literary forms. One would be those historiographic metafictions in which the fictively personal becomes the historically – and thus politically – public in a kind of synecdochic fashion: in Rushdie's *Midnight's Children*, the protagonist cannot and will not separate his self-representation from the representation of his nation, and the result is the politicization of public *and* private experience, of nationality *and* subjectivity. In Nigel Williams's *Star Turn* or John Berger's *G.* the representation of public historical events tends to take on political dimensions within the private fictional world of the characters, but because of metafictional self-consciousness, the synecdoche extends to include the world of the reader.

Another related form of postmodern writing informed by the feminist revaluation of life-writing and its politicization of the personal is the kind of work that sits on the borderline between fiction and personal history, either biographical or autobiographical: Ondaatje's *Running in the Family*, Kingston's *The Woman Warrior* and *China Men*, Banville's *Doctor Copernicus* and *Kepler*. The representation of the self (and the other) in history in this form is also done with intense self-consciousness, thus revealing the problematic relation of the private person writing to the public as well as personal events once lived (by the narrator or someone else).

In order to underline what I see to be the particularly feminist source of inspiration for these postmodern modes of dealing with the private and public politics of representation, I would like to use as examples two works that I think of as both feminist and postmodern (always remembering that the two, however related, must be kept separate) and that overtly enact the specifically political dimension involved in this paradoxical kind of historical narrative representation. Gayl Jones's *Corregidora* is a novel about Ursa, an American blues singer, whose entire life has been shaped by the hatred of the female line of her family for Corregidora, a Brazilian-Portuguese 'slave-breeder and whoremonger' (Jones 1976: 8–9) who fathered her mother and grandmother. The family's personal history has been passed on orally from one woman to the next, from the enslaved to the finally free. The only historical document of the past that the women possess is a photograph of Corregidora: 'Tall, white hair, white beard, white mustache' (10) – a demonic parody of the white Christian God-figure. The story of one black family becomes the microcosmic history of an entire race.

Jones's novel repeatedly tells the story of Corregidora's sexual and racial exploitation, so that the reader too is made to experience the iterative act of fixing memory. This is particularly necessary because Ursa is barren: she will have no daughter to whom she can and must relate the family/racial history. As readers we become her surrogate daughter, but the mode of telling can then no longer be oral. The recourse to oral history was originally necessary because the whites had burned all written evidence of black history. As Ursa's great-grandmother says: *'I'm leaving evidence. And you got to leave evidence too. And your children got to leave evidence. And when it come time to hold up the evidence, we got to have evidence to hold up against them'* (Jones 1976: 14, italics in text). She later adds: *'They can burn the papers but they can't burn conscious, Ursa. And that what makes the evidence. And that's what makes the verdict'* (22). Ursa uses her blues music as well as her narrative to us in order to present both the evidence and the verdict. But first she has to accept that she is indeed one of the 'Corregidora women' even though free and not herself fathered by the slave-breeder: *'I am Ursa Corregidora. I have tears for eyes. I was made to touch my past at an early age'* (77). Through several marriages, she retains that hated but accurate (maternal-line) surname as another form of 'evidence.'

The black men in the story respond with resignation to the white destruction of documents such as black land purchases or proof of spouses bought out of slavery: 'they ain't nothing you can do when they tear the pages out of the book and they ain't no record of it' (Jones 1976: 78). But the women's response to the willed (and political) lacunae of private and public history is to tell the story of oppression over and over again. As Ursa says, *'[t]hey squeezed Corregidora into me, and I sung back in return'* (103), translating the verbal narrative representation into emotion and song. Ursa distinguishes between 'the lived life' and 'the spoken one' (108); but there is also the sung one, not to mention the written ones, both the official public record of historical injustice (destroyed by white men) and the unofficial personal record that is this novel.

At no point here is the private separable from the public. Ursa's female oppression (in white or black society) becomes the metaphor for black oppression and exploitation in America. A male blues singer tells Ursa: 'Sinatra was the first one to call Ray Charles a genius, he spoke of "the genius of Ray Charles." And after that everybody called him a genius. They didn't call him a genius before that though. He *was* a genius but they didn't call him that' (Jones 1976: 169). He adds: 'If a white man hadn't told them, they wouldn't have seen it' (170), and his 'they' includes blacks as well as whites. This is a powerful novel that self-consciously de-naturalizes many aspects of history: the reliability of its recording; the availability of its archive; the politics of its representation of black women who must pass down their oral past 'from generation to generation so we'd never forget. Even though they'd burned everything to play like it didn't never happen' (9).

The power of remembering and forgetting is also the focus of Christa Wolf's narrative of the interweaving of personal and public history and responsibility in *Patterns of Childhood*, an example of the second kind of feminist-inspired postmodern writing about the self and its relation to time and place. A prefatory note tells us that all characters are 'an invention of the narrator' (note: not the author) and that none is identical with anyone real. If, however, we were to note any similarity between fiction and reality, we are told: 'Generally recognizable behavior patterns should be blamed on circumstances.' When the circumstances are the rise of the Nazi Party and the Second World War and the writer is East German, the public and the private are joined from the start; the personal is likely to be political.

The book opens with what might be an archetypally postmodern statement about history: 'What is past is not dead; it is not even past' (Wolf 1980: 3). The narrator addresses herself as 'you' – 'the voice that assumes the task of telling it' (4). 'It' is the story of her childhood, but always as seen from the point of view of subsequent history, both personal and public: 'The present intrudes upon remembrance' (4). The form of the text's narration itself is complex. The writing is said to take place between 1972 and 1975 but it uses as a frame an earlier trip back to her native town in order to study the even more distant past of her 1930s and 1940s childhood. With memory she must cross both temporal and spatial borders – even national ones, for the town she grew up in and fled from (in advance of the Russian army) was once in Germany (Landsberg) but is now, thanks to history, in Poland (Grozów Wielkopolski). The narrator ('you') refers to herself as a child ('she') as Nelly, thereby introducing a degree of distancing through fictive naming and third-person address. This also serves to signal that the child she once was is now deemed almost inaccessible to her thirty years later: the woman and the girl have different knowledge. As the narrator self-consciously writes, we watch her try to deal with both distance and complicity, both the past and the present:

> From the beginning this chapter had been earmarked to deal with the war; like all the other chapters, it has been prepared on sheets with headings such as Past, Present, Trip to Poland, Manuscript. Auxiliary structures, devised to organize the material and to detach it from yourself by this system of overlapping layers. . . . Form as a possibility of gaining distance.
>
> (Wolf 1980: 164)

The narrative of *Patterns of Childhood* is full of passages like this, metafictive representations of the act of trying to tell the story of the past of her self and her country, both in the present and during the trip to Poland, accompanied by her husband, daughter, and brother. The public history actually turns out to be the easier one to relate: 'we either fictionalize or become tongue-tied when it comes to personal matters' (8). But there are also problems with this public dimension. For instance, she wants to use as a guiding epigraph the words of Kazimierz Brandys: 'Fascism . . . as a concept, is larger than the Germans. But they became its classic example' (36). But she dares not, for fear of how her German readers would react. Of course, her self-consciousness here makes her point nevertheless. Her reconstruction of the past from both personal and official memory is not an exculpation or an excuse. She also forbids herself any irony, disgust, or scorn at the expense of those – like her own parents – who went along with the rise of Nazi power (38). She does not allow herself to imagine their thinking: that 'remains undescribed, being inaccessible to the power of imagination' (39). There are limits, then, to the narrative representation of any kind of history, even that of immediate personal experience.

One of the major limits is that of memory itself. The German people had been told about the existence of concentration camps for 'derelict elements' of society – the newspaper accounts exist to prove it – but this was somehow not remembered. The narrator parenthetically wonders: '(A bewildering suspicion: they really had forgotten. Completely. Total war: total amnesia.)' (Wolf 1980: 39). Her own memory too needs supplementing. After a vivid description of a Hitler Youth rally attended by Nelly, the narrator adds: '(The information about the sequence of events was obtained from the 1936 volume of the *General-Anzeiger* in the State Library; the images – "strings of torches," "blazing woodpile" – come from memory.)' (129–30). The problem is that both sources can prove unreliable: 'it's so much easier . . . to invent the past than to remember it' (153). Nevertheless, she still feels the need to consult and cite the documents of the historical archive, such as Goebbels's anti-Semitic radio speech on the occasion of Kristallnacht.

What the narrator comes to realize is that the past 'cannot be described objectively' (Wolf 1980: 164) and that her present will always mediate her past. This does not absolve her from the responsibility of trying to describe it, nevertheless. Writing is 'a duty which surpasses all others, even if it means reopening questions about which everything seems to have been said, and about which the rows of book spines in the libraries are no longer measured in yards, but in miles' (171). Her personal responsibility must be faced; so too must her nation's: 'it may be impossible to be alive today without becoming implicated in the crime' (171). Feeling weighed down by notebooks, diaries, and her notes from reading those miles of books, the narrator must face another obstacle to her recording of both public and private history: the proliferation of archival material.

She also confronts her own desire to distance. Is her objectification of her childhood self as 'Nelly' hypocritical? Is her adult writer's lament about the 'ghastly undertone' (Wolf 1980: 48) of the German language in which she composes a form of guilt for

Nelly's response to the 'glitter words' of the 1930s: 'alien blood,' 'a eugenic way of life' (61)? Why does she want to avoid certain words and expressions? Why is it unbearable to think of 'I' in conjunction with 'Auschwitz'? Her answer points to the moral and political issues of representation in such historical narrative: ' "I" in the past conditional: I would have. I might have. I could have. Done it. Obeyed orders' (230).

History, however, has a short memory – even in families. The narrator's guilt about her personal and national past, about those who were allowed to 'commit murder without remorse by a language stripped of conscience' (Wolf 1980: 237), is contrasted with her daughter's lack of any sense of responsibility: until the trip to Poland she had only known of the war through her history textbook, which mitigated the fading horror of the previous generation. The narrator has no such luxury: she cannot think of any event in her childhood without thinking of what was happening in the public arena at the same time. She cannot even use the German language without facing a responsibility that is both personal and national: the meaning of the word 'verfallen' exists in no other language in the one particular sense of ' "irretrievably lost, because enslaved by one's own, deep-down consent" ' (288). Or the word 'chronic' begins to take on the qualities of a moral category: 'Chronic blindness. And the question cannot be: How can they live with their conscience?, but: What kind of circumstances are those that cause a collective loss of conscience?' (319).

The narrator's awareness that to represent the past in language and in narrative is to construct that past cannot be separated from her awareness of the inextricable links between the personal and the political:

> Ideally the structure of the experience coincides with the structure of the narrative. . . . But there is no technique that permits translating an incredibly tangled mesh whose threads are interlaced according to the strictest laws, into linear narrative without doing it serious damage. To speak about superimposed layers – 'narrative levels' – means shifting into inexact nomenclature and falsifying the real process. 'Life,' the real process, is always steps ahead.
>
> (Wolf 1980: 272)

Besides the postmodern self-consciousness here about the paradoxes and problems of historical representation (and self-
representation), there is also a very feminist awareness of the
value of experience and the importance of its representation in
the form of 'life-writing' – however difficult or even falsifying
that process might turn out to be. It may be the case that we can
'no longer tell exactly what we have experienced' (362) and that
the attempt to represent some version of that is inevitably a
process of '[e]rasing, selecting, stressing' (359), but the constraints must be faced and not used as an excuse for not making
the attempt. It is Christa Wolf's experience as a novelist that
comes to her aid: 'I believe that the mechanism which deals with
the absorption and processing of reality is formed by literature'
(368–9). But the way we represent the result of that absorption
and processing is also formed by our knowledge of past
representations – both historical and literary.

The feminist practices that are so powerful in Christa Wolf's
other, equally self-conscious writing indirectly inform this work
too. Although its focus is not specifically on women's issues, the
formal preoccupations of *Patterns of Childhood* illustrate some of
the things feminisms have brought to postmodernism, sometimes to reinforce already existing concerns, sometimes to
unmask cultural forms in need of 'de-doxification.' I am thinking not only of an increased awareness of gender differences, but
of issues like the complexity of the representation of experience;
the paradox of the inevitable distortions of recording history
and yet the pressing drive to record nevertheless; and the
unavoidable politics of the representation of both the past and
the present.

There is, then, a two-way involvement of the postmodern
with the feminist: on the one hand, feminisms have successfully
urged postmodernism to reconsider – in terms of gender – its
challenges to that humanist universal called 'Man' and have
supported and reinforced its de-naturalization of the separation
between the private and the public, the personal and the
political; on the other hand, postmodern parodic representational strategies have offered feminist artists an effective way of
working within and yet challenging dominant patriarchal discourses. That said, there is still no way in which the feminist and
the postmodern – as cultural enterprises – can be conflated. The

differences are clear, and none so clear as the political one. Chris Weedon (1987) opens her book on feminist practice with the words: 'Feminism is a politics.' Postmodernism is not; it is certainly political, but it is politically ambivalent, doubly encoded as both complicity and critique, so that it can be (and has been) recuperated by both the left and the right, each ignoring half of that double coding.

Feminisms will continue to resist incorporation into postmodernism, largely because of their revolutionary force as political movements working for real social change. They go beyond making ideology explicit and deconstructing it to argue a need to change that ideology, to effect a real transformation of art that can only come with a transformation of patriarchal social practices. Postmodernism has not theorized agency; it has no strategies of resistance that would correspond to the feminist ones. Postmodernism manipulates, but does not transform signification; it disperses but does not (re)construct the structures of subjectivity (Foster 1985: 6). Feminisms must. Feminist artists may use postmodern strategies of parodic inscription and subversion in order to initiate the deconstructive first step but they do not stop there. While useful (especially in the visual arts where the insistence of the male gaze seems hard to avoid), such internalized subversion does not automatically lead to the production of the new, not even new representations of female desire. As one critic asks: 'is it possible to create new erotic codes – and I assume that is what feminism is striving for – without in some ways reusing the old?' (Winship 1987: 127). Perhaps postmodern strategies do, however, offer ways for women artists at least to contest the old – the representations of both their bodies and their desires – without denying them the right to re-colonize, to reclaim both as sites of meaning and value. Such practices also remind us all that every representation always has its politics.

Concluding note: some directed reading

In order to keep referencing to a minimum in the text, I list below some of the major points discussed and suggested readings from the bibliography.

Specific cultural forms

Postmodernism and architecture: Jencks 1977, 1980a, 1980b, 1982; Portoghesi 1974, 1982, 1983; McLeod 1985; Stern 1980; Lerup 1987; Brolin 1976; D. Davis 1987; M. Davis 1985; Jameson 1985; Tafuri 1980.

Postmodernism and film: Creed 1987; Carroll 1985; most issues of *Screen*.

Postmodernism and fiction: McHale 1987; Hutcheon 1988; McCaffery 1986a, 1986b; Newman 1985; Klinkowitz 1985, 1986; Thiher 1984; Stevick 1981, 1985; Mellard 1980; Tanner 1971; Bradbury 1983; Lodge 1977; Ebert 1980; Lauzen 1986; Lee 1988; Malmgren 1985; Porush 1985; Wilde 1981, 1987; Zimmerman 1986.

Postmodernism and poetry: Rawson 1986; Altieri 1973, 1984; Davidson 1975; Perloff 1985; Moramarco 1986; Russell 1985.

Postmodernism and television: Grossberg 1987; Roberts 1987; Eco 1984; Baudrillard 1983; Kaplan 1987.

Postmodernism and photography: Abbas 1984; Crimp 1979, 1980, 1983, 1987; Starenko 1983; Thornton 1979; Andre 1984; Barber 1983/4; Bellavance 1986; Corrigan 1985; Goldberg 1988; Graham 1985; Mulvey 1986; Phillips 1987; Sekula 1982; Solomon-Godeau 1984a, 1984b; Burgin 1982b, 1986a, 1986b; Tagg 1982; Wollen 1978/9.

170   The Politics of Postmodernism

General studies of the concept of the postmodern

In visual arts: D. Davis 1977, 1980; Owens 1982; Crimp 1980, 1983; Buchloh 1984; James 1985; Jameson 1986–7; Kibbins 1983; Krauss 1979, 1985, 1987; Kuspit 1984; Lippard 1976; Paoletti 1985.

In literature and criticism: Arac 1987; Paterson 1986; Köhler 1977; Hassan 1971, 1975, 1980a, 1980b, 1982, 1986, 1987; Hoffmann *et al.* 1977; Graff 1973, 1979, 1981; Bertens 1986; Huyssen 1986; Calinescu 1987; Hutcheon 1988; Russell 1985; Huyssen 1986.

In social and cultural studies: Palmer 1977; Lyotard 1984a, 1984b, 1986; Habermas 1983, 1985a, 1985b; Baudrillard 1983; Kroker and Cook 1986; Bell 1973, 1976; Russell 1985; Benhabib 1984; Trachtenberg 1985; Bauman 1987; Bennett 1987; Collins 1987; Davidson 1975; Jameson 1983, 1984a, 1984c; Kramer 1982; Müller 1979; Owens 1980a, 1980b, 1983, 1984; Foster 1983, 1985; Polkinhorn 1987; Radhakrishnan 1986; Schmidt 1986; Wellbery 1985.

On postmodernism and modernism: Eagleton 1985; Jameson 1984a; Foster 1985; Huyssen 1986; Greenberg 1980; Latimer 1984; Laffey 1987; Silliman 1987; Calinescu 1977: 120–44; Wilde 1981, 1987; Bürger 1987; Garvin 1980; Giddens 1981; Hayman 1978; Malmgren 1987; Nägele 1980/1; Raulet 1984; Rowe 1987; Russell 1982; Scherpe 1986/7; Wellmer 1985; Wolin 1985.

Bibliography

Abbas, M.A. (1984) 'Photography/writing/postmodernism,' *Minnesota Review* n.s. 23: 91–111.

Abrams, M.H. (1981) *A Glossary of Literary Terms*, 4th ed. rev., New York: Holt, Rinehart, & Winston.

Ackroyd, Peter (1985) *Hawksmoor*, London: Hamish Hamilton.

—(1987) *Chatterton*, London: Hamish Hamilton.

Adorno, Theodor (1978) 'On the fetish-character in music and the regression of listening,' in Arato and Gebhardt (1978).

Althusser, Louis (1969) *For Marx*, trans. Ben Brewster, New York: Pantheon.

—(1971) *Lenin and Philosophy and Other Essays*, trans. Ben Brewster, London: New Left Books.

Altieri, Charles (1973) 'From symbolist thought to immanence: the ground of postmodern American poetics,' *boundary 2* 1, 3: 605–41.

—(1984) *Self and Sensibility in Contemporary American Poetry*, Cambridge: Cambridge University Press.

Andre, Linda (1984) 'The politics of postmodern photography,' *Minnesota Review* n.s. 23: 17–35.

Arac, Jonathan (1987) *Critical Genealogies: Historical Situations for Postmodern Literary Studies*, New York: Columbia University Press.

Arato, Andrew and Gebhardt, Eike (eds) (1978) *The Essential Frankfurt School Reader*, New York: Urizen Books.

Art and Ideology (1984) Catalogue, New York: New Museum of Contemporary Art.

Atwood, Margaret (1985) *The Handmaid's Tale*, Toronto: McClelland & Stewart.

Banes, Sally (1985) 'Dance,' in Trachtenberg (1985): 82–100.

Banville, John (1976) *Doctor Copernicus*, New York: Norton.

—(1981) *Kepler*, London: Secker & Warburg.

Barber, Bruce Alistair (1983/4) 'Appropriation/expropriation: convention or intervention?' *Parachute* 33: 29–39.

Barnes, Julian (1984) *Flaubert's Parrot*, London: Jonathan Cape.

Barth, John (1967) 'The literature of exhaustion,' *Atlantic* 220, 2: 29–34.

—(1979) *LETTERS*, New York: Putnam's Sons.

—(1980) 'The literature of replenishment: postmodernist fiction,' *Atlantic* 245, 1: 65–71.

Barthes, Roland (1977a) *Image Music Text*, trans. Stephen Heath, New York: Hill & Wang.

—(1977b) *Roland Barthes by Roland Barthes*, trans. Richard Howard, New York: Hill & Wang.

—(1981) *Camera Lucida: Reflections on Photography*, trans. Richard Howard, New York: Hill & Wang.

Baudrillard, Jean (1976) *L'Echange symbolique et la mort*, Paris: Gallimard.

—(1983) *Simulations*, trans. Paul Foss, Paul Patton, and Philip Beitchman, New York: *Semiotext(e)*.

—(1984) 'The precession of simulacra,' in Wallis (1984): 253–81.

Bauman, Zygmund (1987) *Legislators and Interpreters: On Modernity, Post-Modernity and Intellectuals*, Ithaca, NY: Cornell University Press.

Beal, Graham W.J. (1986) 'A little history,' in *Second Sight*: Biennial IV Catalogue, San Francisco Museum of Modern Art: 1–11.

Bell, Daniel (1973) *The Coming of Post-industrial Society*, New York: Basic.

—(1976) *The Cultural Contradictions of Capitalism*, New York: Basic.

Bellavance, Guy (1986) Review of *Magnificent Obsession*, Galérie Optica, Montreal, *Parachute* 42: 35–6.

Belsey, Catherine (1980) *Critical Practice*, London: Methuen.

Benhabib, Seyla (1984) 'Epistemologies of postmodernism: a rejoinder to Jean-François Lyotard,' *New German Critique* 33: 103–26.

Benjamin, Walter (1968) *Illuminations*, ed. Hannah Arendt, trans. Harry Zohn, New York: Schocken.

Bennett, David (1987) 'Wrapping up postmodernism: the subject of consumption versus the subject of cognition,' *Textual Practice* 1, 3: 243–61.

Berger, John (1972a) *Ways of Seeing*, London: BBC; Harmondsworth: Penguin.

—(1972b) *G.*, New York: Pantheon.

Bernstein, Richard J. (ed.) (1985) *Habermas and Modernity*, Cambridge, Mass.: MIT Press.

Bertens, Hans (1986) 'The postmodern *Weltanschauung* and its relation with modernism: an introductory survey,' in Fokkema and Bertens (1986): 9–51.

Betterton, Rosemary (ed.) (1987) *Looking On: Images of Femininity in the Visual Arts and Media*, London and New York: Pandora.

Bois, Yve-Alain (1986) 'The antidote,' *October* 39: 128–44.

Bois, Yve-Alain, Crimp, Douglas, and Krauss, Rosalind (1987) 'A conversation with Hans Haacke,' in Michelson *et al.* (1987): 175–200.

Bowering, George (1980) *Burning Water*, Don Mills, Ontario: General Publishing.

Boyd, William (1987) *The New Confessions*, London: Hamish Hamilton.

Bradbury, Malcolm (1983) *The Modern American Novel*, Oxford and New York: Oxford University Press.

Braudel, Fernand (1980) *On History*, trans. Sarah Matthews, Chicago, Ill.: University of Chicago Press.

Brecht, Bertolt (1964) *Brecht on Theatre: The Development of an Aesthetic*, ed. and trans. John Willet, New York: Hill & Wang; London: Methuen.

Brolin, Brent (1976) *The Failure of Modern Architecture*, New York: Van Nostrand Reinhold.

Brooks, Peter (1984) *Reading for the Plot: Design and Intention in Narrative*, New York: Random House.

Buchloh, Benjamin H.D. (1984a) 'Figures of authority, ciphers of regression: notes on the return of representation in European painting,' in Wallis (1984): 106–35.

—(1984b) 'Since realism there was . . . ,' in *Art and Ideology* (1984): 5–11.

Bürger, Christa (1987) 'Das Verschwinden der Kunst: Die Postmoderne-Debatte in den USA,' in Bürger and Bürger (1987): 34–55.

Bürger, Christa and Bürger, Peter (eds) (1987) *Postmoderne: Alltag, Allegorie und Avantgarde*, Frankfurt am Main: Suhrkamp.

Burgin, Victor (ed.) (1982a) *Thinking Photography*, London: Macmillan.

—(1982b) 'Photography, phantasy, function,' in Burgin (1982a): 177–216.

—(1986a) *The End of Art Theory: Criticism and Postmodernity*, Atlantic Highlands, NJ: Humanities Press International.

—(1986b) *Between*, Oxford: Basil Blackwell.

Calinescu, Matei (1977) *Faces of Modernity*, Bloomington, Ind.: Indiana University Press.

—(1987) 'Introductory remarks: postmodernism, the mimetic and theatrical fallacies,' in Calinescu and Fokkema (1987): 3–16.

Calinescu, Matei and Fokkema, Douwe (eds) (1987) *Exploring Postmodernism*, Amsterdam and Philadelphia, Pa: John Benjamins.

Canary, Robert H. and Kozicki, Henry (eds) (1978) *The Writing of History: Literary Form and Historical Understanding*, Madison, Wis.: University of Wisconsin Press.

Carroll, Noël (1985) 'Film,' in Trachtenberg (1985): 101–33.

Carter, Angela (1974) *Fireworks: Nine Profane Pieces*, London: Quartet Books.

—(1979) *The Sadeian Woman: An Exercise in Cultural History*, London: Virago.

—(1984) *Nights at the Circus*, London: Picador.

—(1985) *Black Venus*, London: Chatto & Windus and Hogarth Press.

Caute, David (1972) *The Illusion*, New York: Harper & Row.

Chow, Rey (1986/7) 'Rereading mandarin ducks and butterflies: a response to the "postmodern" condition,' *Cultural Critique* 5: 69–93.

Clarkson, David (1987–8) 'Sarah Charlesworth: an interview,' *Parachute* 49: 12–15.

Coetzee, J.M. (1986) *Foe*, Toronto: Stoddart.

Cohen, Leonard (1966) *Beautiful Losers*, Toronto: McClelland & Stewart.

Collingwood, R.G. (1946) *The Idea of History*, Oxford: Clarendon Press.

Collins, James (1987) 'Postmodernism and cultural practice: redefining the parameters,' *Postmodern Screen* issue of *Screen* 28, 2: 11–26.

Coover, Robert (1977) *The Public Burning*, New York: Viking.

Corrigan, Philip (1985) 'In/formation: a short organum for PhotoGraphWorking,' *Photo Communique* (Fall): 12–17.

Cortázar, Julio (1978) *A Manual for Manuel*, trans. Gregory Rabassa, New York: Pantheon.

Coward, Rosalind (1984) *Female Desire*, London: Paladin.

Creed, Barbara (1987) 'From here to modernity: feminism and postmodernism,' *Postmodern Screen* issue of *Screen* 28, 2: 47–67.

Crimp, Douglas (1977) 'Pictures' in catalogue for *Pictures*, Artists Space, New York: Committee for the Visual Arts.

—(1979) 'Pictures,' *October* 8: 75–88.

—(1980) 'The photographic activity of postmodernism,' *October* 15: 91–101.

—(1983) 'On the museum's ruins,' in Foster (1983): 43–56.

—(1987) 'The postmodern museum,' *Parachute* 46: 61–9.

Daitch, Susan (1986) *L.C.*, London: Virago.

Danto, Arthur C. (1965) *Analytic Philosophy of History*, New York: Cambridge University Press.

Davidson, Michael (1975) 'The languages of postmodernism,' *Chicago Review* 27: 11–22.

Davis, Douglas (1977) *Artculture: Essays on the Post-Modern*, New York: Harper & Row.

—(1980) 'Post-everything,' *Art in America* 68: 11, 13–14.

—(1987) 'Late postmodern: the end of style,' *Art in America* n.s. 6 (June): 15–23.

Davis, Lennard J. (1983) *Factual Fictions: The Origins of the English Novel*, New York: Columbia University Press.

—(1987) *Resisting Novels: Ideology and Fiction*, New York and London: Methuen.

Davis, Mike (1985) 'Urban renaissance and the spirit of postmodernism,' *New Left Review* 151: 106–13.

Davis, Natalie Zemon (1983) *The Return of Martin Guerre*, Cambridge, Mass.: Harvard University Press.

Davis, Peter (1988) 'Prince Charles narrowly escapes beheading,' *Esquire* (April): 93–111.

de Certeau, Michel (1975) *L'Ecriture de l'histoire*, Paris: Gallimard.

de Lauretis, Teresa (ed.) (1986a) *Feminist Studies/Critical Studies*, Bloomington, Ind.: Indiana University Press.

—(1986b) 'Feminist studies/critical studies: issues, terms, and contexts,' in de Lauretis (1986a): 1–19.

—(1987) *Technologies of Gender: Essays on Theory, Film, and Fiction*, Bloomington, Ind.: Indiana University Press.

Derrida, Jacques (1974) *Glas*, Paris: Galilée.

—(1976) *Of Grammatology*, trans. Gayatri Spivak, Baltimore, Md: Johns Hopkins University Press.

—(1978) *Writing and Difference*, trans. Alan Bass, Chicago, Ill.: University of Chicago Press.

—(1981) *Dissemination*, trans. Barbara Johnson, Chicago, Ill.: University of Chicago Press.

—(1982) 'Sending: on representation,' trans. Peter and Mary Ann Caws, *Social Research* 49, 2: 294–326.

Difference: On Representation and Sexuality (1984) Catalogue, New York: New Museum of Contemporary Art.

Doctorow, E.L. (1971) *The Book of Daniel*, New York: Bantam.

—(1975) *Ragtime*, New York: Random House.

—(1983) 'False documents,' in Trenner (1983): 16–27.

During, Simon (1987) 'Postmodernism or post-colonialism today,' *Textual Practice* 1, 1: 32–47.

Eagleton, Terry (1985) 'Capitalism, modernism and postmodernism,' *New Left Review* 152: 60–73.

—(1987a) 'The end of English,' *Textual Practice* 1, 1: 1–9.

—(1987b) *Saints and Scholars*, London and New York: Verso.

Ebert, Teresa L. (1980) 'The convergence of postmodern innovative fiction and science fiction,' *Poetics Today* 1, 4: 91–104.

Eco, Umberto (1976) *A Theory of Semiotics*, Bloomington, Ind.: Indiana University Press.

—(1982) 'Critique of the image,' in Burgin (1982a): 32–8.

Eco, Umberto (1983) *The Name of the Rose*, trans. William Weaver, San Diego, Calif., New York, and London: Harcourt Brace Jovanovich.

—(1984) 'A guide to the neo television of the 1980s,' *Framework* 25: 18–25.

Findley, Timothy (1977) *The Wars*, Toronto: Clarke, Irwin.

—(1981) *Famous Last Words*, Toronto: Clarke, Irwin.

Fletcher, Angus (ed.) (1976) *The Literature of Fact*, New York: Columbia University Press.

Fokkema, Douwe and Bertens, Hans (eds) (1986) *Approaching Postmodernism*, Amsterdam and Philadelphia, Pa: John Benjamins.

Foley, Barbara (1983) 'From *U.S.A.* to *Ragtime*: notes on the forms of historical consciousness in modern fiction,' in Trenner (1983): 158–78.

—(1986) *Telling the Truth: The Theory and Practice of Documentary Fiction*, Ithaca, NY and London: Cornell University Press.

Folland, Tom (1988) Review of Astrid Klein at the Ydessa Gallery, *Parachute* 50: 59–60.

Forster, E.M. (1927) *Aspects of the Novel*, London: Edward Arnold.

Foster, Hal (ed.) (1983) *The Anti-Aesthetic: Essays on Postmodern Culture*, Port Townsend, Wash.: Bay Press.

—(1984) 'Re: post,' in Wallis (1984): 188–201.

—(1985) *Recodings: Art, Spectacle, Cultural Politics*, Port Townsend, Wash.: Bay Press.

Foucault, Michel (1970) *The Order of Things: An Archaeology of the Human Sciences*, New York: Pantheon.

—(1972) *The Archaeology of Knowledge and the Discourse on Language*, trans. A.M. Sheridan Smith, New York: Pantheon.

—(1977) *Language, Counter-Memory, Practice: Selected Essays and Interviews*, trans. Donald F. Bouchard and Sherry Simon, Ithaca, NY: Cornell University Press.

—(1980) *The History of Sexuality: Volume I: An Introduction*, trans. Robert Hurley, New York: Vintage.

Fowles, John (1969) *The French Lieutenant's Woman*, Boston, Mass., and Toronto: Little, Brown; London: Jonathan Cape.

—(1985) *A Maggot*, Toronto: Collins; London: Jonathan Cape.

Friedberg, Anne (1988) 'Mutual indifference: feminism and postmodernism,' unpublished manuscript.

Fuentes, Carlos (1976) *Terra Nostra*, trans. Margaret Sayers Peden, New York: Farrar, Straus, & Giroux.

Gablik, Suzi (1984) *Has Modernism Failed?* London and New York: Thames & Hudson.

Gagnon, Monika (1987) 'Work in progress: Canadian women in the visual arts 1975–1987,' in Tregebov (1987): 100–27.

García Márquez, Gabriel (1970) *One Hundred Years of Solitude*, trans. Gregory Rabassa, New York: Avon.

—(1982) *Chronicle of a Death Foretold*, trans. Gregory Rabassa, New York: Ballantine.

Garvin, Harry R. (ed.) (1980) *Romanticism, Modernism, Postmodernism*, Lewisburg, Pa: Bucknell University Press; London: Associated University Press.

Gass, William H. (1985) *Habitations of the Word: Essays*, New York: Simon & Schuster.

Gauss, Kathleen McCarthy (1985) *New American Photography*, Los Angeles: Los Angeles County Museum of Art.

Giddens, Anthony (1981) 'Modernism and post-modernism,' *New German Critique* 22: 15–18.

Goldberg, Vicki (1988) 'The borrowers: how they play the game of appropriation today,' *American Photographer* (May): 24–5.

Gossman, Lionel (1978) 'History and literature: reproduction or signification,' in Canary and Kozicki (1978): 3–39.

Graff, Gerald (1973) 'The myth of the postmodernist breakthrough,' *TriQuarterly* 26: 383–417.

—(1979) *Literature Against Itself*, Chicago, Ill.: University of Chicago Press.

—(1981) 'Under our belt and off our back: Barth's *LETTERS* and postmodern fiction,' *TriQuarterly* 52: 150–64.

Graham, Robert (1985) 'Ritual and camera,' *Parachute* 39: 31–2.

Grass, Günter (1962) *The Tin Drum*, trans. Ralph Manheim, New York: Pantheon.

Gray, Alasdair (1969, 1981) *Lanark: A Life in Four Books*, New York: Harper & Row.

Green, Jonathan (1984) *American Photography: A Critical History 1945 to the Present*, New York: Harry N. Abrams.

Greenberg, Clement (1980) 'Modern and post-modern,' *Arts Magazine* 54, 6: 64–6.

Grossberg, Laurence (1987) 'The indifference of television,' *Postmodern Screen* issue of *Screen* 28, 2: 28–46.

Haacke, Hans (1986–7) 'Museums, managers of consciousness,' in Wallis (1986–7a): 60–72.

Habermas, Jürgen (1983) 'Modernity – an incomplete project,' in Foster (1983): 3–15.

—(1985a) 'Neoconservative culture criticism in the United States and West Germany: an intellectual movement in two political cultures,' in Bernstein (1985): 78–94.

—(1985b) 'Questions and counterquestions,' in Bernstein (1985): 192–216.

Harland, Richard (1987) *Superstructuralism: The Philosophy of*

Structuralism and Post-Structuralism, London and New York: Methuen.

Hassan, Ihab (1971) 'POSTmodernISM,' *New Literary History* 3, 1: 5–30.

——(1975) *Paracriticisms: Seven Speculations of the Times*, Urbana, Ill.: University of Illinois Press.

——(1980a): *The Right Promethean Fire: Imagination, Science, and Cultural Change*, Urbana, Ill.: University of Illinois Press.

——(1980b) 'The question of postmodernism,' in Garvin (1980): 117–26.

——(1982) *The Dismemberment of Orpheus: Toward a Postmodern Literature*, 2nd edn, Madison, Wis.: University of Wisconsin Press.

——(1986) 'Pluralism in postmodern perspective,' *Critical Inquiry* 12, 3: 503–20.

——(1987) *The Postmodern Turn: Essays in Postmodern Theory and Culture*, n.p.: Ohio State University Press.

Hayman, David (1978) 'Double distancing: an attribute of the "postmodern"avant-garde,' *Novel* 12, 1: 33–47.

Hayward, Philip and Kerr, Paul (1987) 'Introduction,' *Postmodern Screen* issue of *Screen* 28, 2: 2–8.

Heath, Stephen (1982) *The Sexual Fix*, London: Macmillan.

Hoban, Russell (1980) *Riddley Walker*, London: Picador.

Hodgins, Jack (1977) *The Invention of the World*, Toronto: Macmillan.

Hoffman, Gerhard, Hornung, Alfred, and Kunow, Rüdiger (1977) '"Modern," "postmodern," and "contemporary" as criteria for the analysis of twentieth-century literature,' *Amerikastudien* 22: 19–46.

Humm, Peter, Stigant, Paul, and Widdowson, Peter (eds) (1986) *Popular Fictions: Essays in Literature and History*, London and New York: Methuen.

Hutcheon, Linda (1985) *A Theory of Parody: The Teachings of Twentieth-Century Art Forms*, London and New York: Methuen.

——(1988) *A Poetics of Postmodernism: History, Theory, Fiction*, New York and London: Routledge.

Huyssen, Andreas (1986) *After the Great Divide: Modernism, Mass Culture, Postmodernism*, Bloomington, Ind.: Indiana University Press.

Jacobs, Jane (1961) *Death and Life of Great American Cities*, New York: Vintage.

James, Carol Plyley (1985) '"No, says the signified": the "logical status" of words in painting,' *Visible Language* 19, 4: 439–61.

Jameson, Fredric (1972) *The Prison-House of Language: A Critical Account of Structuralism and Russian Formalism*, Princeton, NJ: Princeton University Press.

——(1979) 'Marxism and historicism,' *New Literary History* 11, 1: 41–73.

—(1981) *The Political Unconscious: Narrative as a Socially Symbolic Act*, Ithaca, NY: Cornell University Press.
—(1983) 'Postmodernism and consumer society,' in Foster (1983): 111–25.
—(1984a) 'Postmodernism, or the cultural logic of late capitalism,' *New Left Review* 146: 53–92.
—(1984b) 'Foreword,' in Lyotard (1984a): vii–xxi.
—(1984c) 'The politics of theory: ideological positions in the post-modernism debate,' *New German Critique* 33: 53–65.
—(1985) 'Architecture and the critique of ideology,' in Ockman (1985): 51–87.
—(1986) 'On magic realism in film,' *Critical Inquiry* 12, 2: 301–25.
—(1986–7) 'Hans Haacke and the cultural logic of postmodernism,' in Wallis (1986–7a): 38–50.
Jencks, Charles (1977) *The Language of Post-Modern Architecture*, London: Academy.
—(1980a) *Post-Modern Classicism: The New Synthesis*, London: Academy.
—(1980b) *Late-Modern Architecture and Other Essays*, London: Academy.
—(1982) *Architecture Today*, New York: Abrams.
Jones, Gayl (1976) *Corregidora*, New York: Random House.
Kaplan, E. Ann (1983) 'Is the gaze male?' in Snitow *et al.* (1983): 309–27.
—(1987) *Rocking Around the Clock: Music, Television, Post-Modernism and Consumer Culture*, London and New York: Methuen.
Kennedy, William (1975) *Legs*, Harmondsworth: Penguin.
Kermode, Frank (1966–7) *The Sense of an Ending*, London and New York: Oxford University Press.
—(1979) *The Genesis of Secrecy: On the Interpretation of Narrative*, Cambridge, Mass. and London: Harvard University Press.
Kibbins, Gary (1983) 'The enduring of the artsystem,' *Open Letter* 5th series, 5–6: 126–39.
Kingston, Maxine Hong (1976) *The Woman Warrior: Memories of a Girlhood Among Ghosts*, New York: Knopf.
—(1980) *China Men*, New York: Ballantine.
Klinkowitz, Jerome (1985) *Literary Subversions: New American Fiction and the Practice of Criticism*, Carbondale and Edwardsville, Ill.: Southern Illinois University Press.
—(1986) 'Writing under fire: postmodern fiction and the Vietnam War,' in McCaffery (1986a): 79–92.
Kogawa, Joy (1981) *Obasan*, Toronto: Lester & Orpen Dennys.
Köhler, Michael (1977) '"Postmodernismus": Ein begriffsgeschichtlicher Überblick,' *Amerikastudien* 22, 1: 8–18.
Kramer, Hilton (1982) 'Postmodern: art and culture in the 1980s,' *New Criterion* 1, 1: 36–42.

Krauss, Rosalind (1979) 'John Mason and post-modernist sculpture: new experiences, new words,' *Art in America* 67, 3: 120–7.

—(1985) *The Originality of the Avant-Garde and Other Modernist Myths*, Cambridge, Mass. and London: MIT Press.

—(1987) 'Notes on the index: seventies art in America,' in Michelson *et al.* (1987): 2–15.

Kroker, Arthur and Cook, David (1986) *The Postmodern Scene: Excremental Culture and Hyper-Aesthetics*, Montreal: New World Perspectives.

Kruger, Barbara (1982) ' "Taking" pictures: photo-texts by Barbara Kruger,' *Screen* 23, 2: 90–4.

Kuhn, Annette (1985) *The Power of the Image: Essays on Representation and Sexuality*, London: Routledge & Kegan Paul.

Kuspit, Donald B. (1984) 'Symptoms of critique: Nancy Spero and Francesco Torres,' in *Art and Ideology* (1984): 21–8.

LaCapra, Dominick (1983) *Rethinking Intellectual History: Texts, Contexts, Language*, Ithaca, NY: Cornell University Press.

—(1985) *History and Criticism*, Ithaca, NY: Cornell University Press.

—(1987) *History, Politics, and the Novel*, Ithaca, NY: Cornell University Press.

Laffey, John (1987) 'Cacophonic rites: modernism and postmodernism,' *Historical Reflections/Réflexions Historiques* 14, 1: 1–32.

Latimer, Dan (1984) 'Jameson and post-modernism,' *New Left Review* 148: 116–27.

Lauzen, Sarah E. (1986) 'Notes on metafiction: every essay has a title,' in McCaffery (1986a): 93–116.

Lee, Alison (1988) 'Realism doesn't . . . ,' Ph.D. dissertation, McMaster University.

Lerup, Lars (1987) *Planned Assaults*, Montreal: Canadian Center for Architecture.

Levine, Sherrie (1987) 'Five comments,' in Wallis (1987): 92–3.

Linker, Kate (1984) 'Representation and sexuality,' in Wallis (1984): 390–415.

Lippard, Lucy R. (1971) 'Sexual politics, art style,' *Art in America* 59, 5: 19–20.

—(1976) *From the Center: Feminist Essays on Women's Art*, New York: Dutton.

—(1980) 'Sweeping exchanges: the contribution of feminism to the art of the 1970s,' *Art Journal* 40, 1–2: 362–5.

—(1984) 'Give and take: ideology in the art of Suzanne Lacy and Jerry Kearns,' in *Art and Ideology* (1984): 29–38.

Lodge, David (1977) *The Modes of Modern Writing: Metaphor, Metonymy, and the Typology of Modern Literature*, London: Edward Arnold.

Lukács, Georg (1962) *The Historical Novel*, trans. Hannah and Stanley Mitchell, London: Merlin.

Lyotard, Jean-François (1981) 'Theory as art: a pragmatic point of view,' trans. Robert A. Vollrath, in Steiner (1981): 71–7.

—(1984a) *The Postmodern Condition: A Report on Knowledge*, trans. Geoff Bennington and Brian Massumi, Minneapolis, Minn.: University of Minnesota Press.

—(1984b) 'Answering the question: what is postmodernism?' trans. Régis Durand, in Lyotard (1984a): 71–82.

—(1984c) 'The *différend*, the referent, and the proper name,' trans. Georges Van Den Abbeele, *Diacritics* 14, 3: 4–14.

—(1986) *Le Postmoderne expliqué aux enfants: Correspondance 1982–1985*, Paris: Galilée.

MacCabe, Colin (1978/9) 'The discursive and the ideological in film: notes on the conditions of political intervention,' *Screen* 19, 4: 29–43.

McCaffery, Larry (ed.) (1986a) *Postmodern Fiction: A Bio-bibliographical Guide*, New York: Greenwood Press.

—(1986b) 'Introduction,' in McCaffery (1986a): ix–xxviii.

McHale, Brian (1987) *Postmodernist Fiction*, London and New York: Methuen.

McLeod, Mary (1985) 'Architecture,' in Trachtenberg (1985): 19–52.

Mailer, Norman (1970) *Of a Fire on the Moon*, Boston, Mass.: Little, Brown.

Malen, Lenore (1988) 'The politics of gender,' introduction to *The Politics of Gender* catalogue, Queensborough Community College, CUNY Bayside, NY: 7–11.

Malmgren, Carl Darryl (1985) *Fictional Space in the Modernist and Postmodernist American Novel*, Lewisburgh, Pa: Bucknell University Press.

—(1987) '"From work to text," the modernist and postmodernist *Künstlerroman*,' *Novel* 21, 1: 5–28.

Marzorati, Gerald (1986) 'Art in the (re)making,' *Art News* (May): 91–9.

Mellard, James M. (1980) *The Exploded Form: The Modernist Novel in America*, Urbana, Ill.: University of Illinois Press.

Michelson, Annette, Krauss, Rosalind, Crimp, Douglas, and Copjec, Joan (eds) (1987) *October: The First Decade, 1976–1986*, Cambridge, Mass. and London: MIT Press.

Miller, Nancy K. (1986) 'Changing the subject: authorship, writing, and the reader,' in de Lauretis (1986a): 102–20.

Mink, Louis O. (1978) 'Narrative form as a cognitive instrument,' in Canary and Kozicki (1978): 129–49.

—(1987) *Historical Understanding*, ed. Brian Fay, Eugene O. Golub, and Richard T. Vann, Ithaca, NY: Cornell University Press.

Mitchell, W.J.T. (1986) *Iconology: Image, Text, Ideology*, Chicago, Ill.: University of Chicago Press.

Moramarco, Fred (1986) 'Postmodern poetry and fiction: the connective links,' in McCaffery (1986a): 129–41.

Müller, Heiner (1979) 'Reflections on post-modernism,' *New German Critique* 16: 55–7.

Mulvey, Laura (1975) 'Visual pleasure and narrative cinema,' *Screen* 16, 3: 6–18.

—(1986) 'Magnificent obsession,' *Parachute* 42: 6–12.

Myers, Kathy (1987) 'Towards a feminist erotica,' in Betterton (1987): 189–202.

Nägele, Rainer (1980/1) 'Modernism and postmodernism: the margins of articulation,' *Studies in 20th Century Literature* 5: 5–25.

Nead, Lynda (1983) 'Representation, sexuality and the female nude,' *Art History* 6, 2: 227–36.

Newman, Charles (1985) *The Post-Modern Aura: The Act of Fiction in an Age of Inflation*, Evanston, Ill.: Northwestern University Press.

Nichols, Bill (1981) *Ideology and the Image: Social Representation in the Cinema and Other Media*, Bloomington, Ind.: Indiana University Press.

Nietzsche, Friedrich (1957) *The Use and Abuse of History*, trans. Adrian Collins, Indianapolis, Ind. and New York: Liberal Arts Press and Bobbs-Merrill.

Ockman, J. (ed.) (1985) *Architecture, Criticism, Ideology*, Princeton, NJ: Princeton Architectural Press.

Ondaatje, Michael (1976) *Coming Through Slaughter*, Toronto: Anansi.

—(1982) *Running in the Family*, Toronto: McClelland & Stewart.

Owens, Craig (1980a) 'The allegorical impulse: toward a theory of postmodernism. Part I,' *October* 12: 67–86.

—(1980b) 'The allegorical impulse: toward a theory of postmodernism. Part II,' *October* 13: 59–80.

—(1982) 'Representation, appropriation & power,' *Art in America* 70, 5: 9–21.

—(1983) 'The discourse of others: feminists and postmodernism,' in Foster (1983): 57–82.

—(1984) 'Posing,' in *Difference* (1984): 6–17.

Palmer, Richard E. (1977) 'Postmodernity and hermeneutics,' *boundary 2* 5, 2: 363–93.

Paoletti, John T. (1985) 'Art,' in Trachtenberg (1985): 53–79.

Parker, Rozsika and Pollock, Griselda (eds) (1987a) *Framing Feminism: Art and the Women's Movement 1970–85*, London and New York: Pandora.

—(1987b) 'Fifteen years of feminist action: from practical strategies to strategic practices,' in Parker and Pollock (1987a): 3–78.

Paterson, Janet (1986) 'Le Roman "postmoderne": mise au point et perspectives,' *Canadian Review of Comparative Literature* 13, 2: 238–55.

Peirce, C.S. (1931–58) *Collected Papers*, 8 vols, ed. Charles Hartshorne and Paul Weiss, Cambridge, Mass.: Harvard University Press.

Perloff, Marjorie (1985) *The Dance of the Intellect: Studies in the Poetry of the Pound Tradition*, Cambridge: Cambridge University Press.

Phillips, Christopher (1987) 'The judgment seat of photography,' in Michelson *et al.* (1987): 257–93.

Polkinhorn, Harry (1987) 'The failure of a postmodern aesthetic,' *Poetics Journal* 7: 63–70.

Portoghesi, Paolo (1974) *Le inibizioni dell'architettura moderna*, Bari: Laterza.

—(1982) *After Modern Architecture*, trans. Meg Shore, New York: Rizzoli.

—(1983) *Postmodern: The Architecture of the Postindustrial Society*, New York: Rizzoli.

Porush, David (1985) *The Soft Machine: Cybernetic Fiction*, New York and London: Methuen.

Puig, Manuel (1978, 1979) *Kiss of the Spider Woman*, trans. Thomas Colchie, New York: Random House.

Pynchon, Thomas (1961, 1963) *V.*, New York: Bantam.

—(1965) *The Crying of Lot 49*, New York: Bantam.

—(1973) *Gravity's Rainbow*, New York: Viking.

Radhakrishnan, R. (1986) 'Reality, the text, and postmodern representation: a question in theory, or theory in question,' in McCaffery (1986a): 229–44.

Raulet, Gérard (1984) 'From modernity as one-way street to postmodernity as dead end,' *New German Critique* 33: 155–77.

Rawson, Claude (1986) 'A poet in the postmodern playground,' *The Times Literary Supplement*, 4 July: 723–4.

Reed, Ishmael (1969) *Yellow Back Radio Broke-Down*, Garden City, NY: Doubleday.

—(1972) *Mumbo Jumbo*, Garden City, NY: Doubleday.

—(1976) *Flight to Canada*, New York: Random House.

—(1982) *The Terrible Twos*, New York: St Martin's/Marek.

Rees, A.L. and Borzello, Frances (eds) (1986) *The New Art History*, London: Camden Press.

Roa Bastos, Augusto (1986) *I the Supreme*, trans. Helen Lane, New York: Aventura.

Roberts, John (1987) 'Postmodern television and visual arts,' *Postmodern Screen* issue of *Screen* 28, 2: 118–27.

Rorty, Richard (1981) 'Nineteenth-century idealism and twentieth-century textualism,' *Monist* 64: 155–74.

184 The Politics of Postmodernism

Rorty, Richard (1984) 'Habermas, Lyotard et la postmodernité,' *Critique* 442: 181–97.
Rosenberg, Harold (1973) *Discovering the Present: Three Decades in Art, Culture and Politics*, Chicago, Ill.: University of Chicago Press.
Rosler, Martha (1981) *3 Works*, Halifax, NS: Nova Scotia College of Art and Design.
—(1984) 'Lookers, buyers, dealers, and makers: thoughts on audience,' in Wallis (1984): 310–39.
Rosso, Stefano (1983) 'A correspondence with Umberto Eco,' trans. Carolyn Springer, *boundary 2* 12, 1: 1–13.
Rowe, John Carlos (1987) 'Modern art and the invention of postmodern capital,' *American Quarterly* 39, 1: 155–73.
Rushdie, Salman (1981) *Midnight's Children*, London: Picador.
—(1983) *Shame*, London: Picador.
Russell, Charles (1980) 'The context of the concept,' in Garvin (1980): 181–93.
—(1982) 'Subversion and legitimation: the avant-garde in postmodern culture,' *Chicago Review* 33, 2: 54–9.
—(1985) *Poets, Prophets, and Revolutionaries: The Literary Avant-garde from Rimbaud through Postmodernism*, New York and Oxford: Oxford University Press.
Said, Edward (1975) *Beginnings: Intention and Method*, New York: Basic.
—(1983) *The World, the Text, and the Critic*, Cambridge, Mass.: Harvard University Press.
Scherpe, Klaus R. (1986/7) 'Dramatization and de-dramatization of "the end": the apocalyptic consciousness of modernity and postmodernity,' *Cultural Critique* 5: 95–129.
Schmidt, Burghart (1986) *Postmoderne – Strategien des Vergessens: ein kritischer Bericht*, Darmstadt und Neuwied: Luchterhand.
Schreiber, LeAnne (1987) 'Talking to . . . Barbara Kruger,' *Vogue*, October: 260 and 268.
Scott, Chris (1982) *Antichthon*, Montreal: Quadrant.
Sekula, Allan (1982) 'On the invention of photographic meaning,' in Burgin (1982a): 84–109.
—(1987) 'Reading an archive,' in Wallis (1987): 114–27.
Siegle, Robert (1986) *The Politics of Reflexivity: Narrative and the Constitutive Poetics of Culture*, Baltimore, Md and London: Johns Hopkins University Press.
Silliman, Ron (1987) '"Postmodernism": sign for a struggle, the struggle for the sign,' *Poetics Journal* 7: 18–39.
Sims, Lowry (1984) 'Body politics: Hannah Wilke and Kaylynn Sullivan,' *Art and Ideology*: 45–56.
Siska, William C. (1979) 'Metacinema: a modern necessity,' *Literature/Film Quarterly* 7, 1: 285–9.

Sloterdijk, Peter (1987) *Critique of Cynical Reason*, trans. Michael Eldred, Minneapolis, Minn.: University of Minnesota Press.

Smith, Paul (1988) *Discerning the Subject*, Minneapolis, Minn.: University of Minnesota Press.

Snitow, Ann, Stansell, Christine, and Thompson, Sharon (eds) (1983) *Powers of Desire: The Politics of Sexuality*, New York: Monthly Review Press.

Solomon-Godeau, Abigail (1984a) 'Photography after art photography,' in Wallis (1984): 74–85.

—(1984b) 'Winning the game when the rules have been changed: art photography and postmodernism,' *Screen* 25, 6: 88–102.

Sontag, Susan (1967) *Against Interpretation and Other Essays*, New York: Dell.

—(1977) *On Photography*, New York: Farrar, Straus, & Giroux.

Spanos, William V. (1987) *Repetitions: The Postmodern Occasion in Literature and Culture*, Baton Rouge, La: Louisiana State University Press.

Squiers, Carol (1987) 'Diversionary (syn)tactics: Barbara Kruger has her way with words,' *ARTnews* 86, 2: 76–85.

Starenko, Michael (1983) 'What's an artist to do? A short history of postmodernism and photography,' *Afterimage* (January): 4–5.

Steiner, Wendy (ed.) (1981) *Image and Code*, Ann Arbor, Mich.: University of Michigan Press.

Stephanson, Anders (1987) 'Regarding postmodernism – a conversation with Fredric Jameson,' *Social Text* 17: 29–54.

Stern, Robert (1980) 'The doubles of post-modern,' *Harvard Architectural Review* 1: 75–87.

Sterne, Laurence (1967) *The Life and Opinions of Tristram Shandy*, Harmondsworth: Penguin.

Stevick, Philip (1981) *Alternative Pleasures: Postrealist Fiction and the Tradition*, Urbana, Ill.: University of Illinois Press.

—(1985) 'Literature,' in Trachtenberg (1985): 135–56.

Stimpson, Catherine R. (1988) 'Nancy Reagan wears a hat: feminism and its cultural consensus,' *Critical Inquiry* 14, 2: 223–43.

Sukenick, Ronald (1985) *In Form: Digressions on the Act of Fiction*, Carbondale and Edwardsville, Ill.: Southern Illinois University Press.

Süskind, Patrick (1986) *Perfume: The Story of a Murderer*, trans. John E. Woods, New York: Knopf.

Swan, Susan (1983) *The Biggest Modern Woman of the World*, Toronto: Lester & Orpen Dennys.

Swift, Graham (1983) *Waterland*, London: Heinemann.

Tafuri, Manfredo (1980) *Theories and History of Architecture*, London: Granada.

Tagg, John (1982) 'The currency of the photograph,' in Burgin (1982a): 110–41.

Tanner, Tony (1971) *City of Words: American Fiction 1950–1970*, New York: Harper & Row.

Thiher, Allen (1984) *Words in Reflection: Modern Language Theory and Postmodern Fiction*, Chicago, Ill.: University of Chicago Press.

Thomas, Audrey (1984) *Intertidal Life*, Toronto: Stoddart.

Thomas, D.M. (1981) *The White Hotel*, Harmondsworth: Penguin.

Thornton, Gene (1979) 'Post-modern photography: it doesn't look "modern" at all,' *ARTnews* 78, 4: 64–8.

Tickner, Lisa (1984) 'Sexuality and/in representation: five British artists,' in *Difference* (1984): 19–30.

—(1987) 'The body politic: female sexuality and women artists since 1970,' in Parker and Pollock (1987a): 263–76.

Trachtenberg, Stanley (ed.) (1985) *The Postmodern Moment: A Handbook of Contemporary Innovation in the Arts*, Westport, Conn.: Greenwood Press.

Tregebov, Rhea (ed.) (1987) *Work in Progress: Building Feminist Culture*, Toronto: Women's Press.

Trenner, Richard (ed.) (1983) *E. L. Doctorow: Essays and Conversations*, Princeton, NJ: Ontario Review Press.

Vargas Llosa, Mario (1984) *The War of the End of the World*, trans. Helen R. Lane, New York: Farrar, Straus, & Giroux.

—(1986) *The Perpetual Orgy: Flaubert and Madame Bovary*, trans. Helen Lane, New York: Farrar, Straus, & Giroux.

Vattimo, Gianni (1985) *La fine della modernità: Nichilismo ed ermeneutica nella cultura post-moderna*, Milan: Garzanti.

Veyne, Paul (1971) *Comment on écrit l'histoire*, Paris: Seuil.

Waller, Marguerite (1987) 'Academic Tootsie: the denial of difference and the difference it makes,' *Diacritics* 17, 1: 2–20.

Wallis, Brian (ed.) (1984) *Art After Modernism: Rethinking Representation*, New York: New Museum of Contemporary Art; Boston, Mass.: Godine.

—(ed.) (1986–7a) *Hans Haacke: Unfinished Business*, New York: New Museum of Contemporary Art; Cambridge, Mass. and London: MIT Press.

—(1986–7b) 'Institutions trust institutions,' in Wallis (1986–7a): 51–9.

—(ed.) (1987) *Blasted Allegories: An Anthology of Writings by Contemporary Artists*, New York: New Museum of Contemporary Art; Cambridge, Mass.: MIT Press.

Ward, Andrea (1987) 'Interview with Frederic [sic] Jameson,' *Impulse* 13, 4: 8–9.

Webster, Frank (1980) *The New Photography: Responsibility in Visual Communication*, London: Calder.

Weedon, Chris (1987) *Feminist Practice and Poststructuralist Theory*, Oxford: Basil Blackwell.

Wellbery, David E. (1985) 'Postmodernism in Europe: on recent German writing,' in Trachtenberg (1985): 229–49.

Wellmer, Albrecht (1985) 'On the dialectic of modernism and post-modernism,' trans. David Roberts, *Praxis International* 4, 4: 337–62.

White, Hayden (1973) *Metahistory: The Historical Imagination in Nineteenth-Century Europe*, Baltimore, Md: Johns Hopkins University Press.

—(1976) 'The fictions of factual representation,' in Fletcher (1976): 21–44.

—(1978a) 'The historical text as literary artifact,' in Canary and Kozicki (1978): 41–62.

—(1978b) *Tropics of Discourse: Essays in Cultural Criticism*, Baltimore, Md: Johns Hopkins University Press.

—(1980) 'The value of narrativity in the representation of reality,' *Critical Inquiry* 7, 1: 5–27.

—(1984) 'The question of narrative in contemporary historical theory,' *History and Theory* 23, 1: 1–33.

—(1986) 'Historical pluralism,' *Critical Inquiry* 12, 3: 480–93.

—(1987) *The Content of the Form: Narrative Discourse and Historical Representation*, Baltimore, Md and London: Johns Hopkins University Press.

Wiebe, Rudy (1973) *The Temptations of Big Bear*, Toronto: McClelland & Stewart.

Wilde, Alan (1981) *Horizons of Assent: Modernism, Postmodernism, and the Ironic Imagination*, Baltimore, Md: Johns Hopkins University Press.

—(1987) *Middle Grounds: Studies in Contemporary American Fiction*, Philadelphia, Pa: University of Pennsylvania Press.

Williams, Nigel (1985) *Star Turn*, London and Boston, Mass.: Faber & Faber.

Williams, Raymond (1960) *Culture and Society 1780–1950*, Garden City, NY: Doubleday.

Winship, Janice (1987) ' "A girl needs to get street-wise": magazines for the 1980s,' in Betterton (1987): 127–41.

Wolf, Christa (1980) *Patterns of Childhood*, trans. Ursule Molinaro and Hedwig Rappolt, New York: Farrar, Straus, & Giroux.

—(1982) *No Place on Earth*, trans. Jan Van Heurck, New York: Farrar, Straus, & Giroux.

—(1984) *Cassandra: A Novel and Four Essays*, trans. Jan Van Heurck, London: Virago.

Wolin, Richard (1985) 'Modernism versus postmodernism,' *Telos* 62: 9–29.

Wollen, Peter (1978/9) 'Photography and aesthetics,' *Screen* 19, 4: 9–28.

Zimmerman, Bonnie (1986) 'Feminist fiction and the postmodern challenge,' in McCaffery (1986a): 175–88.

Index

Abrams, M. H. 18
Ackroyd, Peter 119; *Chatterton* 49, 95–8, 117; *Hawksmoor* 42, 58
Adorno, Theodor 13
advertising 42, 44, 118, 121, 124, 125, 128, 130, 135, 137, 154
Allen, Woody 9, 107, 109–10, 113
Althusser, Louis 6, 33, 108, 133, 134, 138
Anderson, Laurie 135
Annales school 63
Arac, Jonathan 170
architecture *see* postmodernism in architecture
archive *see* document(ary)
Ashbery, John 10
Atwood, Margaret 20, 154
autobiography *see* life-writing
avant-garde 9, 26, 27, 134

Banes, Sally 9
Banville, John: *Doctor Copernicus* 53, 71, 73, 105, 161; *Kepler* 161

Barber, Bruce 169
Barnes, Julian: *Flaubert's Parrot* 80
Barth, John 11, 85–6
Barthes, Roland 3, 23, 37, 40–1, 44, 61, 91, 123, 124–5, 133, 139
Baudrillard, Jean 7, 10, 11, 33, 34, 82, 120, 121, 144, 169
Beal, Graham W. J. 105
Bell, Daniel 170
Belsey, Catherine 108
Benhabib, Seyla 170
Benjamin, Walter 31, 35, 42, 91, 120, 139
Bennett, David 170
Berger, John 20, 45, 155; *G.* 47, 69, 74, 80, 105
Bertens, Hans 170
biography *see* life-writing
black *see* race
Bois, Yve-Alain 45, 140
Bowering, George: *Burning Water* 77
Boyd, William: *The New Confessions* 74

Bradbury, Malcolm 169
Braudel, Fernand 63
Brecht, Bertolt 42, 73, 88, 128,
    154
Brolin, Brent 169
Brooks, Peter 49, 51
Buchloh, Benjamin H. D. 120,
    170
Bürger, Christa 170
Burgin, Victor 3, 15–16, 19, 23,
    39, 43, 100, 102–3, 118, 119,
    122, 125, 127, 128, 131, 134,
    135–6, 137, 139, 155, 169

Calinescu, Matei 170
capitalism 2, 13, 25–6, 28, 43,
    46, 61, 93, 103, 113, 114, 119,
    122, 127–8, 135, 137, 139–40,
    144, 155
Carter, Angela 8, 20, 39, 94,
    150, 154, 155–6; 'Black
    Venus' 53, 145–9; 'The Loves
    of Lady Purple' 32–3; Nights
    at the Circus 98
Caute, David 2
Charlesworth, Sarah 44
Chow, Rey 38
class 4–5, 23, 39, 46, 61, 112,
    133, 137, 139, 141, 156
Coetzee, J. M. 51; Foe 76
Cohen, Leonard: Beautiful Losers
    51
Collingwood, R. G. 56, 67
consumer capitalism see
    capitalism
Coover, Robert: The Public
    Burning 36, 71, 77, 88, 92
Cortázar, Julio: Hopscotch 90; A
    Manual for Manuel 87–8
Coward, Rosalind 144
Creed, Barbara 19, 153, 169
Crimp, Douglas 19, 43, 169,
    170

Daitch, Susan 22; L.C. 154
Danto, Arthur C. 71
Davis, Douglas 12, 121, 169, 170
Davis, Lennard J. 42, 49, 76
Davis, Natalie Zemon 71, 115
Davis, Peter 36–7
deconstruction see
    poststructuralism
de Lauretis, Teresa 8, 14, 154
De Palma, Brian 114–15
Derrida, Jacques 3, 14, 24, 32,
    37, 85, 125, 131, 151
desire 46, 141–68
discourse 4, 7, 23–4, 33, 36, 43,
    61, 66, 67, 74, 81, 84, 88, 108,
    113, 116, 118, 120, 138,
    144–5, 150, 155
Doctorow, E. L. 4, 80; The Book
    of Daniel 69–70, 71, 81; Ragtime
    36, 57, 71, 81, 95
document(ary) 7, 29, 43, 44, 45,
    50, 57, 58, 64, 71–2, 75–6,
    78–92, 95–7, 106, 109, 110,
    113, 116, 118, 120, 121, 126–7,
    133, 134, 163–7
Dos Passos, John: USA 95
Douglas, Stan 46
During, Simon 38

Eagleton, Terry 2, 18, 27, 28,
    59, 170; Saints and Scholars
    59–61
Eco, Umberto 3–4, 119, 169;
    The Name of the Rose 42, 63,
    94–5
erotic see desire
Esquire 36–7
ethnicity 10, 22, 23, 39, 40, 46,
    141

Fellini, Federico 107, 112
feminisms 2, 6, 7, 9, 10, 14, 17,
    19–21, 22–3, 37–8, 39, 45,

50–1, 69, 76, 98–9, 101–2,
110–11, 122, 129, 133–4,
136–8, 139, 140, 141–68
fiction *see* postmodernism in
fiction
Fiedler, Leslie 10
film *see* postmodernism in film
Findley, Timothy: *Famous Last
Words* 67, 82; *The Wars* 47
Foley, Barbara 58
formalism 7, 26, 28, 29, 41, 43,
44, 45, 80, 115, 121, 122, 127,
128, 129
Foster, Hal 17–18, 28, 45, 94,
139, 168, 170
Foucault, Michel 3, 14, 24, 32,
37, 56, 66, 136
Fowles, John 39; *The French
Lieutenant's Woman* 51, 53, 83,
84, 86, 112, 113; *A Maggot*
38–9, 53, 82, 83, 89, 90
Friedberg, Anne 13, 14
Fuentes, Carlos: *Terra Nostra* 77

Gagnon, Monika 21
García Márquez, Gabriel 51;
Chronicle of a Death Foretold
80; *One Hundred Years of
Solitude* 65, 70
Gass, William H. 83
gay issues 6, 7, 21, 22, 23, 39,
46, 133
Geltner, Gail 151–2
gender issues *see* feminisms
General Idea 46
Giddens, Anthony 170
Glass, Phil 9
Gossman, Lionel 87
Graff, Gerald 10, 170
Grass, Gunter 4; *The Tin Drum*
65, 104
Gray, Alasdair: *Lanark* 85
Greenaway, Peter: *A Zed and

Two Noughts 116–17
Greenberg, Clement 170

Haacke, Hans 21, 42, 45, 46,
118, 127–8, 130, 135, 137,
139–40
Habermas, Jürgen 24–6, 170
Harrison, Margaret 150
Hassan, Ihab 10, 11, 16, 18, 28,
37, 170
Hayman, David 170
Heartfield, John 42–3, 45
Heath, Stephen 51, 155
high art 3, 35, 43, 105, 112, 118,
120, 121, 124, 126, 129, 132,
136, 140, 150, 154, 161
historiographic metafiction *see*
postmodernism in fiction
history 2, 5–6, 7, 10, 11–12, 14,
15, 17, 18, 24–5, 27, 35, 36, 39,
46, 47–61, 62–92, 93–4, 95,
97, 100–1, 102, 103–4,
105–6, 109, 113–14, 115–17,
119, 122, 146–9, 153, 160–8
Hoban, Russell: *Riddley Walker*
58
Hodgins, Jack: *The Invention of
the World* 90
humanism 2, 13, 23, 38, 62, 108,
116, 122–3, 143, 153, 157, 167
Hunter, Alexis 152
Huyssen, Andreas 15, 20, 27,
28, 170

ideology 3, 4, 6, 7, 10, 16, 17,
21, 23, 26, 28–9, 31, 33, 35, 42,
45, 50, 53, 54, 67, 74, 76,
88–9, 93, 101, 107, 108, 113,
117, 121, 122, 123, 124, 132,
133, 137, 138–9, 143, 144,
153, 168
imperialism *see* post-colonial
intertextuality *see* parody

irony 1, 3, 13, 15, 17, 18, 27, 43, 44, 46, 49, 50, 58, 59, 85, 88, 93, 94, 95, 98, 99, 100–1, 103, 105, 107, 108, 113, 114, 119, 123, 130, 147, 149, 152, 156

Jacobs, Jane 12
Jameson, Fredric 2, 11, 15, 24, 25–7, 28, 34, 50, 60, 64–5, 74, 94, 107, 113–14, 124, 169, 170
Jean-Louis, Don 135
Jencks, Charles 9, 169
Jones, Gayl: *Corregidora* 47, 50, 161–3

Kaplan, E. Ann 151, 169
Kelly, Mary 21, 134, 150, 157
Kennedy, William: *Legs* 58–9
Kermode, Frank 11, 79
Kingston, Maxine Hong 20, 50, 154; *China Men* 47, 81, 88–9, 161; *The Woman Warrior* 23, 161
Klinkowitz, Jerome 169
Kolbowski, Silvia 42, 100, 139, 152, 154, 155
Kramer, Hilton 2, 170
Krauss, Rosalind 8, 170
Kroker, Arthur 11, 170
Kruger, Barbara 19, 39, 43, 45, 100, 106, 118, 119, 122, 124, 125, 128–30, 135, 136–7, 138, 140, 152, 154, 155, 156–8, 160
Kuhn, Annette 22, 44
Kuspit, Donald B. 170

Lacan, Jacques 14, 108, 131, 133–4
LaCapra, Dominick 8, 50, 56, 57, 62–3, 81, 100
Laffey, John 170
Lawlor, Michael 43

Lee, Alison 169
Leo, Vincent 106
Lerup, Lars 169
Levine, Sherrie 14, 43, 45, 98–9, 156
liberal humanism *see* humanism
life-writing 22–3, 40–1, 160–8
Linker, Kate 129, 131
Lippard, Lucy R. 158, 170
Lodge, David 169
Lukács, Georg 27, 60, 77
Lyotard, Jean-François 4, 7, 11, 14, 24–6, 56, 67, 86, 153, 170

MacCabe, Colin 138
McHale, Brian 11, 47, 59, 169
Mailer, Norman: *Of a Fire on the Moon* 82
Malen, Lenore 102
Malmgren, Carl Darryl 169, 170
Marxism 2, 6, 14, 17, 28, 57, 59–61, 64–5, 69, 70, 108, 113, 133, 134, 138, 144, 158, 159
mass culture/mass media 3, 9–10, 15, 18, 22, 28–9, 33, 35, 42, 43, 44, 100, 102, 105, 118, 120, 121, 124, 129, 132, 135–6, 140, 144, 152, 154, 157, 161
metafiction *see* postmodernism in fiction
Mitchell, W. J. T. 121
modernism 7, 11–12, 14, 15, 18, 19, 26, 27–8, 29, 34, 41, 42, 43, 44, 45, 50, 51, 64, 93, 99, 100, 103, 107, 109–10, 122, 123–4, 128, 129, 143, 152
modernity 24–5
Müller, Heiner 2, 170
Mulvey, Laura 19, 133, 151, 169

Nägele, Rainer 170
narrative 7, 8, 14–15, 17, 29, 31,
    35–6, 40–1, 42, 47–61,
    62–92, 128, 160–8
neoconservative 2, 13, 16–17,
    98, 119
New Art History 46
Newman, Charles 2, 11, 16, 29,
    169
Nichols, Bill 124
Nietzsche, Friedrich 61, 74
nostalgia 13, 98, 113, 114, 117,
    119

Ondaatje, Michael: *Coming
    Through Slaughter* 47, 91;
    Running in the Family 23, 161
orality 89–91, 162–3
Osten, Suzanne: *The Mozart
    Brothers* 9, 110–11
Owens, Craig 19, 95, 125, 142,
    170

Palmer, Richard E. 170
paratextuality 82–92
Parker, Rozsika and Griselda
    Pollock 160
parody 2, 3, 7, 9, 12, 13, 15, 18,
    35, 53, 58, 61, 65, 89–90,
    93–117, 126, 128–9, 146, 147,
    150, 151–60, 168
pastiche 17, 93, 94, 98, 100, 107,
    113, 114
Paterson, Janet 170
patriarchy 2, 13, 22, 37, 103,
    119, 134, 142, 144, 153, 155,
    160
Peirce, C. S. 130–1
Perloff, Marjorie 64, 169
photography *see* postmodernism
    in photography
poetry *see* postmodernism in
    poetry

politics *see* postmodernism
Portoghesi, Paolo 9, 169
postcolonial 6, 37–8, 53, 65, 66,
    104, 130, 145–9
postmodernism: in architecture
    1, 2, 8, 11–12, 16, 17, 71, 107,
    119; debates over 16–18,
    23–9, 38; definitions of 1–2,
    3–4, 6–8, 10, 11, 15, 16, 18;
    and feminisms *see* feminisms;
    in fiction 1, 7, 14–15, 20, 21,
    27, 28, 35–7, 38–9, 42, 47–61,
    62–92, 93–8, 101–2, 104, 105,
    145–9, 160–1; in film 1, 8–9,
    21, 40, 44, 107–11; genre/
    media border crossing 9, 17,
    18–20, 35, 36–7, 71–2, 112,
    114–15, 118–40; and history
    see history; and modernism *see*
    modernism; modernity *see*
    modernity; and other arts 1,
    9, 16, 40, 44; in photography
    1, 7, 14, 19, 21–2, 28, 29–30,
    35, 39, 42–6, 63–4, 91–2,
    98–9, 100, 102–3, 105–6,
    118–40, 152–60; in poetry 1,
    9, 64; and postmodernity *see*
    postmodernity; in television
    10, 121–2; and theory 14,
    19–20, 118–19, 120, 131,
    132–4; in visual arts generally
    (including painting) 16,
    20–2, 44, 99, 104–5
postmodernity 23–6
poststructuralism 3, 6, 19, 39,
    81, 108, 133, 144
Prince, Richard 43
psychoanalysis 19, 85, 108, 131,
    132, 133–4
Puig, Manuel 8, 47; *Kiss of the
    Spider Woman* 85, 112
Pynchon, Thomas 63;
    V. 68

race 5, 6, 10, 17, 21, 22, 23, 39,
    45, 46, 104, 115, 133, 141, 147,
    156, 161–3
Ramos, Mel 152
realism 7, 10, 15, 27, 29, 34, 36,
    41, 42, 44, 45, 53, 77–8, 89–90,
    96, 98, 107, 109, 120, 121
Reed, Ishmael 51, 104
representation *see*
    postmodernism
Roa Bastos, Augusto: *I the
    Supreme* 47–9, 57, 64
romanticism 14, 19, 63, 64, 143,
    145
Rorty, Richard 24
Rosenberg, Harold 157
Rosler, Martha 19, 42, 43, 45,
    105–6, 118, 126–7, 130, 137,
    139
Rowe, John Carlos 170
Rush, Richard: *The Stunt Man*
    110
Rushdie, Salman 8, 47, 51, 94;
    Midnight's Children 57, 63,
    65–6, 68–9, 75–6, 86, 104,
    161; *Shame* 67, 71–2, 77–8, 104
Russell, Charles 2, 7, 169, 170

Said, Edward 117
Saura, Carlos: *Carmen* 112–13
Schell, Maximilian: *Marlene* 9,
    115–16
Scott, Chris: *Antichthon* 86
Scott, Nigel 43
Sekula, Allan 4, 19, 169
self-reflexivity 2, 3, 6, 7, 14, 15,
    18, 29, 35–6, 39, 41, 52, 59–60,
    61, 64, 71, 76, 82–3, 85, 89,
    97, 101, 107, 110, 111, 113,
    133, 135, 161
sexual orientation *see* gay issues
Sherman, Cindy 14, 43, 150,
    156, 158–9

Siegle, Robert 35–6
simulacrum 11, 23, 33–4, 82,
    120, 144
Siska, William C. 107
Sleigh, Sylvia 102
Sloterdijk, Peter 11, 19, 37
Smith, Paul 39
Solomon-Godeau, Abigail 93,
    106, 169
Sontag, Susan 10, 44, 109, 122
Spanos, William V. 18
Spero, Nancy 160
Staeck, Hans 46
Starenko, Michael 43, 169
Stern, Robert 169
Sterne, Laurence: *Tristram
    Shandy* 63, 65, 84, 104
Stevick, Philip 169
Stimpson, Catherine R. 31, 38,
    141, 144–5, 160
story telling *see* narrative
subjectivity 13–14, 23, 38–9,
    40–1, 108–9, 110, 113, 116,
    117, 122, 133–4, 135–6, 137,
    142, 143, 144, 145–9, 154–5,
    156, 157, 158
Sukenick, Ronald 90
surfiction 27
Süskind, Patrick: *Perfume* 52–3,
    54
Swift, Graham: *Waterland* 49,
    54–6, 57, 64, 72–3

Tafuri, Manfredo 169
Tanner, Tony 169
Tansey, Mark 99, 104–5
Tel Quel 27
Thiher, Allen 169
Thomas, Audrey 20, 154;
    Intertidal Life 86
Thomas, D. M.: *The White Hotel*
    63, 80, 87, 105
Tickner, Lisa 33, 145, 158

totalization 24–5, 37, 62–70, 95
Trachtenberg, Stanley 9, 27, 170

Vargas Llosa, Mario: *The Perpetual Orgy* 37; *The War of the End of the World* 53
Vattimo, Gianni 4, 24
Veyne, Paul 57

Waller, Marguerite 159
Webster, Frank 123
Weedon, Chris 168
Wellbery, David 4, 170
Wellmer, Albrecht 170
White, Hayden 7, 50, 54, 56, 67–8, 74–5, 80
Wiebe, Rudy: *The Temptations of Big Bear* 51, 90–1
Wilde, Alan 11, 18, 169, 170
Wilke, Hannah 137–8, 150, 158–60
Williams, Nigel: *Star Turn* 4–6, 161
Williams, Raymond 56
Wolf, Christa 20–1; *Cassandra* 51, 79, 101–2; *No Place on Earth* 20; *Patterns of Childhood* 23, 163–7
women's issues *see* feminisms

Yates, Marie 134